THIS BOOK BELONGS TO

The Library of

....

....

I can't tell you how grateful I am that you decided to read my book. My most heartfelt thanks that you took time out of your life to choose my work and I hope you find benefit within these pages.

There are so many books available today that offer similar content so that makes it even more humbling that you decided to buying mine.

Tell me what you thought! I am eager to hear your opinion and ideas on what you read as are others who are looking for a good book to buy. Leave a review on Amazon.com so others can benefit from your wisdom!

With much thanks.

Table of Contents

SUMMARY

The Art and Craft of Crochet is a comprehensive guidebook that delves into the intricate world of crochet. This book is a treasure trove of knowledge for both beginners and experienced crocheters alike, offering a wealth of information and inspiration.

The author, an expert in the field, takes readers on a journey through the history and evolution of crochet, providing valuable insights into the origins of this timeless craft. From its humble beginnings to its current status as a popular form of artistic expression, the author explores the various techniques, styles, and trends that have shaped crochet over the years.

One of the standout features of this book is its detailed and easy-to-follow instructions. The author breaks down the crochet process step-by-step, ensuring that even those with no prior experience can grasp the fundamentals. From choosing the right yarn and hook size to mastering basic stitches and creating intricate patterns, this book covers it all.

Moreover, The Art and Craft of Crochet goes beyond the basics and delves into more advanced techniques. Readers will learn how to create complex stitches, experiment with different yarn weights and textures, and even incorporate beads and other embellishments into their projects. The author also provides tips and tricks for troubleshooting common issues and achieving professional-looking results.

In addition to the technical aspects, this book also celebrates the artistic side of crochet. It showcases a wide range of stunning projects, from delicate lace doilies to cozy blankets and fashionable garments. Each project is accompanied by detailed instructions, clear diagrams, and beautiful photographs, allowing readers to visualize the final product and gain inspiration for their own creations.

The Art and Craft of Crochet also emphasizes the therapeutic and meditative qualities of crochet. The author highlights the calming and stress-relieving benefits of this craft, making it an ideal hobby for those seeking relaxation and mindfulness. The book includes anecdotes and personal stories from crocheters around the world, further emphasizing the sense of community and connection that crochet can foster.

Overall, The Art and Craft of Crochet is a must-have resource for anyone interested in this timeless craft. Whether you are a beginner looking to learn the basics or an experienced crocheter seeking new challenges and inspiration, this book has something to offer. With its comprehensive instructions, stunning projects, and celebration of the artistic and therapeutic aspects of crochet, it is sure to become a beloved companion on your crochet journey.

Choosing the right materials is a crucial step in any project or task. The materials used can greatly impact the overall quality, durability, and functionality of the end product. Therefore, it is essential to carefully consider various factors when selecting materials.

One important factor to consider is the intended purpose of the project. Different materials have different properties and characteristics that make them suitable for specific applications. For example, if you are building a structure that requires strength and stability, you may opt for materials such as steel or concrete. On the other hand, if you are creating a lightweight and flexible product, materials like plastic or aluminum may be more suitable.

Another factor to consider is the environmental conditions that the materials will be exposed to. Some materials may be more resistant to moisture, heat, or corrosion, making them ideal for outdoor or high-temperature applications. It is important to assess the potential risks and challenges that the materials may face in order to choose ones that can withstand these conditions and maintain their integrity over time.

Cost is also a significant consideration when choosing materials. Different materials come with varying price tags, and it is important to find a balance between quality and affordability. While it may be tempting to opt for cheaper materials, it is crucial to consider the long-term costs and potential consequences of using subpar materials. Investing in higher-quality materials may save you money in the long run by reducing maintenance and replacement costs.

Furthermore, it is important to consider the availability and accessibility of the materials. Some materials may be readily available in your area, while others may need to be sourced from distant locations, resulting in higher transportation costs and longer lead times. It is important to assess the feasibility and practicality of obtaining the chosen materials within your project's timeline and budget.

Lastly, it is essential to consider any regulatory or safety requirements when selecting materials. Certain industries or applications may have specific regulations or standards that dictate the types of materials that can be used. It is important to ensure compliance with these requirements to avoid legal issues and ensure the safety of the end-users.

In conclusion, choosing the right materials is a critical step in any project. By considering factors such as the intended purpose, environmental conditions, cost, availability, and regulatory requirements, you can make informed decisions that will result in a high-quality and successful end product. Taking the time to carefully select materials will ultimately contribute to the overall success and longevity of your project.

Working in the round refers to a technique used in various crafts, such as knitting, crochet, and sewing, where the work is done in a continuous spiral without turning the piece. This technique is commonly used to create seamless items, such as hats, socks, and amigurumi.

When working in the round, the first step is to cast on or create a foundation row of stitches. This can be done using various methods, such as the long-tail cast on in knitting or the magic ring in crochet. Once the foundation row is complete, the work is joined in a circle by connecting the first and last stitches.

One of the main advantages of working in the round is that it eliminates the need for seams. This creates a clean and seamless finish, which is especially desirable for items like hats and socks that are worn directly against the skin. Additionally, working in the round allows for continuous knitting or crocheting without the interruption of turning the work at the end of each row.

There are different techniques for working in the round, depending on the craft being used. In knitting, circular needles or double-pointed needles are commonly used. Circular needles have two needle tips connected by a flexible cable, allowing for the knitting of larger items, such as sweaters or blankets. Double-pointed needles, on the other hand, have pointed tips on both ends and are used for smaller projects, like socks or mittens.

In crochet, a circular project can be worked using a regular crochet hook or a specialized tool called a crochet hook with a cable. The latter allows for the creation of larger items, similar to circular knitting needles. Alternatively, a technique called the magic ring can be used to create a tight and adjustable starting loop for crochet projects worked in the round.

Working in the round requires some adjustments in terms of stitch placement and pattern reading. For example, when knitting in the round, the right side of the work is always facing out, so patterns that involve both knit and purl stitches need to be modified. Similarly, in crochet, the direction of the stitches may need to be adjusted to maintain the desired pattern.

Overall, working in the round is a versatile technique that allows for the creation of seamless and continuous projects in various crafts. It offers a clean and professional finish, making it a popular choice for many crafters.

Understanding crochet terminology is essential for anyone interested in learning how to crochet. Crochet terminology refers to the specific words and abbreviations used in crochet patterns and instructions. These terms are used to describe different stitches, techniques, and actions that are necessary to create various crochet projects.

One of the first things to understand about crochet terminology is the different types of stitches. Common stitches include the chain stitch (abbreviated as ch), single crochet (sc), double crochet (dc), and treble crochet (tr). Each stitch has its own abbreviation, which is used in patterns to indicate which stitch to use.

In addition to stitches, crochet terminology also includes terms for different techniques and actions. For example, the term turn is used to indicate that you should turn your work around to continue crocheting in the opposite direction. The term join is used to indicate that you should connect two pieces of crochet together, often using slip stitches.

Understanding crochet terminology is important because it allows you to follow crochet patterns accurately. Crochet patterns are written using a combination of words, abbreviations, and symbols. By understanding the terminology, you can decipher the instructions and create the desired project.

Crochet terminology can sometimes be confusing, especially for beginners. However, there are resources available to help you learn and understand the different terms. Crochet books, online tutorials, and crochet communities are all great sources of information and support.

Once you have a good understanding of crochet terminology, you will be able to read and interpret crochet patterns with ease. This opens up a world of possibilities for creating beautiful and intricate crochet projects. Whether you want to make blankets, scarves, hats, or even amigurumi toys, understanding crochet terminology is the first step towards success.

In conclusion, understanding crochet terminology is crucial for anyone interested in learning how to crochet. It allows you to follow crochet patterns accurately and create beautiful projects. While it may take some time and practice to become familiar with the different terms, the effort is well worth it. So, grab your crochet hook and yarn, and start exploring the wonderful world of crochet!

Single stitch patterns are a type of knitting or crochet pattern that involve using only one type of stitch throughout the entire project. These patterns are often simple and easy to follow, making them perfect for beginners or those looking for a quick and straightforward project.

One common example of a single stitch pattern is the garter stitch. This stitch is created by knitting every row, resulting in a fabric that has a bumpy texture on both sides. The garter stitch is often used for scarves, blankets, and other items where a thick and warm fabric is desired.

Another popular single stitch pattern is the stockinette stitch. This stitch is created by alternating between knitting one row and purling the next. The result is a smooth and flat fabric with a distinct V pattern on one side and a bumpy texture on the other. The stockinette stitch is commonly used for sweaters, hats, and other garments where a more polished and professional look is desired.

Single stitch patterns can also include more intricate designs, such as cables or lace. These patterns often involve manipulating the stitches in various ways to create unique textures and patterns. Cables, for example, are created by crossing stitches over each other, resulting in a twisted and raised design. Lace patterns, on the other hand, involve creating deliberate holes and spaces in the fabric, resulting in a delicate and airy look.

Overall, single stitch patterns offer a wide range of possibilities for knitters and crocheters. Whether you're a beginner looking to practice your skills or an experienced crafter looking for a quick and satisfying project, these patterns are a great choice. With their simplicity and versatility, single stitch patterns are sure to keep you engaged and inspired.

Cable stitch patterns are a popular and versatile knitting technique that adds texture and interest to any project. These patterns involve crossing stitches over each other to create intricate designs that resemble twisted cables. They can be used to create a wide range of items, from cozy sweaters and scarves to blankets and hats.

There are countless cable stitch patterns to choose from, each with its own unique look and level of difficulty. Some patterns feature simple, single cable twists, while others incorporate multiple cables and complex crossings. The possibilities are endless, allowing knitters to experiment and create their own personalized designs.

To create cable stitch patterns, you will need a cable needle, which is a short, double-pointed needle used to hold stitches temporarily while you work on other stitches. The cable needle is used to hold the stitches in front or back of your work, allowing you to cross them over each other and create the cable effect.

One of the most basic cable stitch patterns is the 2/2 Right Cross. This pattern involves crossing two stitches to the right over two other stitches. To work this pattern, you would slip the first two stitches onto a cable needle and hold them at the back of your work. Then, you would knit the next two stitches from the left-hand needle. Finally, you would knit the two stitches from the cable needle. This creates a neat and symmetrical cable twist.

Another popular cable stitch pattern is the Honeycomb Cable. This pattern creates a beautiful, textured design that resembles a honeycomb. It involves crossing stitches over each other in a specific pattern to create the honeycomb effect. This pattern requires a bit more attention and concentration, but the end result is well worth the effort.

Cable stitch patterns can be incorporated into a variety of knitting projects. They can be used as a focal point on a sweater or cardigan, or as a decorative border on a scarf or blanket. They can also be combined with other stitch patterns, such as ribbing or lace, to create unique and interesting designs.

When working with cable stitch patterns, it is important to keep track of your rows and stitches. It can be helpful to use stitch markers or a row counter to help you stay organized. Additionally, it is important to maintain an even tension while knitting, as this will ensure that your cables are neat and well-defined.

Tunisian crochet is a unique and versatile crochet technique that originated in Tunisia. It is also known as Afghan crochet or Tricot crochet. Unlike traditional crochet, Tunisian crochet uses a longer hook with a stopper on the end, similar to a knitting needle. This allows for the creation of a fabric that is thicker and denser than regular crochet.

The process of Tunisian crochet involves working with multiple loops on the hook at once. The first row is created by picking up loops from the foundation chain, and subsequent rows are worked by picking up loops from the previous row. This creates a fabric that has a distinct grid-like appearance, similar to knitting.

One of the key features of Tunisian crochet is the ability to create intricate and textured stitch patterns. The longer hook allows for the creation of longer stitches, such as the Tunisian simple stitch, Tunisian knit stitch, and Tunisian purl stitch. These stitches can be combined in various ways to create beautiful and unique designs.

Tunisian crochet is often used to create blankets, scarves, shawls, and other accessories. The dense fabric created by this technique provides warmth and durability, making it perfect for cozy winter projects. Additionally, the grid-like structure of Tunisian crochet makes it ideal for colorwork and intarsia, allowing for the creation of intricate patterns and designs.

While Tunisian crochet may seem intimidating at first, it is actually quite easy to learn. Many crochet enthusiasts find that it is a natural progression from traditional crochet, as it builds upon the basic crochet stitches. There are numerous resources available, including books, online tutorials, and classes, that can help beginners get started with Tunisian crochet.

In conclusion, Tunisian crochet is a fascinating and versatile crochet technique that allows for the creation of thick and textured fabrics. With its unique stitch patterns and ability to create intricate designs, it is a popular choice among crochet enthusiasts. Whether you are a beginner or an experienced crocheter, Tunisian crochet offers endless possibilities for creativity and exploration.

Understanding pattern construction is a crucial skill in various fields, including fashion design, architecture, and graphic design. It involves the ability to analyze and deconstruct existing patterns, as well as the knowledge and creativity to create new ones.

Pattern construction begins with the analysis of existing patterns. This involves examining the elements and principles of design used in the pattern, such as line, shape, color, and texture. By understanding how these elements are arranged and combined, one can gain insights into the overall structure and composition of the pattern.

Once the existing pattern has been analyzed, the next step is to deconstruct it. This involves breaking down the pattern into its individual components, such as motifs, repeats, and borders. By understanding how these components are organized and interconnected, one can gain a deeper understanding of the pattern's construction and potential variations.

After deconstructing the pattern, the next step is to create a new pattern. This requires a combination of knowledge and creativity. The knowledge comes from understanding the principles and techniques of pattern construction, such as symmetry, balance, and proportion. The creativity comes from the ability to think outside the box and come up with unique and innovative designs.

Creating a new pattern involves making decisions about various aspects, such as the overall layout, the choice of motifs, the arrangement of repeats, and the use of color and texture. These decisions are guided by the desired aesthetic, functionality, and context of the pattern. For example, a pattern for a fabric design may need to consider factors such as the type of fabric, the intended use of the fabric, and the target audience.

Pattern construction also requires attention to detail. It involves precision in measuring and marking, as well as accuracy in cutting and sewing. A small mistake in any of these steps can result in a flawed pattern.

Therefore, patience and meticulousness are essential qualities for successful pattern construction.

In conclusion, understanding pattern construction is a valuable skill that can be applied in various fields. It involves the ability to analyze and deconstruct existing patterns, as well as the knowledge and creativity to create new ones. It requires attention to detail and a combination of technical skills and artistic vision. By mastering pattern construction, one can unlock endless possibilities for creating visually appealing and functional designs.

Crochet accessories refer to a wide range of items that are made using the technique of crochet. Crochet is a method of creating fabric by interlocking loops of yarn or thread using a crochet hook. It is a versatile craft that allows for the creation of various accessories that can be both functional and decorative.

One of the most popular crochet accessories is the crochet hat. Crocheted hats come in different styles and designs, ranging from simple beanies to intricate slouchy hats. They can be made using different types of yarn, allowing for endless possibilities in terms of color and texture. Crochet hats are not only fashionable but also provide warmth and protection during colder seasons.

Another commonly made crochet accessory is the scarf. Crocheted scarves are known for their unique and intricate patterns. They can be made using different stitches and techniques, resulting in a wide variety of designs. Crochet scarves are not only stylish but also provide warmth and comfort, making them a popular choice during the winter months.

Crochet bags are also popular accessories that are both practical and stylish. Crocheted bags can be made in different sizes and shapes, allowing for customization based on individual preferences. They can be used for various purposes, such as carrying groceries, books, or personal belongings. Crochet bags are often adorned with decorative elements, such as buttons or tassels, adding a touch of uniqueness to each piece.

In addition to hats, scarves, and bags, crochet accessories also include items such as gloves, headbands, and shawls. Crocheted gloves provide warmth and protection for the hands, while headbands add a stylish touch to any outfit. Crocheted shawls are versatile accessories that can be worn in different ways, providing both warmth and elegance.

Crochet accessories are not only limited to clothing items but also extend to home decor. Crocheted blankets, pillows, and coasters are popular choices for adding a cozy and handmade touch to any living space. These items can be made using different crochet techniques, resulting in unique and personalized designs.

Overall, crochet accessories offer a wide range of options for individuals who enjoy the art of crochet. From hats and scarves to bags and home decor items, there is something for everyone. The versatility and creativity of crochet allow for endless possibilities in terms of design and customization. Whether for personal use or as gifts for loved ones, crochet accessories are a beautiful and practical way to showcase the artistry and craftsmanship of crochet.

Fixing common mistakes is an important aspect of any task or project. It helps to ensure that the final result is of high quality and meets the desired standards. Common mistakes can occur due to various reasons such as lack of attention to detail, miscommunication, or simply not having enough knowledge or experience in the particular area.

One common mistake that often occurs is overlooking small errors or typos. These may seem insignificant, but they can have a negative impact on the overall quality of the work. It is important to carefully review and proofread the content to catch any spelling or grammatical errors. This can be done by using spell-check tools or by having someone else review the work.

Another common mistake is not following the given instructions or guidelines. This can lead to a deviation from the intended outcome and may result in a subpar final product. It is crucial to thoroughly read and understand the instructions before starting the task. If there are any doubts or uncertainties, it is advisable to seek clarification from the relevant authority or supervisor.

Miscommunication is also a common source of mistakes. This can occur when there is a lack of clear and effective communication between team members or stakeholders. It is important to establish open lines of communication and ensure that everyone involved is on the same page. Regular meetings, progress updates, and clear documentation can help minimize miscommunication and prevent mistakes from occurring.

Furthermore, lack of knowledge or experience in a particular area can lead to mistakes. It is important to acknowledge one's limitations and seek assistance or guidance when needed. This can be done by consulting experts, conducting research, or undergoing training to acquire the necessary skills and knowledge.

In conclusion, fixing common mistakes is crucial for ensuring the quality and success of any task or project. By paying attention to detail, following instructions, improving communication, and acquiring the necessary knowledge and skills, one can effectively address and rectify common mistakes. This will ultimately lead to a higher quality final product and a more successful outcome.

One way to enhance your crochet skills and connect with fellow crochet enthusiasts is by joining crochet communities. These communities provide a platform for individuals to share their love for crochet, exchange ideas, and learn from one another.

When you join a crochet community, you gain access to a wealth of knowledge and expertise. Members often share their patterns, tips, and tricks, allowing you to expand your crochet repertoire. Whether you're a beginner or an experienced crocheter, there is always something new to learn and discover within these communities.

Additionally, being part of a crochet community offers a sense of belonging and camaraderie. You can connect with like-minded individuals who share your passion for crochet, creating a supportive network of fellow crafters. This can be particularly beneficial if you don't have many crochet enthusiasts in your immediate social circle. Through online forums, social media groups, or local crochet meetups, you can find a community that suits your preferences and engage in meaningful discussions about your favorite craft.

Furthermore, joining crochet communities opens up opportunities for collaboration and inspiration. You can participate in crochet-alongs, where members work on the same project simultaneously, sharing their progress and offering guidance along the way. This collaborative environment fosters creativity and encourages you to step out of your comfort zone, trying new techniques and experimenting with different yarns and patterns.

In addition to the educational and social benefits, crochet communities often organize events, workshops, and competitions. These events provide opportunities to showcase your skills, learn from experts in the field, and even win prizes. Participating in such activities can boost your confidence as a crocheter and motivate you to continue honing your craft.

Lastly, joining crochet communities can also lead to potential business opportunities. If you aspire to turn your crochet hobby into a small business, these communities can serve as a valuable platform to promote and sell your handmade creations. You can gain exposure to a wider audience, receive feedback on your products, and even collaborate with other members on joint ventures.

In conclusion, joining crochet communities offers numerous benefits, including access to valuable knowledge, a sense of belonging, collaboration opportunities, inspiration, and potential business prospects. So, if you're passionate about crochet and want to take your skills to the next level, consider becoming part of a crochet community.

Crocheting is not just a hobby; it is a journey of self-discovery and creative exploration. As you sit down with your crochet hook and yarn, you embark on a path that leads to personal growth and artistic expression. Looking back on this journey, you realize how far you have come and how much you have learned.

When you first picked up a crochet hook, you were filled with excitement and curiosity. The simple act of creating loops with yarn seemed like magic, and you were eager to unravel the mysteries of this craft. You started with basic stitches, clumsily working your way through the patterns, but with each stitch, you gained confidence and skill.

As time went on, you began to experiment with different yarns and colors, discovering the endless possibilities that crochet offered. You found joy in selecting the perfect yarn for each project, carefully considering its texture, weight, and color. The yarn became your paintbrush, and the crochet hook your tool for shaping and molding your creations.

With each completed project, you felt a sense of accomplishment and pride. Whether it was a cozy blanket, a delicate doily, or a trendy hat, each piece represented hours of dedication and love. You learned to appreciate the value of patience and perseverance, as some projects required countless hours of stitching and unraveling before reaching perfection.

But crochet is not just about the finished product; it is about the process itself. As you sat down to crochet, you found solace and tranquility in the rhythmic motion of your hands. The repetitive nature of the stitches became a form of meditation, allowing you to escape the stresses of daily life and find inner peace.

As your skills grew, so did your creativity. You began to experiment with different stitch patterns, combining them in unique and unexpected ways. You started designing your own patterns, bringing your imagination to life through yarn and hook. Each new project became an opportunity to push your boundaries and explore new techniques.

But crochet is not just about the individual projects; it is about the connections you make along the way. You joined crochet groups and attended workshops, surrounded by fellow enthusiasts who shared your passion. Through these interactions, you discovered a community of like-minded individuals who understood the joy and satisfaction that crochet brings.

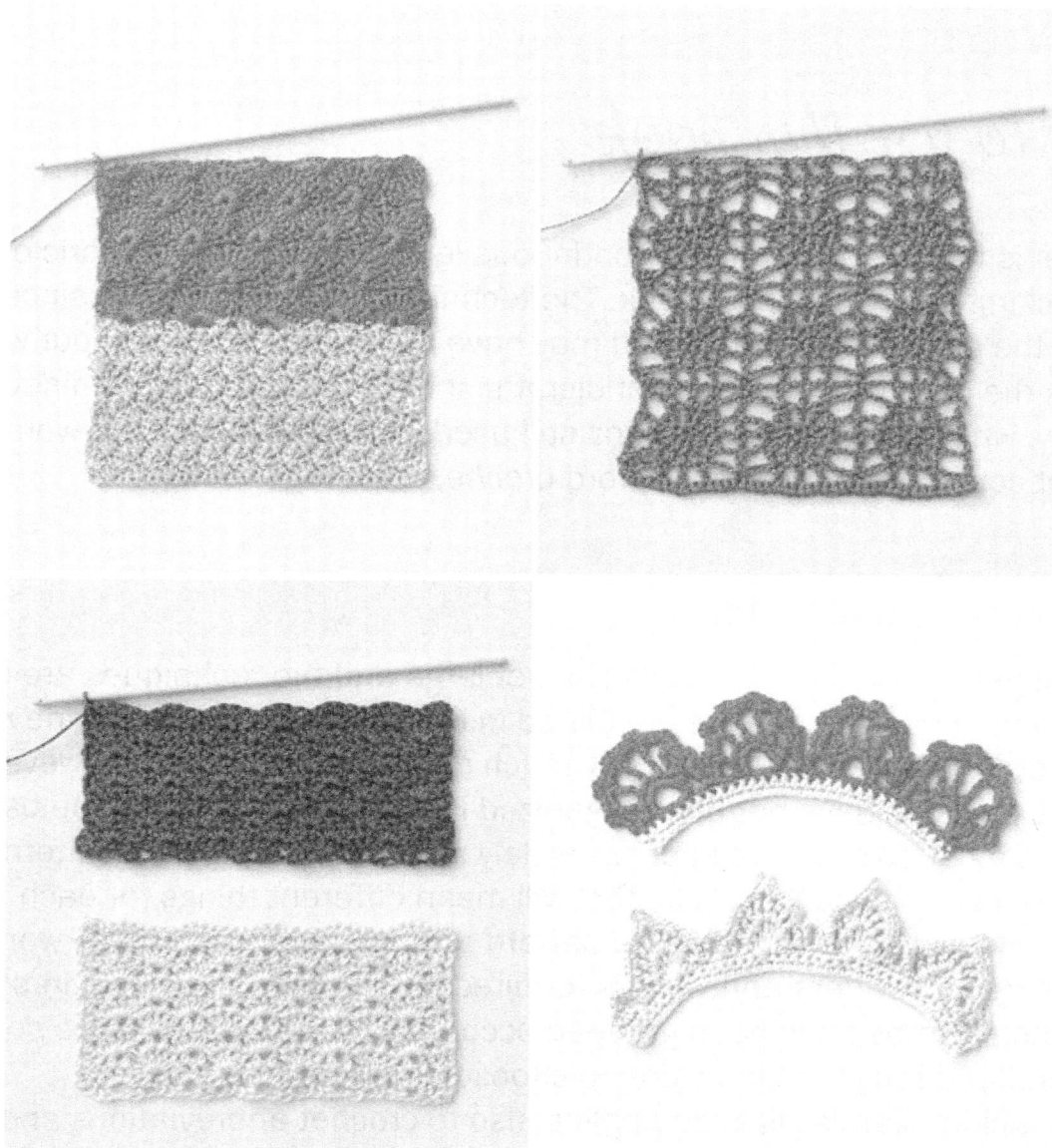

Swatches (clockwise from top left): Textured 15 and 16, Lace 7, Edging 11 and 12, and Fan 1 and 2

How to use this book

Crochet is formed by working a continuous length of yarn into a fabric of interlocking stitches using a hook. The technique has been known since the end of the eighteenth century and may have developed from tambour work. As was the case with so many handicrafts, it flourished during the nineteenth century, when many of the patterns still used were developed. The word crochet comes from the French word *croche*, meaning "hook."

Terms and symbols

The range of basic crochet stitches is not large and the techniques are easy to master. These stitches are combined in many ways to create a wide range of patterns. Crochet developed very much as a household craft, however, and the patterns have not been organized in any way. Apart from the basic stitches, most do not have specific, widely recognized names. Even terms such as "fan," "picot," and "cluster" will mean different things for each pattern, so always read the whole pattern through before you begin work and make sure you understand what is required in that particular case. In this book the patterns have been grouped according to their appearance so that you can flip through each section to choose a pattern.

This lack of standardization applies also to crochet abbreviations and symbols. A list of common abbreviations, including all those used in this book, is given here. The symbols used in the stitch charts are shown here. Charts were not traditionally used for crochet, but they are becoming more common; and they are included in this book for more complicated patterns.

Swatches

Each pattern in the book has been crocheted, and a full-size photograph is included to give an idea of its appearance. This will, however, vary slightly, depending on the yarn and size of hook used and how tightly you work.

These swatches were worked using pearl cotton and a size C/2 (2.5) hook.

Many swatches begin with a foundation row of single crochet to provide a neat edge. This row is not included in the instructions or charts, as it is not part of the pattern.

The swatches show the result for a right-handed crocheter (if you are left-handed, see here).

Starting to crochet

This chapter covers the basic reference material you need to start crocheting: information on yarns and hooks, and lists of the terms, abbreviations, and symbols used in crochet patterns.

Yarns and hooks

In order to crochet you need two things: yarn and a hook. By choosing different types and thicknesses of yarn and different sizes of hooks you can achieve a wide range of effects. For example, a thin yarn and large hook will give a lacy look while a thicker yarn and smaller hook will result in a firmer, stiffer fabric.

Yarns

Crochet can be worked using a wide variety of materials, ranging from the usual cotton and wool yarns to novelty items used for more unusual pieces. As long as a material is flexible enough to be manipulated by the hook and twisted into the stitch shapes, it can be used for crochet.

If your chosen yarn or thread comes in skeins, however, you will need to wind it into a ball before you start crocheting.

Following are just some of the materials that can be used for crochet work.

Crochet cotton is a fine, smooth yarn that has been mercerized (treated with alkali to improve strength and luster). It comes in a wide range of thicknesses, from 60 (very fine) to 5 (the thickest). It has traditionally been used for crochet work, including table runners and doilies, throws, garments, and edgings for embroidery.

Pearl cotton, or perle cotton, is a softer, less tightly twisted thread usually sold for embroidery. It comes in a variety of thicknesses (3, 5, 8, and 12, with 3 the thickest). The swatches in this book were made using pearl cotton.

Knitting yarns, including cotton, wool, silk, and synthetics, are also often used for crochet work. Firmly spun ones are easier to use and give a neater finish. However, softer, more loosely spun yarns can produce beautiful results if you are willing to persevere. Wool is very popular for crochet work, especially for garments and rugs.

Metallic embroidery threads can be used alone or incorporated into other work.

Woven fabric, cut into strips about 1 inch (2.5 cm) wide and folded so the edges are hidden, can be used with a large hook. Fine cotton fabric and single crochet will give the best results. Leather can also be cut into strips for crocheting.

String and raffia can be used for crocheting items such as handbags.

Soft wire can also be used to create sculptural effects and jewelry.

Hooks

Crochet hooks come in a range of materials. The small ones used with fine yarns are generally metal (steel or coated aluminum), but hooks can also be plastic, bamboo, or wood. Which type you use is a matter of personal preference.

Always use hooks that are in good condition. Rusty or tarnished steel hooks may stain the yarn, while nicks in plastic or wooden ones will catch on the yarn and damage it.

There are three sizing systems used for crochet hooks: the American system, the metric system developed in Europe, the Imperial system developed in the UK.

The tables at right are a guide to the most common sizes (larger and smaller hooks are also available). The equivalencies shown are not exact, and, indeed, different brands can also vary slightly in size.

Experiment to determine the hook to use to get the effect you want. You may also need to use a slightly smaller or larger hook than that specified in a pattern to achieve the correct gauge.

Hook sizes
(plastic, wood and bamboo, and aluminum)

American	Metric (mm)	Imperial
B/1	2.25	14
C/2	2.75	12
D/3	3.25	10
E/4	3.5	9
F/5	3.75	8
G/6	4.5	7
H/8	5.0	6
I/9	5.5	5
J/10	6.0	4
K/10½	6.5	3
*	7.0	2
*	7.5	1
L/11	8.0	0

Steel hook sizes

American	Metric (mm)	Imperial

14	0.6	6
13	0.75	5
12	1	4
10	1.25	3
8	1.5	2½
6	1.75	2
4	2	1
2	2.25	0
1	2.5	00
0	3	000

*no U.S. equivalent

International symbols

As well as standard text, crochet patterns can also be shown in symbols. Some crocheters prefer to use these as a guide when working a pattern, but read the written instructions as well to be sure you understand exactly what is required to work the crochet pattern.

Also check the list of symbols in the book you are using, because despite being called "international" symbols, the symbols have not been standardized and different books may use slightly different symbols. Even books published in the same country will use different symbols. The chart shows the symbols that are used throughout this book.

Symbols used in this book

Specific instructions for making specialty stitches are included in individual stitch patterns.

Symbol Stitch or instruction

Symbol	Stitch or instruction
⌒	chain (ch)
·	slip stitch (Sl st)
+	single crochet (sc)
‡	extended single crochet (Esc)
T	half double crochet (hdc)
†	double crochet (dc)
‡	treble (tr)
‡	double treble (dtr)
⌇	front post single crochet (FPsc)
⌇	front post double crochet (FPdc)

(symbol)	back post double crochet (BPdc)
(symbol)	Knot stitch (KS)
(symbol)	locking stitch (lks)
(symbol)	bullion stitch (bullion st)
(symbol)	broomstick loop stitch (ls)
(symbol)	extended loop stitch (Els)
(symbol)	bouclé loop stitch (bls)
(symbol)	(5 double crochet) popcorn (pc)
(symbol)	(4 half double crochet) puff
(symbol)	(5 double crochet) bobble
(symbol)	finger (or yarn) loop
(symbol)	(single crochet) spike
(symbol)	stitch worked in front loop only (added below stitch symbol)
(symbol)	stitch worked in back loop only (added below stitch symbol)
→	direction of next row
×	do not turn work
▶	start
▪	fasten off
▷	add new yarn

Abbreviations

The following abbreviations are commonly used in crochet patterns.

alt	alternate
beg	begin/beginning
BLO	back loop only
bls	bouclé loop stitch
BPdc	back post double crochet
BPsc	back post single crochet
C	crossed stitch
CC	contrasting color
Cdc	crossed double crochet
ch	chain/chain stitch
ch-sp	chain-space
CL	cluster
cont	continue
dc	double crochet
dc2tog	double crochet two together
dec	decrease/decreasing
dsc	double single crochet
dtr	double treble
ea	each
Els	extended loop stitch
Esc	extended single crochet
est	established
FLO	front loop only
FPdc	front post double crochet
FPsc	front post single crochet
FPtr	front post treble
hdc	half double crochet

inc	increase
KS	Knot stitch
lks	locking stitch
lp	loop
ls	loop stitch
MC	main color
och	overlaid chain
pat st	pattern stitch
pc	popcorn
q tr	quadruple treble
rem	remain/remaining
rev dc	reverse double crochet
rev sc	reverse single crochet
rf	relief stitch
rnd(s)	round(s)
RS	right side
sc	single crochet
sc2tog	single crochet two together
Sl st	slip stitch
sp(s)	space(s)
st(s)	stitch(es)
tch	turning chain
Tks	Tunisian knit stitch
tog	together
Tps	Tunisian purl stitch
tr	treble
trtr	treble (or triple) treble (also ttr)
tr2tog	treble two together
Tss	Tunisian simple stitch
WS	wrong side
yo	yarn over hook (also yoh)

Joined symbols

Where a number of symbols are joined at the top, this indicates that the stitches are worked as a cluster, and stitches are subtracted.

Where they are joined at the base, they are all worked into the same space, as for fans and shells, and stitches are added.

Cluster

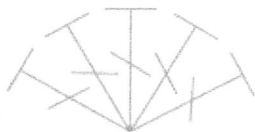

Stitches worked into same space

Crochet term usage

Although many of the same terms are used for crochet stitches throughout the English-speaking world, they mean different things depending on whether they are used in American or English (Australian, Canadian) patterns. If you are using an English pattern, remember to convert the stitches or your piece will be bigger and you will have difficulty following the instructions.

American	English	Symbol
ch (chain)	ch (chain)	◯
Sl st (slip stitch)	sl st (slip stitch)	•
sc (single crochet)	dc (double crochet)	+
hdc (half double crochet)	htr (half treble)	
dc (double crochet)	tr (treble)	
tr (treble)	dtr (double treble)	

dtr (double treble)   ttr (triple treble)

Following a pattern

A number of symbols and other abbreviations are used to indicate that you should repeat the following stitches. For example, the pattern might read *dc in the next 3 sts, ch 6, rep from *

5 times This means you should repeat the three double crochets and six chain stitches five times (that is, work them six times in all, once and then another five times). Other symbols such as *, ★, and † can be used in the same way. In other patterns the material to be repeated may be enclosed in parentheses: (dc in next 3 st, ch 4) 4 times or brackets: [dc in next 3 st, ch 4] 4 times Parentheses or brackets can also be used to indicate that a number of stitches are worked into one stitch.

Tip When you are making a large piece of crochet, it can be frustrating to come to the end of the first row and find that you have miscounted the number of chains in the foundation row. If you leave a long yarn end when you make the initial slip knot, you can undo the knot and work enough chains to complete the pattern, before completing the first row.

For example: (tr, ch 1, tr) in ch-sp or:

[tr, ch 1, tr] in ch-sp means that the treble, chain stitch, and treble are all worked in the same chain-space.

Essential crochet facts

1 The chain stitch on the hook is never counted as a stitch.

2 Read the pattern through before starting in order to make sure you understand all the instructions.

3 Always insert the hook from front to back unless the instructions say otherwise.

4 Always insert the hook under the top two loops of a stitch, unless you're working on the first row or the pattern says otherwise.

5 There should always be one loop left on the hook when a stitch or pattern is completed unless the instructions say otherwise.

6 Turning chains (the chain stitches at the end of a row) should make a stitch the same height as the other stitches in that row or the edge of the piece may not lie flat. Experiment and make your turning chains tighter or looser as needed.

7 Turning chains should be worked into as instructed.

Crochet techniques

This chapter presents the various techniques used in crochet work. Along with the basic stitches and formations in the following chapter, they form the basis of all crochet.

Holding the yarn (two alternatives for method 1)

When crocheting it is important to hold the yarn and hook correctly so that the work proceeds smoothly.

The hook is held between the thumb and index finger either like a pen or like a knife (see diagrams). It is held in the right hand (or left hand if you are left-handed).

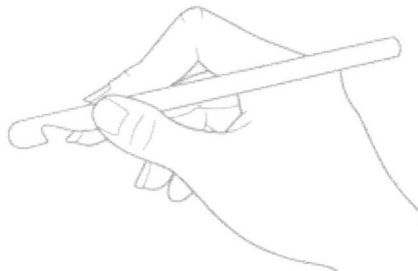

Holding the hook

The yarn is held in the free hand. Again, you have a choice of methods to control the yarn while it feeds smoothly through your fingers. Choose the one that feels most comfortable.

Method 1 Place the yarn over your index finger and around the other fingers in either way shown above. You will then be able to hold the crochet work between the thumb and middle finger (diagram A).

Method 2 Place the yarn over your middle finger, under the ring finger, and once around your little finger. You will then hold the crochet work between the thumb and index finger (diagram B).

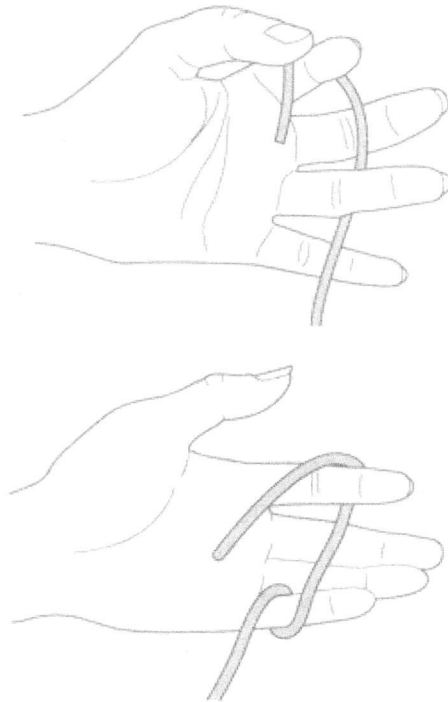

Holding the hook and yarn (two alternatives for method 1)

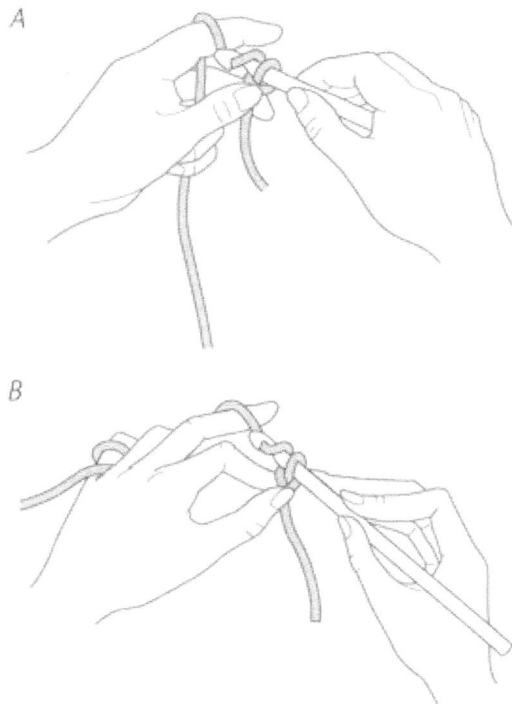

A

B

Holding the yarn and crochet work (methods 1 and 2)

You are now ready to begin crocheting. All crochet begins with a row of chain stitches. Follow these instructions to make the required number of chain stitches.

Working in rows

The basic stitches may be worked in rows. Usually the work is turned at the end of the row so that you are always working from right to left.

When you are working in rows, chain stitches are used to elevate the yarn and hook to the next row. These are called turning chains, and the last turning chain forms the first stitch of the new row. Once the turning chains have been worked, the piece is turned around and the new row is worked back in the opposite way to the preceding row. At the end of that row again work turning chains and turn the work, remembering to work into the original turning chain at the end of the row (unless the pattern says otherwise). Working into the turning chain can be difficult, so it is a good idea to make the final turning chain a little looser than the other stitches.

three turning chains

When working in double crochet, make three turning chains at the end of each row before turning the work.

three turning chains

When working in double crochet, make three turning chains at the end of each row before turning the work.

Number of turning chains required

Stitch	Chains
Single crochet	1
Extended single crochet	2
Half double crochet	2
Double crochet	3
Treble crochet	4

Double treble crochet	5
Treble treble crochet	6

Inserting the hook

To make stitches the crochet hook may be inserted into a stitch of the previous row or into the space between stitches (called the chain-space; see diagram). Work into the stitch unless the pattern instructs you to work into the chain-space. The hook is usually inserted under both loops of the stitch but is sometimes inserted under only one. Inserting under only one loop creates a ridge on the fabric. If you insert the hook under only the front loop, a ridge forms on the back of the work. If you insert the hook under only the back loop, a ridge forms on the front (see diagrams). Ridges can be used to create patterns in the work.

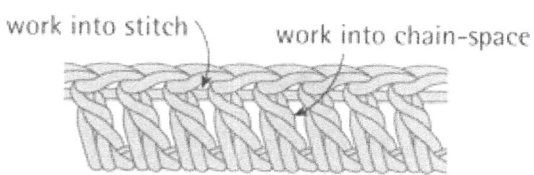

work into stitch   work into chain-space

Working into the stitch or chain-space

In crochet, the post is the vertical part of the stitch; the bar is the horizontal part. Raised, or post, stitches are made by inserting the hook around the leg, or post, of the stitch below. To make spike stitches the hook is inserted one or more rows below, either directly below the stitch to be worked or to one side to make an angled stitch (see diagram).

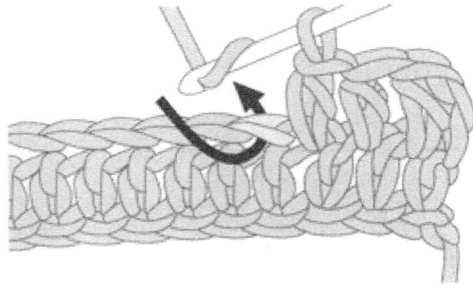

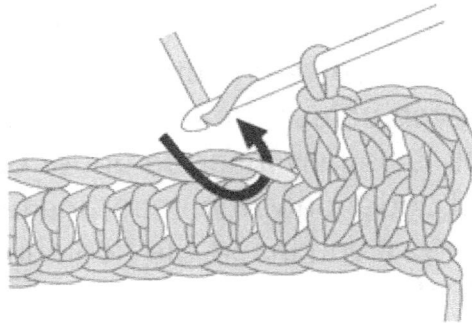

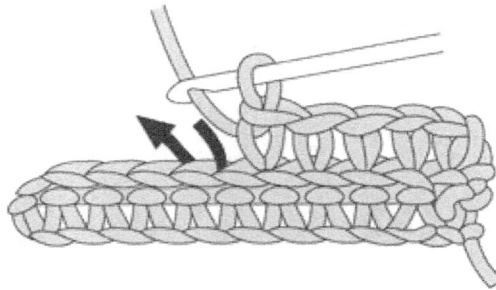

Working under both loops (top), under the front loop (center), and under the back loop (bottom)

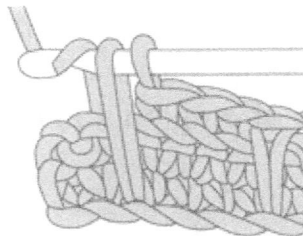

Single crochet spike stitch

Working in rounds

Crochet can also be worked in rounds. To do this you begin with a ring of chain stitches and always work in the same direction: the work is not turned when you work in rounds. To make a flat piece of crochet such as a medallion, you increase the number of stitches in each round. If you work rounds without increasing the number of stitches, you will produce a tube.

1 Make a slip knot and row of chain stitches as usual. When the required number of chain stitches has been made, join the last one to the first with a slip stitch.

2 Work chain stitches to create the height needed for the next round and then hook to the next round in the same way as when working rows. (The same numbers of chain stitches are required; see chart.)

3 Work stitches into the chains of the ring, increasing as instructed. Close the ring by making a slip stitch into the last chain of the round.

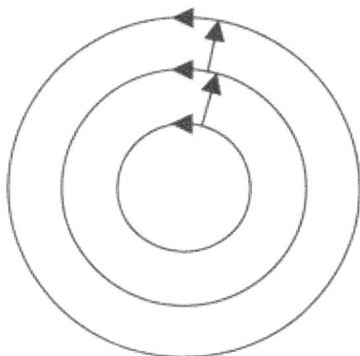

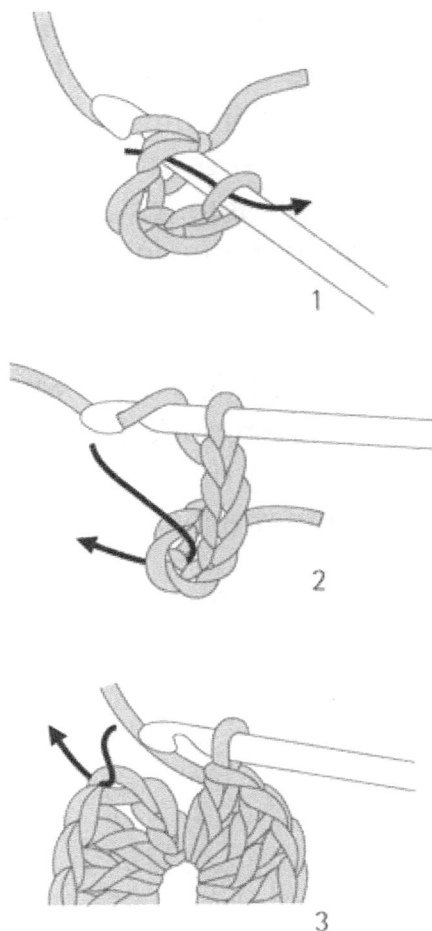

Working in rounds

Tip Be sure you have the correct number of chain stitches for the foundation row before you continue working. Count them as you make them and then count them again to double check. Remember, do not include the slip knot or the loop on the hook in your count.

Working a closed center

When working a shape with a closed center, begin by wrapping the yarn one or more times around your left index finger (see diagram 1). Work the first stitch into this loop (see diagram 2). Gently slip the loop off your finger and work the rest of the round; then pull on the yarn tail to tighten the center (see diagram 3).

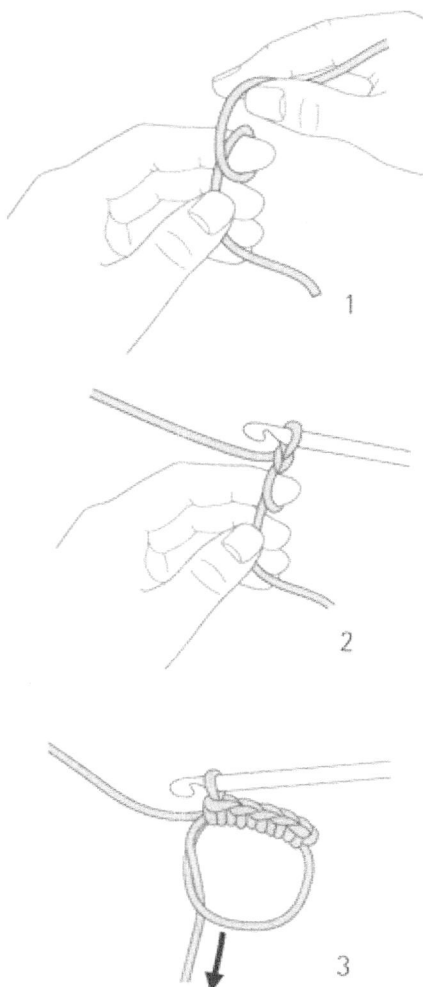

Making a yarn, or finger, loop for a motif with a closed center

Tubular crochet

Almost any crochet pattern can be adapted to tubular crochet, which has the advantage of doing away with bulky seams. It can be used for hats, handbags, skirts, napkin rings, and even bolsters. Tubular crochet is worked in the same way as working in rounds, but without changing the number of stitches, although the tube can, of course, be shaped. For example, a hat may be worked partly as a tube and then the number of stitches decreased to close the top.

To work tubular crochet, make the required number of chain stitches and form a ring with a slip stitch into the first chain stitch. Then work chains and rounds to the required length.

Fastening off

Once the last stitch of the work is completed, work one chain stitch and cut the yarn, leaving at least 4 inches (10 cm). Pull the yarn through the loop, tightening it carefully.

When working in rounds, you need to hide the yarn. To do this, insert the hook through the last slip stitch from back to front and pull the yarn through to the back of the work.

Increasing and decreasing

Crochet pieces are shaped by increasing or decreasing the number of stitches at various points in the rows. Stitches are increased by working two or more stitches into the same stitch or chain-space. The multiple stitches may be worked at the end of a row or anywhere along it. There are several ways to decrease the number of stitches:

• Work into two or more stitches together, making a cluster (a group of stitches joined into one stitch at the top).
• Work slip stitches into the stitches you have to decrease or at the end of the row.
• Skip the stitches you have to decrease.

Checking gauge

The gauge of a piece refers to how many stitches and rows you work in a given square. It is determined by the thickness of the yarn, the size of the hook, and how tightly you work the stitches. When the piece you are working needs to be a particular size, it is important to work a gauge swatch before you begin. If necessary, you can then adjust the size of the stitches, usually by changing the size of the hook. Keep making gauge swatches until you get the correct gauge. When measuring for gauge, lay the piece flat and iron or block as recommended for the particular yarn. Place straight pins in the work 4 inches (10 cm) apart. Count the number of stitches between the pins and then repeat the process to count the rows (see photos).

Counting the stitches to determine the stitch gauge

Counting the rows to determine the row gauge

Joining yarn

When you need to begin a new ball of yarn, hold the end of the ball to one side and place the start of the new ball beside it. Thread the new yarn through your fingers and continue crocheting. This can be done at any point in the stitch, but it is usual to do so just before the final yarn over hook (yo or yoh). This means the new yarn is drawn through the two loops of old yarn, leaving the loop of new yarn on the hook (see diagrams). Once the piece is completed, the yarn tails can be fastened off or tied together on the wrong side of the work. The same method can be used to change yarns when working in several colors.

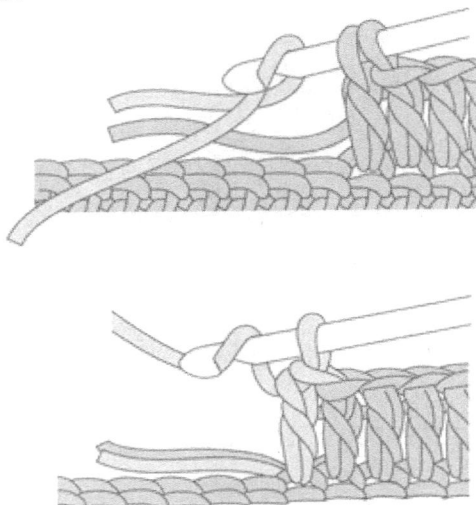

Joining new yarn

Working in several colors

Working in several colors is simple in crochet, although for a smooth result you need to use the same thickness of yarn throughout. Remember, too, that if you are changing colors at the end of a row, the turning chains should match the color of the new row.

There are two main methods used for changing colors. Often the pattern will specify which to use.

Large blocks of color

When you are working in large blocks of color, yarns can be changed as described in "Joining yarn" at left. Cut the old yarn, leaving a tail of 4–6 inches (10–15 cm), and work both tails into the back of the work.

Changing color frequently

When colors change frequently, however, it is easier and neater to carry the unused yarns over rather than fasten them off and start new ones each time. To do this you need to work them into the crochet. Don't leave them loose on the back of the work or they will catch and pull, ruining the evenness of the work.

To carry over yarns, have the right side of the work facing you. Bring the unused yarn to the back, insert the hook into the stitch, and bring the unused yarn over the hook. Bring the working yarn over the hook and complete the stitch as usual. This encloses the unused yarn in the stitch, thus hiding it. Continue working in this way, changing yarns back and forth as required.

This method can be used with any number of unused yarns, but be careful to keep them on the wrong side of the work. The yarns will become tangled as they cross over each other, so work slowly and take time to disentangle them as you go.

A blanket of granny squares (Medallion 2)

Combining yarns

When you are choosing yarns for multicolored work, you need to bear in mind the same considerations as for any work using more than one yarn. Different textures and thicknesses can result in uneven work, so use the same type and thickness of yarn throughout unless you want a textured result.

Using several colors, even of the same yarn, may also affect your gauge, especially if you are carrying unused yarns over. If you are combining patterned and plain pieces in the same work, you need to make allowances for this, perhaps by altering the size of the hook used.

Joining techniques

There are a number of different methods for joining together crocheted motifs such as medallions and other shapes. Whichever you use, in order to obtain a neat result it is essential to position the motifs carefully so that the pattern matches across the join. Check, too, that each motif is right side up.

The motifs can then be joined with sewing or crochet stitches. The best method in each case is usually specified in the pattern, and crocheted joins may sometimes be incorporated into it.

Sewing stitches

Motifs can be joined using a tapestry needle and whipstitches (see diagram at top). To get a neat look, use the same yarn as you used for the crochet.

Crochet stitches

Crochet stitches can be worked along the join or used at appropriate points.

If shapes are worked individually and then joined, a common method is to use a row of single crochet (see diagram at center). Decorative joins can also be used, such as a series of simple chain arches or zigzags (see diagram at bottom). They become part of the overall pattern of the piece.

When shapes are worked in rows and joined together during the crocheting process, slip stitches can be used where appropriate. For a looser effect, single crochet stitches can be used instead. If picots are to be joined, work half the number of chain stitches and then a slip stitch into the corresponding picot on the existing shape before completing the picot.

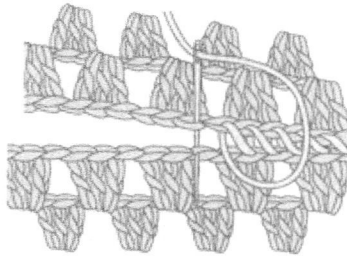

Whipstitch

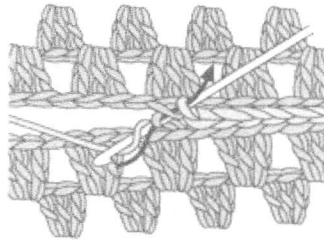

Single crochet

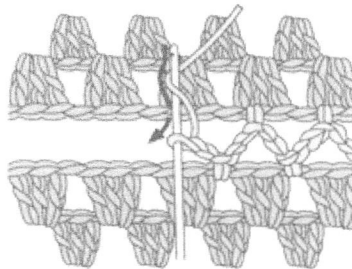

Chain arches

Joining crocheted motifs

Textural effects

In addition to the textured effects that are created by some crochet patterns themselves, texture can be added to crocheted pieces by the addition of beads, ribbons, and so on.

Adding beads

Beads can be threaded onto the yarn and incorporated so that they sit in the spaces of a stitch pattern. To pull a bead through into the stitch, remove the spaces of a stitch pattern. To pull a bead through into the stitch, remove the hook from the yarn and insert it through the bead and into the loop at the end of the crochet. Pull the loop through the bead. If the hook is too large to fit through the bead, change to a smaller hook just to pull the loop through the bead. Push the bead against the previous stitch so that you can maintain an even tension in the work.

It will be easier to thread very small beads if you dab the end of the yarn with nail polish.

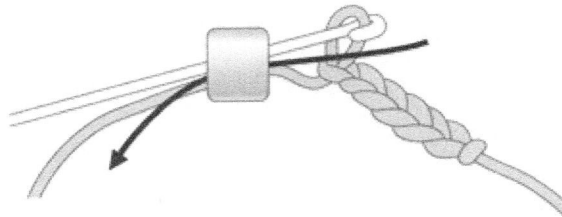

Beads can be used to add texture and variety to crochet work.

Threading a bead

Adding ribbons

Most crochet fabric is loose enough so that ribbons can be woven through to provide contrasting texture or color. Secure the ends of the ribbon on the edge of the crocheted piece or in the seams with a few stitches using sewing thread.

Ribbons can also be used to join crocheted pieces. There are two methods:

- One or two lengths of ribbon can be threaded through the two crocheted pieces in a zigzag fashion. If two pieces are used, they can be tied in a bow or decorative knot at either end.
- A number of short lengths of ribbon can be used. Each is threaded from one crocheted piece to the other and tied in a bow or knot.

Whichever method is used, make sure the ribbon is not pulled too tight or it will distort the crocheted pattern.

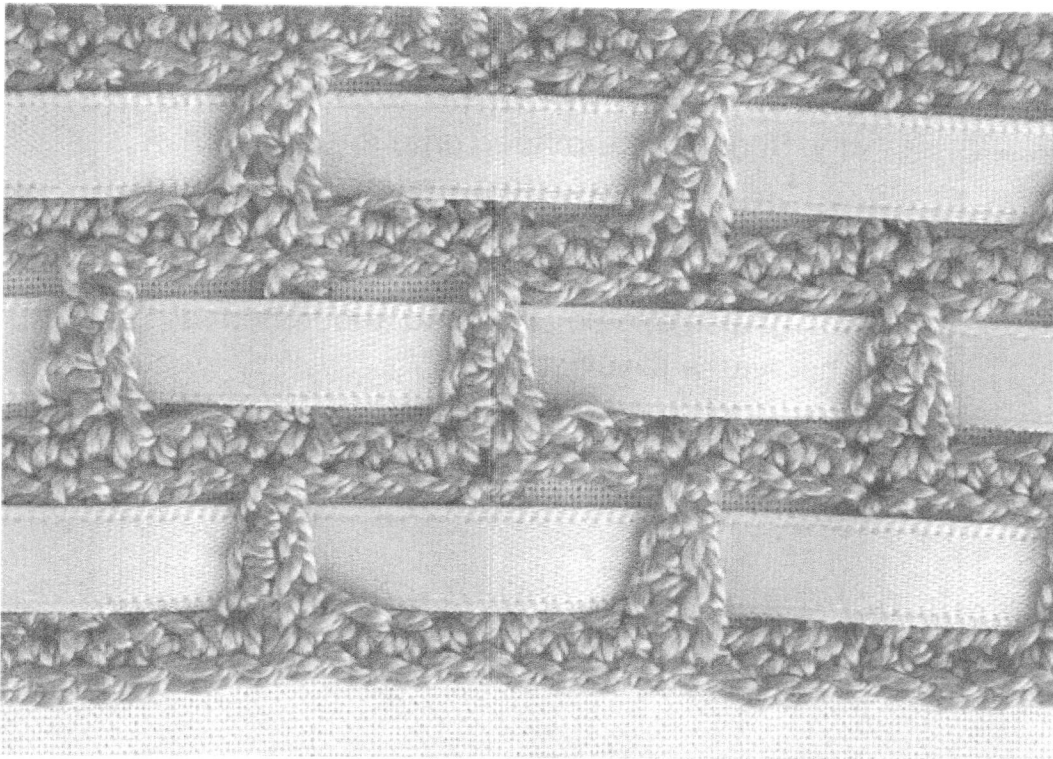

Weaving ribbon through an open pattern gives a neat and decorative result. Here, narrow satin ribbon is woven over and under the posts in Trellis 3 *pattern.*

Crochet jewelry

Crochet techniques can be used with beads to produce beautiful and unusual jewelry items.

Crochet jewelry was popular during the 1920s, when flappers wore long, beaded ropes. The ropes were worn looped around the neck and tied in front, often with beaded tassels on the end. To make these ropes, a large number of seed beads were threaded onto a ball of silk or pearl cotton. Slip stitches or single crochet was used to make a very long, very narrow tube (see "Tubular crochet"), with a bead slipped into place as each stitch was completed. This technique is again popular for beaded jewelry.

Very fine, flexible wire is also used for crochet jewelry. Beads are threaded onto the fine wire. A row of chain stitches is then worked, with a bead positioned between each stitch or after every second or third stitch. Multiple strands of beaded chains can be produced and fastened together with a jewelry clasp.

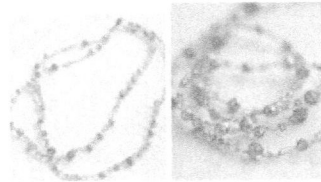

Making a buttonhole

If you are making an item that will be fastened with buttons, you need to work buttonholes into the crocheted fabric.

The easiest way to make a horizontal buttonhole is to substitute chain stitches for the pattern stitches at the appropriate place. The stitches of the next row can then be worked into the chain stitches without disrupting the pattern. The number of chain stitches used depends on

The number of chain stitches used depends on the size of the button.

For a vertical buttonhole, work across the pattern until the position for the buttonhole is reached and then work back and forth until the hole is the required height, finishing at the inner (hole) edge. Work slip stitches down the edge to the last complete row. Work back and forth across the unworked stitches, finishing on the outside edge, and then work complete rows.

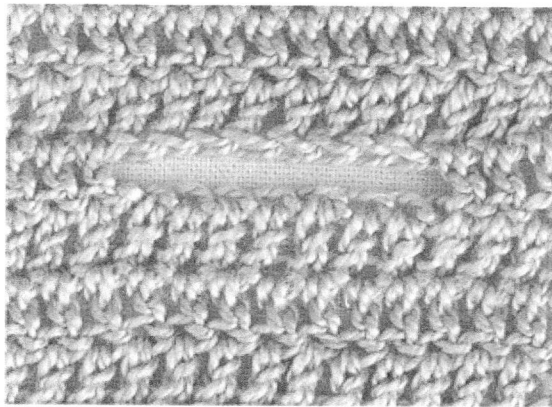

Assembling crochet pieces

Clothing and other shaped items may be made in several pieces that are then joined together. As when joining crocheted motifs, position the pieces carefully so that patterns match across the join. There are a number of different methods that can be used.

Crocheted seams

Work with the same hook and yarn used for making the pieces and join the edges together with a row of slip stitches. If you want the seam to be on the wrong side, work with the right sides of the pieces together. Work consistently (e.g., into every second stitch or every third) and into the same number of stitches along both edges so that the seam is flat. Do not pull the stitches too tight or the seam will pucker. Single crochet seams may be worked in the same way.

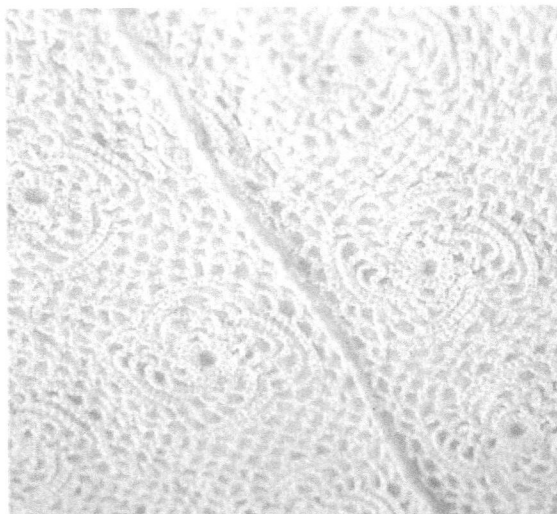

A single crochet seam

Sewn seams

A tapestry needle and yarn that matches the crochet can be used to sew edges together. A row of backstitch just below the edge chains will give a strong seam for garments, handbags, and similar items.

For a flat seam that does not create a ridge, place the edges together and stitch back and forth as shown in this diagram.
To avoid puckering, do not pull too tightly. This is the best way to join delicate pieces.

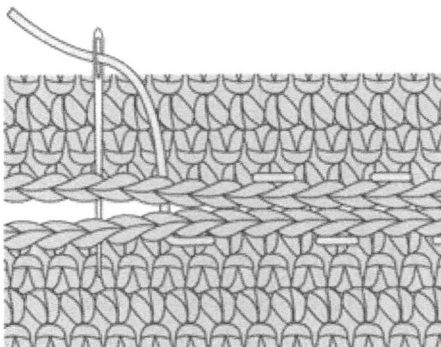

A flat seam

Attaching edgings

Crocheted edgings can be worked directly onto crocheted fabric or, if separate, can be attached with a row of single crochet.

The best method of attaching crocheted edgings to woven fabric is to prepare the fabric by hem-stitching. To hem-stitch, take a threaded needle under four or five threads of crocheted fabric and encircle the group of threads, then return the needle to the starting point, pulling the threads together firmly. Repeat with the next group of threads, creating actual holes on either side of the pulled groups of threads (see diagram). Make the holes large enough for the crochet hook to fit through easily. The edging can then be worked directly onto the fabric.

A wing needle can be used on most sewing machines to make the holes, but hem-stitching gives a better result. If the edging has already been made, hand stitch it to the fabric, as machine stitching will distort it.

Edgings for towels and other utilitarian items should be washed to allow for shrinkage before they are attached.

A crochet fringe

To make a crochet fringe, cut a piece of thick cardboard to the same width as the desired fringe. Work one row of single crochet. Work two more rows of single crochet, this time taking the yarn up over the cardboard and down behind it before working each stitch.

Caring for crochet items

Because most crochet is rather loose in texture, items need to be treated carefully during cleaning. Always follow the instructions on the yarn wrapper, which will tell you whether the yarn is dye-fast and how items made from it can be cleaned.

Washing

If you are uncertain about how a crocheted item should be cleaned, hand washing in warm, soapy water is the best method to use; but check first for color fastness. Crochet cottons are generally fast-dyed. If desired, items made from crochet cotton can be starched to add extra body. Follow the instructions on the starch container. Spray starches are often a good choice.

Some metallic threads and wires should not be washed or dry-cleaned (always check the yarn label). Use a soft brush to clean these pieces.

Drying

Most items should be air-dried flat in the shade to prevent stretching and color fading. Lay them on a clean, flat surface; make sure they are shaped correctly with, for example, scallops all the same size. Some items may need to be blocked (pinned into shape) so that they retain their shape. In that case, lay them on a board that has been covered with several clean towels and use straight pins at regular intervals around the edges. Make sure the pins are not rusty or they will stain the work. Then let the piece air-dry.

Ironing

Iron the piece while it is still damp. Cover it with several clean dish towels and iron very lightly, allowing the steam to remove any creases. Heavy ironing may distort the piece.

Alternatively, the piece can be covered with a clean dish towel and something heavy can be placed on top so that its weight removes creases from the crochet.

Storing items

Crochet items should always be stored flat. If the items are hung up, the stitches will stretch and the shape will be distorted. Treasured pieces can be placed in a cloth bag, drawer, or acid-free cardboard box. Do not use plastic bags, as natural fibers may sweat and the plastic will trap the moisture.

Crochet pieces should be kept away from direct light, excessive humidity, and extreme temperature changes. Protect woolen items by including a natural insect repellent such as lavender, cedar chips, or camphor; but keep the repellent out of direct contact with the items.

Basic stitches and formation

This chapter gives detailed instructions on how to make each of the basic crochet stitches and formations. Once mastered, they can be used to construct any crochet pattern.

BASIC STITCHES

The basic crochet stitches are few in number and easily perfected with a little practice.

   To produce even work, keep the tension consistent and not too tight so that the hook can be drawn smoothly through the loop.

CHAIN/CHAIN STITCH (ch)

Make a slip knot by winding the yarn around the hook as shown and drawing the yarn through the loop.

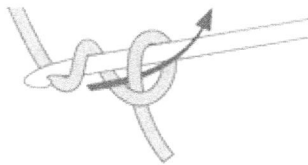

Make a yarn over (yo) by bringing the yarn over the hook from back to front.

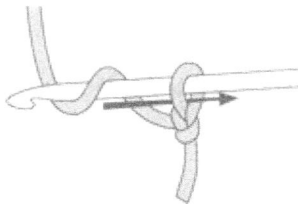

Draw the yarn through the loop on the hook to make a chain stitch.

Work chain stitches evenly.

Continue repeating step 2 until the required number of chain stitches has been made. *The loop on the hook is not counted as a stitch.* The diagram below shows four chain stitches.

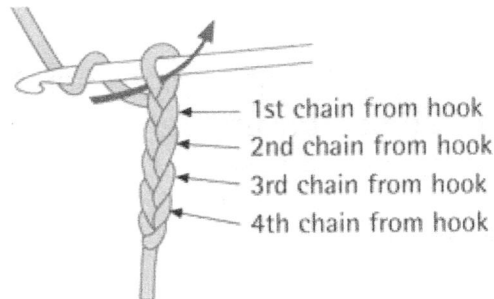

1st chain from hook
2nd chain from hook
3rd chain from hook
4th chain from hook

SLIP STITCH (Sl st)

Make the number of chain stitches required. Insert the hook into the chain stitch stated in the pattern.

Yarn over (yo) and draw the yarn through both loops. There should be one loop left on the hook.

SINGLE CROCHET (sc)

Make the number of chain stitches required. Insert the hook into the second chain stitch from the hook (or as stated in the pattern).

Yarn over (yo) and pull up one loop. There should be two loops left on the hook.

Yo and draw the yarn through both loops. There should be one loop left on the hook.

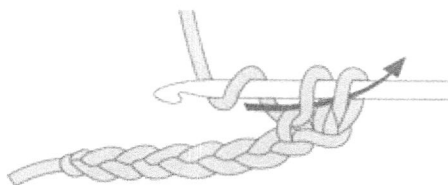

TURNING CHAINS

Your pattern may say to skip the first few chain stitches. These "turning chains" will be the same height as the stitches you will be working for that row (see Number of turning chains required).

HALF DOUBLE CROCHET (hdc)

Make the number of chain stitches required. Yarn over (yo) and insert the hook into the third chain stitch from the hook (or as stated in the pattern).

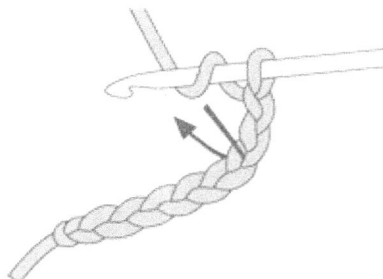

Yo and pull up one loop. There should be three loops left on the hook.

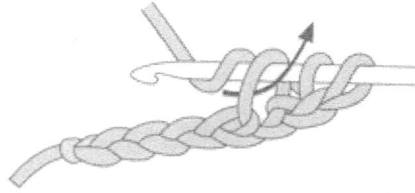

Yo and draw the yarn through three loops. There should be one loop left on the hook.

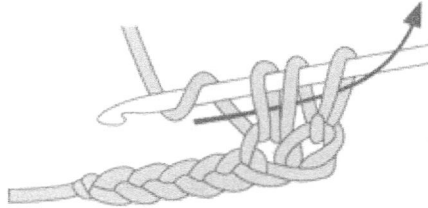

EXTENDED SINGLE CROCHET

Extended single crochet (Esc), or double single crochet (dsc), is a variant of single crochet that can be used when a slightly longer stitch is required.

1 Make the number of chain stitches required. Insert the hook into the third chain stitch from the hook.

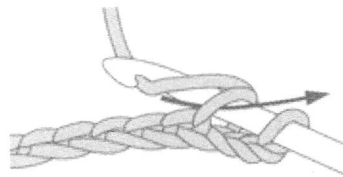

2 Yarn over (yo) and pull up one loop. There should be two loops left on the hook.

3 Yo and draw the yarn through one loop. There should again be two loops left on the hook.

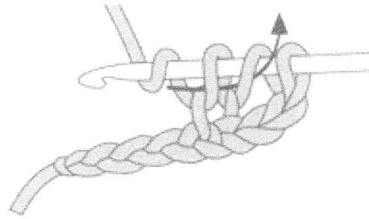

4 Yo and draw the yarn through both loops. There should be one loop left on the hook.

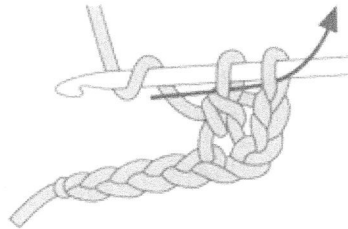

DOUBLE CROCHET (dc)

Make the number of chain stitches required. Yarn over (yo) and insert the hook into the fourth chain stitch from the hook (or as stated in the pattern).

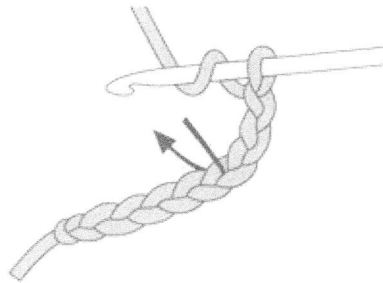

Yo and pull up one loop. There should be three loops left on the hook.

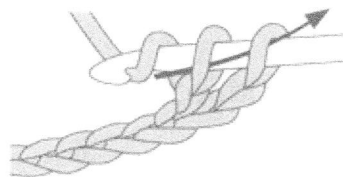

Yo and draw the yarn through two loops. There should be two loops left on the hook.

Yo and draw the yarn through two loops. There should be one loop left on the hook.

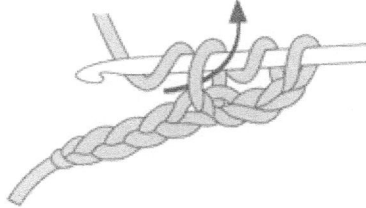

TREBLE CROCHET (tr)

In older patterns this stitch is sometimes called a longer treble crochet.

Make the number of chain stitches required. Yarn over (yo) twice and insert the hook into the fifth chain stitch from the hook (or as stated in the pattern).

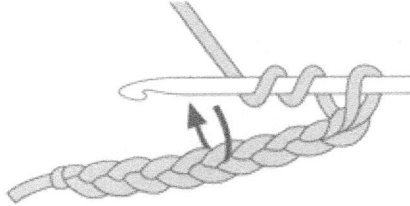

Yo and pull up one loop. There should be four loops left on the hook.

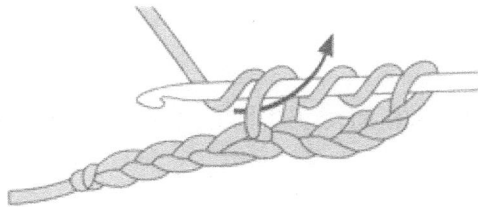

Yo and draw the yarn through two loops. There should be three loops left on the hook.

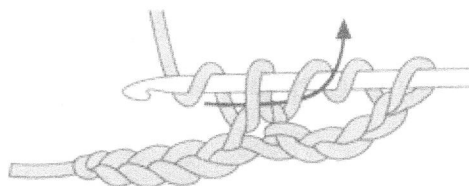

Yo and draw the yarn through two loops. There should be two loops left on the hook.

Yo and draw the yarn through two loops. There should be one loop left on the hook.

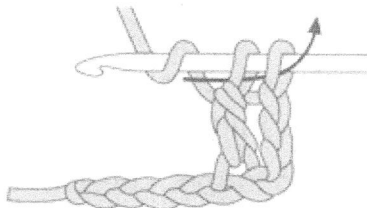

> **Tip** The treble system can be used to make stitches of any length, for example, a quadruple treble (quad tr) is made by starting with yo five times and inserting the hook into the eighth chain from the hook.

DOUBLE TREBLE (dtr)

A double treble is made in the same way as a treble except that you begin with yarn over hook three times.

Make the number of chain stitches required. Yarn over (yo) three times and insert the hook into the sixth chain stitch from the hook (or as stated in the pattern).

Yo and pull up one loop. There should be five loops left on the hook.

Yo and draw the yarn through two loops. There should be four loops left on the hook.

Yo and draw the yarn through two loops. There should be three loops left on the hook.

Yo and draw the yarn through two loops. There should be two loops left on the hook.

Yo and draw the yarn through two loops. There should be one loop left on the hook.

TREBLE TREBLE (ttr)

A treble treble, or triple treble, is made in the same way as a double treble except that you begin with yarn over hook four times.

Make the number of chain stitches required. Yarn over (yo) four times and insert the hook into the seventh chain stitch from the hook (or as stated in the pattern).

Yo and pull up one loop. There should be six loops left on the hook.

Yo and draw the yarn through two loops. There should be five loops left on the hook.

Yo and draw the yarn through two loops. There should be four loops left on the hook.

Yo and draw the yarn through two loops. There should be three loops left on the hook.

Yo and draw the yarn through two loops. There should be two loops left on the hook.

Yo and draw the yarn through two loops. There should be one loop left on the hook.

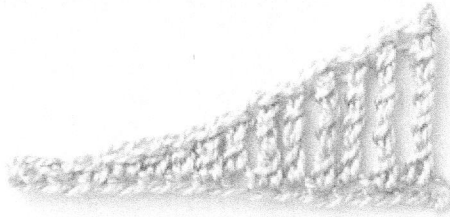

The swatch shows the height of the various stitches. From left to right (two of each are shown): slip stitch, single crochet, half double crochet, double crochet, treble crochet, double treble crochet.

FRONT POST DOUBLE CROCHET (FPdc)

Raised stitches are made by inserting the hook around the leg, or post, of the indicated stitch on the row below. They are not used in the first row of work.

Make three turning chains. Yarn over (yo) and insert the hook around the appropriate post from front to back and right to left.

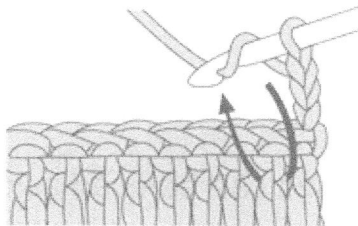

Yo and complete the double crochet. A ridge forms on the back of the work. Continue working front post double crochet stitches in this way as required.

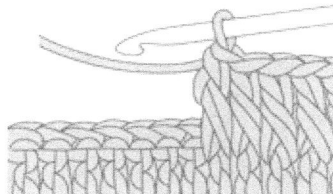

BACK POST DOUBLE CROCHET (BPdc)

Make three turning chains. Yarn over (yo) and insert the hook around the appropriate post from back to front and right to left.

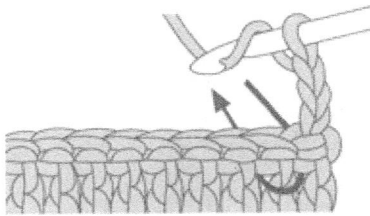

Yo and complete the double crochet. A ridge forms on the front of the work. Continue working back post double crochet stitches in this way as required.

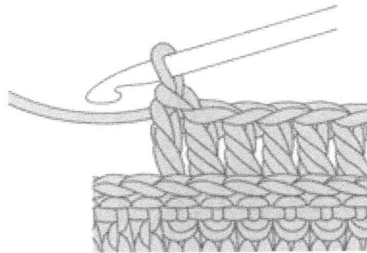

Tip Any of the basic stitches can be worked as raised stitches in this way.

FOUNDATION CHAIN

A row of single crochet stitches can be used as a foundation, or base, chain. It can be easier to count and to work back into than a normal chain, as well as being more flexible.

Work two single chain stitches. Insert the hook into the second chain from the hook and work one single crochet.

Insert the hook under the left-hand thread of the single crochet and work another single crochet. Repeat as required.

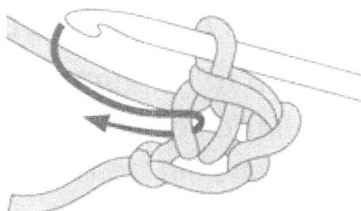

BEGINNER'S CROCHET

Although crochet patterns can look intricate and complex, almost all are made using only three or four different stitches. Beginners will find they can create a variety of work using only four stitches: chain stitch, slip stitch, single crochet, and double crochet. These can be combined in many ways to create interesting and complex patterns.

These basic stitches are not difficult to learn, but time spent practicing the basic movements so that the yarn flows smoothly and the tension is even will be worthwhile. If the stitches and tension are consistent, the crocheted fabric will look attractive, even though only a few stitches have been used. Leaving the loops a little loose will help, too, because if you pull them closed too tightly you will have difficulty drawing the hook through them.

Start by working some of the patterns collected in the "Single crochet rows" and "Double crochet rows" sections, and then you can move on to more elaborate patterns with confidence.

REVERSE SINGLE CROCHET (Rev sc)

Also known as crab stitch and corded edging, reverse single crochet is made by working single crochet in the reverse direction (from left to right). It is used for decorative texture and to make a firm edging.

Work a row of single crochet on the right side. Do not turn the work.

Insert the hook through the stitch to the right and hook the yarn, keeping the hook facing downward. Pull the yarn through, at the same time twisting the hook to face upward. There should be two loops on the hook.

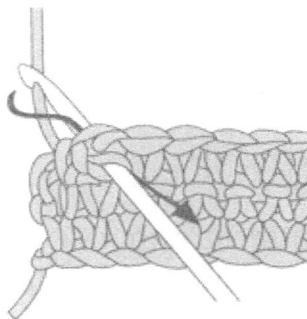

Yarn over (yo) and draw the yarn through both loops to complete the single crochet.

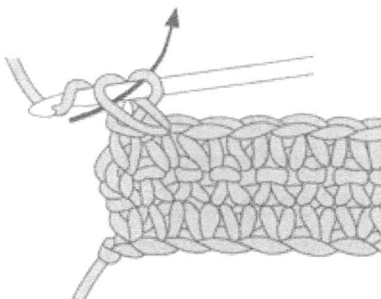

Repeat step 2.

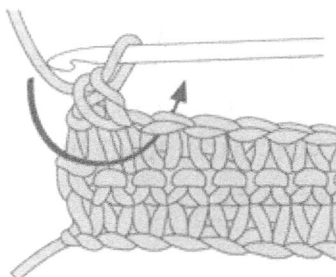

Continue working to the right. The stitches twist to create the decorative effect.

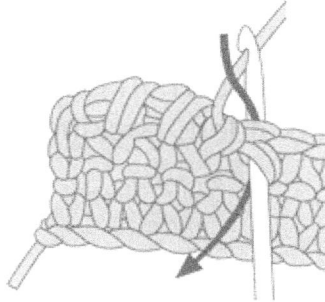

KNOT STITCH (KS)

Knot stitch, also known as Solomon's knot and Love knot, consists of a long chain stitch with a single crochet in the back loop.

Make a chain stitch and lengthen it to about ⅛–⅝ inch (10–15 mm).

Hold the long stitch between the index finger and thumb. Yarn over (yo) and pull up a normal chain stitch. There should be one loop left on the hook.

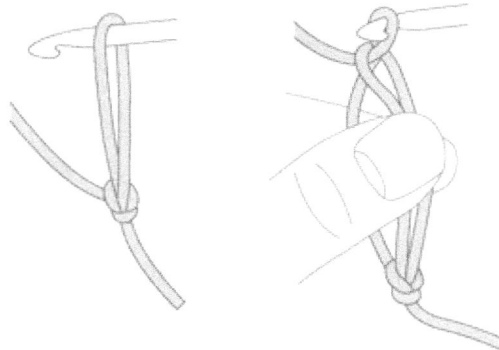

Insert the hook under the new (third) "leg," yo and pull up one loop. There should be two loops left on the hook.

Yo and draw the yarn through both loops.

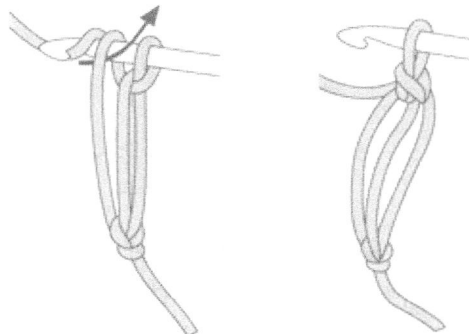

LOCKING STITCH (lks)

This can be used to lock any long stitch in place.
Follow steps 2–4 of Knot stitch at left. Locking stitch is also used in broomstick lace patterns.

BULLION STITCH (bullion st)

Bullion stitch is also known as Roll stitch. As in embroidery, a bullion is made by wrapping the yarn around the hook, up to ten times, and drawing the yarn through.

Wrap the yarn around the hook the required number of times. It should not be too tight. Insert the hook as instructed, yarn over (yo) and pull up one loop.

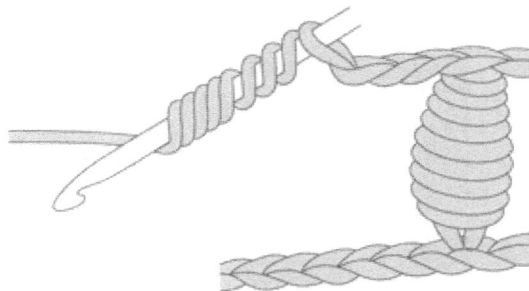

Yo and draw the yarn carefully through all of the loops on the hook.

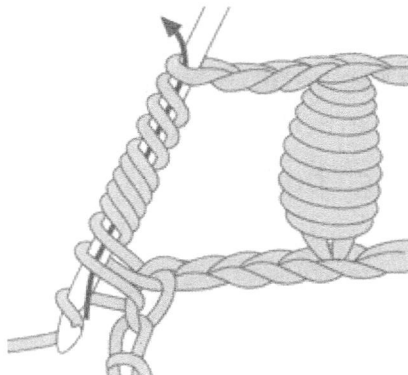

OVERLAID CHAIN (och)

Overlaid chains can be used with any crochet fabric that has a regular gridlike form, including single crochet and double crochet fabrics. This weaving technique is also known as full-surface crochet.

With the yarn at the back of the work, insert the hook from the front. Draw the yarn through so there is one loop on the hook.

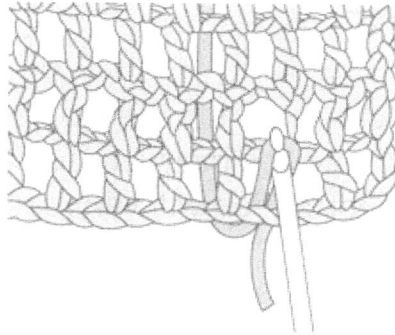

Insert the hook into the next grid opening and draw the yarn through the fabric and the loop on the hook.

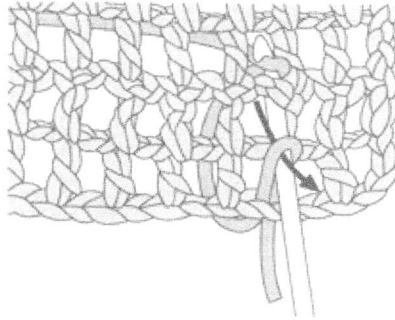

BASIC FORMATIONS

The basic formations are groups of stitches joined in standard ways. When working a pattern, always read the instructions carefully, as the number and type of stitches in the formation will vary.

CLUSTER (CL)

A cluster is a group of two or more stitches of any type joined together at the top. The last loop of each stitch is left on the hook until all are joined at the end. For example, to make a cluster of three double crochet stitches:

Work one double crochet until there are two loops left on the hook.

Work a second double crochet until there are three loops left on the hook.

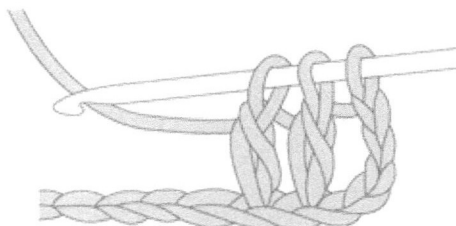

Tip Pay particular attention to where the legs of the stitches in a cluster are to go since they may be worked into adjacent stitches (as shown here) or spaced with stitches between them.

Work a third double crochet until there are four loops left on the hook. Yarn over (yo) and draw the yarn through all of the loops.

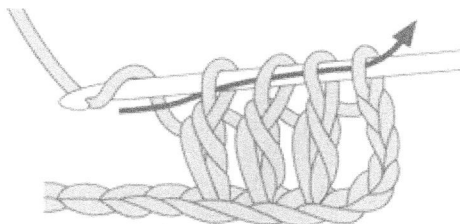

There should be one loop left on the hook.

WORKING STITCHES TOGETHER

Stitches worked "together" are worked in the same way as for a cluster.

POPCORN (pc)

A popcorn is a cluster of stitches worked into the same stitch and then grouped and closed at the top. The number and type of stitches used can vary. For example, to make a popcorn with four double crochet stitches:

Work four double crochets into the same stitch.

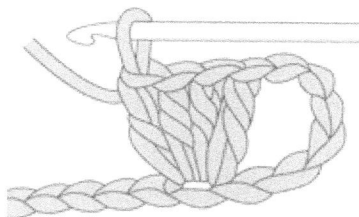

Take the hook out of the working loop and insert the hook under the top two loops of the first double crochet stitch made and back through the working loop.

Draw the working loop through the stitch to close the popcorn.

PUFF

A puff is usually a group of half double crochets worked into the same stitch and joined at the top. For example, to make a puff of three half double crochets:

Yarn over (yo), insert the hook into the stitch, and pull up one loop. Repeat twice. There should be seven loops on the hook. The loops should all be about ¼ inch (1 cm) long.

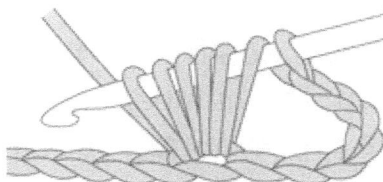

Yo and draw the yarn through all of the loops. There should be one loop left on the hook.

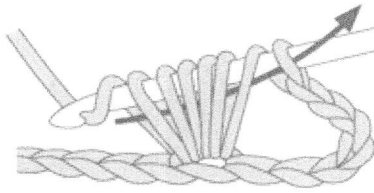

Work one slip stitch to close the puff.

BOBBLE

A bobble is a group of long stitches (double crochets and even longer) worked into the same stitch and joined at the top. The best effect is achieved when the stitches before and after a bobble are shorter and when it is worked on the wrong side. For example, to make a bobble of three double crochets:

Work one double crochet until there are two loops left on the hook.

Work a second double crochet into the same stitch until there are three loops on the hook.

Work a third double crochet into the same stitch until there are four loops on the hook.

Yo and draw the yarn through all of the loops. There should be one loop left on the hook.

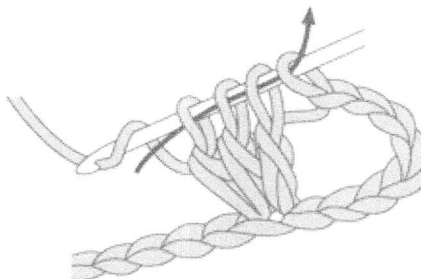

Work a slip stitch to close the bobble.

PICOT (p)

A picot consists of three or more chain stitches made into a ring with a slip stitch or, sometimes, a single crochet. For example, to make a chain-three picot closed by a slip stitch on a row of single crochet:

Work three chain stitches and insert the hook through the last stitch.

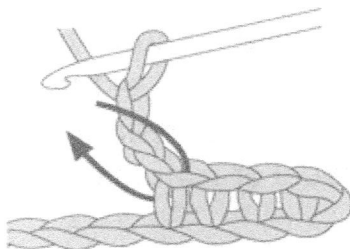

Yarn over (yo) and pull the yarn through. There should be one loop left on the hook. Continue working and making picots as directed.

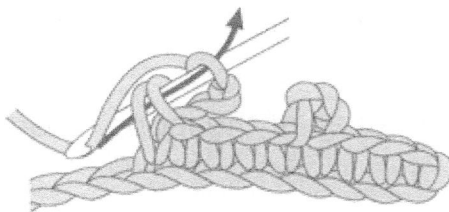

Crochet stitch patterns

The basic stitches and formations may be worked in rows or combined in a wide variety of patterns to create crocheted fabric. The selection of patterns presented in this chapter shows some of the possible variations.

SINGLE CROCHET ROWS

Rows of single crochet stitches form simple, repeated patterns. They are easy to work and make dense, firm fabrics that are durable. These fabrics keep their shape well.

Single crochet rows can be worked in any yarn. Thicker cottons and wools, which produce especially durable fabrics, are often chosen.

SINGLE CROCHET

Ch: required sts

Row 1: Sc in 2nd ch from hook, 1 sc in each ch, turn.

Row 2: Ch 1, skip first sc, 1 sc in each sc, 1 sc in last st, turn.

Repeat Row 2.

EXTENDED SINGLE CROCHET

Ch: required sts + 1

Row 1: Esc in 3rd ch from hook, 1 Esc in each ch, turn.

Row 2: Ch 2, skip first Esc, 1 Esc in each Esc, 1 Esc in 2nd ch of tch, turn.

Repeat Row 2.

See extended single crochet (Esc).

TAPESTRY CROCHET

Tapestry crochet is generally worked in tight single crochets, using a number of colors and following charted patterns. The different-colored yarns are carried over on the back of the work and a thick cotton yarn is used, thus producing a stiff, tapestrylike fabric. The technique first became popular in Africa and South

America.

*Single crochet rows **(top) and** Extended single crochet rows*

From top: Front loop single crochet rows, Back loop single crochet rows, Front and back loop single crochet rows, **and** Alternate single crochet rows

FRONT LOOP SINGLE CROCHET

Ch: required sts

Row 1: Sc in 2nd ch from hook, 1 sc in each ch, turn.

Row 2: Ch 1, skip first sc, 1 sc in front loop of each sc, 1 sc in last st, turn.

Repeat Row 2.

See working into front loops.

BACK LOOP SINGLE CROCHET

Ch: required sts

Row 1: Sc in 2nd ch from hook, 1 sc in each ch, turn.

Row 2: Ch 1, skip first sc, 1 sc in back loop of each sc, 1 sc in last st, turn.

Repeat Row 2.

See working into back loops.

FRONT AND BACK LOOP SINGLE CROCHET

Ch: required sts

Row 1: Sc in 2nd ch from hook, 1 sc in each ch, turn.

Row 2: Ch 1, skip first sc, 1 sc in front loop of each sc, 1 sc in last st, turn.

Row 3: Ch 1, skip first sc, 1 sc in back loop of each sc, 1 sc in last st, turn.

Repeat Rows 2 and 3.

See working into front and back loops.

ALTERNATE SINGLE CROCHET

Ch: even number

Row 1: Sc in 2nd ch from hook, 1 sc in each ch, turn.

Row 2: Ch 1, skip first sc, *1 sc in back loop of next sc, 1 sc in front loop of next sc, repeat from* , 1 sc in last st, turn.

Repeat Row 2.

See working into front and back loops.

> **Tip-** Try keeping your ball of yarn in an empty cardboard tissue box or other clean container as

you crochet. It will then unroll freely but won't roll away and become dirty.

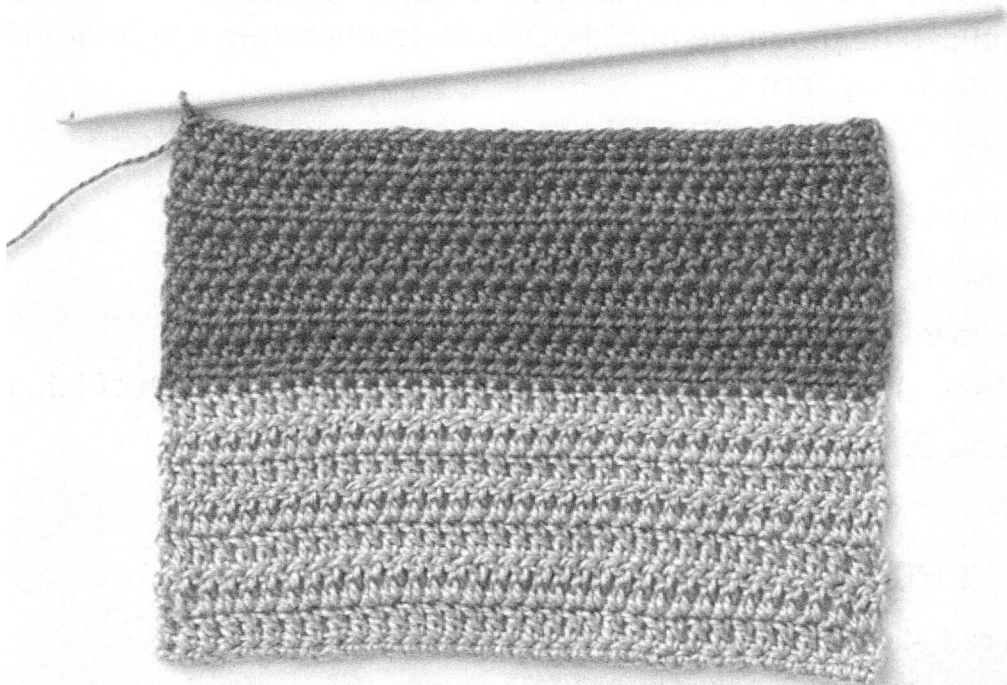

Half double crochet rows **(top) and** *Double crochet rows*

: DOUBLE CROCHET ROWS

Rows of double crochet stitches again form simple, repeated patterns. The resulting fabric is less firm than single crocheted fabric, but it is still fairly stable and can be produced quickly. Double crochet rows can be worked successfully in any yarn.

HALF DOUBLE CROCHET

Ch: required sts + 1

Row 1: Hdc in 3rd ch from hook, 1 hdc in each ch, turn.

Row 2: Ch 2, skip first hdc, 1 hdc in each hdc, 1 hdc in 2nd ch of tch, turn.

Repeat Row 2.

DOUBLE CROCHET

Ch: required sts + 2

Row 1: Dc in 4th ch from hook, 1 dc in each ch, turn.

Row 2: Ch 3, skip first dc, 1 dc in each dc, 1 dc in 3rd ch of tch, turn.

Repeat Row 2.

MAKING A CROCHET SAMPLER

A traditional method of learning to embroider was to stitch a sampler that contained examples of a number of different stitches. A crochet sampler can be made in the same way, and it is an excellent way of learning to crochet or developing your repertoire of stitch patterns.

Work individual squares of crochet, each using a different stitch pattern. Beginners can use the different types of single crochet and double crochet rows, while experienced workers can choose from any of the patterns in this book. These squares can then be joined to make a scarf, blanket, or other item, even a wall hanging. For a subtle look, work all the squares in the same or complementary colors, or choose a variety of colors to make a bright and cheery piece.

There are only two things to consider carefully before you start. First, use the same type and thickness of yarn throughout, unless you want an uneven look. Second, think carefully about the size of the squares to be worked. The simpler patterns can be made to any size, but some of the more elaborate patterns that repeat over a number of stitches will only be effective in larger squares.

From top: Treble crochet rows, Double treble crochet rows, Front loop double crochet rows, **and** Back loop double crochet rows

TREBLE CROCHET

Ch: required sts + 3

Row 1: Tr in 5th ch from hook, 1 tr in each ch, turn.

Row 2: ch 4, skip first tr, 1 tr in each tr, 1 tr in 4th ch of tch, turn.

Repeat Row 2.

DOUBLE TREBLE CROCHET

Ch: required sts + 4

Row 1: Dtr in 6th ch from hook, 1 dtr in each ch, turn.

Row 2: Ch 5, skip first dtr, 1 dtr in each dtr, 1 dtr in 5th ch of tch, turn.

Repeat Row 2.

FRONT LOOP DOUBLE CROCHET

Ch: required sts + 2

Row 1: Dc in 4th ch from hook, 1 dc in each ch, turn.

Row 2: Ch 3, skip first dc, 1 dc in front loop of each dc, 1 dc in 3rd ch of tch, turn.

Repeat Row 2.

BACK LOOP DOUBLE CROCHET

Ch: required sts + 2

Row 1: Dc in 4th ch from hook, 1 dc in each ch, turn.

Row 2: Ch 3, skip first dc, 1 dc in back loop of each dc, 1 dc in 3rd ch of tch, turn.

Repeat Row 2.

See working into front and back loops.

> **Tip** Yarn quantities given in crochet instructions are always approximate. Depending on how tightly or loosely you work, you may need more or less yarn.

Front and back loop double crochet rows **(top)**, *Alternate double crochet rows* **(center), and** *Paired half double crochet rows*

FRONT AND BACK LOOP DOUBLE CROCHET

Ch: required sts + 2

Row 1: Dc in 4th ch from hook, 1 dc in each ch, turn.

Row 2: Ch 3, skip first dc, 1 dc in front loop of each dc, 1 dc in 3rd ch of tch, turn.

Row 3: Ch 3, skip first dc, 1 dc in back loop of each dc, 1 dc in 3rd ch of tch, turn.

Repeat Rows 2 and 3.

ALTERNATE DOUBLE CROCHET

Ch: even number

Row 1: Dc in 4th ch from hook, 1 dc in each ch, turn.

Row 2: Ch 3, skip first dc, *1 dc in back loop of next dc, 1 dc in front loop of next dc, repeat from* , 1 dc in 3rd ch of tch, turn.

Repeat Row 2.

See working into front and back loops.

PAIRED HALF DOUBLE CROCHET

Ch: required sts + 2

Row 1: Hdc2tog inserting hook in 3rd and 4th ch from hook, *hdc2tog inserting hook in same ch as last st then in next ch, repeat from* , turn.

Row 2: Ch 2, hdc2tog inserting hook in first and 2nd hdctog, *hdc2tog inserting hook in same place as last st then in next hdc2tog, repeat from* with last hdc in top of tch, turn.

Repeat Row 2.

See work stitches together.

Crossed double crochet rows (top) and Post double crochet rib

CROSSED DOUBLE CROCHET

Crossed double crochet (Cdc): Skip next 2 dc, 1 dc in same place as base of next dc, 1 dc in 2nd dc of 2 skipped dc, 1 dc in same place as base of first skipped dc. Ch: multiple of 6 + 7

Row 1: Dc in 4th ch from hook, 1 dc in each ch, turn.

Row 2: Ch 3, skip first dc, 1 dc in each dc, 1 dc in 3rd ch of tch, turn.

Row 3: Ch 3, skip first dc, *work 1 Cdc over next 3 dc, 1 dc in each of next 3 dc, repeat from* , work 1 Cdc over last 3 dc, 1 dc in 3rd ch of tch, turn.

Row 4: As Row 2.

Row 5: Ch 3, skip first dc, *1 dc in each of next 3 dc, work 1 Cdc over next 3 dc, repeat from* , 1 dc in each of last 3 dc, 1 dc in 3rd ch of tch, turn.

Repeat Rows 2–5.

POST DOUBLE CROCHET RIB

Ch: even number

Row 1: Dc in 4th ch from hook, 1 dc in each ch, turn.

Row 2: Ch 2, skip first dc, *1 FPdc around next dc, 1 BPdc around next dc, repeat from* , 1 FPdc around tch, turn.

Row 3: Ch 2, skip first dc, *1 FPdc around next dc, 1 BPdc around next dc, repeat from* , 1 FPdc around tch, turn.

Repeat Row 3.

See front post double crochet (FPdc) and back post double crochet (BPdc).

Tip- When working into the base of the next crochet stitch, you are working into the row below.

Front post double crochet rows (top), Back post double crochet rows (center), and Crossed half double crochet rows

FRONT POST DOUBLE CROCHET

Ch: required sts + 2

Row 1: Dc in 4th ch from hook, 1 dc in each ch, turn.

Row 2: Ch 2, skip first dc, *1 FPdc around next dc, repeat from* , 1 FPdc around tch, turn.

Row 3: Ch 2, skip first dc, *1 FPdc around next dc, repeat from* , 1 FPdc around tch, turn.

Repeat Row 3.

BACK POST DOUBLE CROCHET

Ch: required sts + 2

Row 1: Dc in 4th ch from hook, 1 dc in each ch, turn.

Row 2: Ch 2, skip first dc, *1 BPdc around next dc, repeat from* , 1 BPdc around tch, turn.

Row 3: Ch 2, skip first dc, *1 BPdc around next dc, repeat from* , 1 BPdc around tch, turn.

Repeat Row 3.

See front post double crochet (FPdc) **and** back post double crochet (BPdc).

CROSSED HALF DOUBLE CROCHET

Ch: odd number

Row 1: Hdc2tog inserting hook in 3rd and 4th ch from hook, *ch 1, hdc2tog inserting hook in next ch-2, repeat from* to last ch, ch 1, 1 hdc in last ch, turn.

Row 2: Ch 2, hdc2tog inserting hook in first and 2nd ch-sps, *ch 1, hdc2tog inserting hook in same ch-sp as last st then in next ch-sp, repeat from* with last hdc under ch-2 at beginning of previous row, ch 1, 1 hdc in 2nd ch of tch, turn.

Repeat Row 2.

See work stitches together.

*Raised double crochet ridges **(top)** and Relief double crochet rows*

RAISED DOUBLE CROCHET RIDGES

Ch: required sts + 2

Row 1: Dc in 4th ch from hook, 1 dc in each ch, turn.

Row 2: Ch 2, skip first dc, *1 FPdc around next dc, repeat from* , 1 FPdc around tch, turn.

Row 3: Ch 2, skip first dc, *1 BPdc around next dc, repeat from* , 1 BPdc around tch, turn.

Row 4: Ch 2, skip first dc, *1 FPdc around next dc, repeat from* , 1 FPdc around tch, turn.

Repeat Rows 3 and 4.

RELIEF DOUBLE CROCHET

Ch: odd number

Row 1: Dc in 4th ch from hook, 1 dc in each ch, turn.

Row 2: Ch 1, skip first dc, 1 sc in each dc, 1 sc in 2nd ch of tch, turn.

Row 3: Ch 2, skip first sc, *1 FPdc around dc below next sc, skip this sc, 1 sc in next sc, repeat from* , 1 sc in last ch, turn.

Row 4: Ch 1, skip first sc, *1 sc in FPdc, 1 sc in sc, repeat from* , 1 sc in last FPdc, 1 sc in 2nd ch of tch, turn.

Row 5: Ch 2, skip first sc, *1 FPdc around FPdc below next sc, skip this sc, 1 sc in next sc, repeat from* , 1 sc in last ch, turn.

Repeat Rows 4 and 5.

See front post double crochet (FPdc) and back post double crochet (BPdc).

Tip- It is a good idea to read straight through the instructions for any pattern before you start work. This gives you an overall picture of how the piece will progress and so makes following the instructions much easier.

Solid 1 (top), Solid 2 (center), and Solid 3

: SOLID PATTERNS

These patterns produce firm, durable fabric that incorporates an overall design. They range from simple to elaborate, and most look best in cotton yarns. The density of the pattern will depend on the yarn and size of hook chosen.

SOLID 1

Ch: even number

Row 1: Sc in 2nd ch from hook, *ch 1, skip 1 ch, 1 sc in next ch, repeat from* , turn.

Row 2: Ch 1, skip first sc, *1 sc in ch-sp, ch 1, skip 1 sc, repeat from* , 1 sc in tch, turn.

Repeat Row 2.

SOLID 2

Ch: even number

Row 1: Dc in 2nd ch from hook, *1 sc in next ch, 1 dc in next ch, repeat from* , turn.

Row 2: Ch 1, skip first dc, *1 dc in sc, 1 sc in dc, repeat from* , 1 dc in tch, turn.

Repeat Row 2.

SOLID 3

Ch: odd number

Row 1: (Sc, ch 1, 1 sc) in 3rd ch from hook, *skip 1 ch, (1 sc, ch 1, 1 sc) in next ch, repeat from* to last 2 ch, skip 1 ch, 1 sc in last ch, turn.

Row 2: Ch 2, skip 2 sc, (1 sc, ch 1, 1 sc) in each ch-sp, 1 sc in 2nd ch of tch,

turn.
Repeat Row 2.

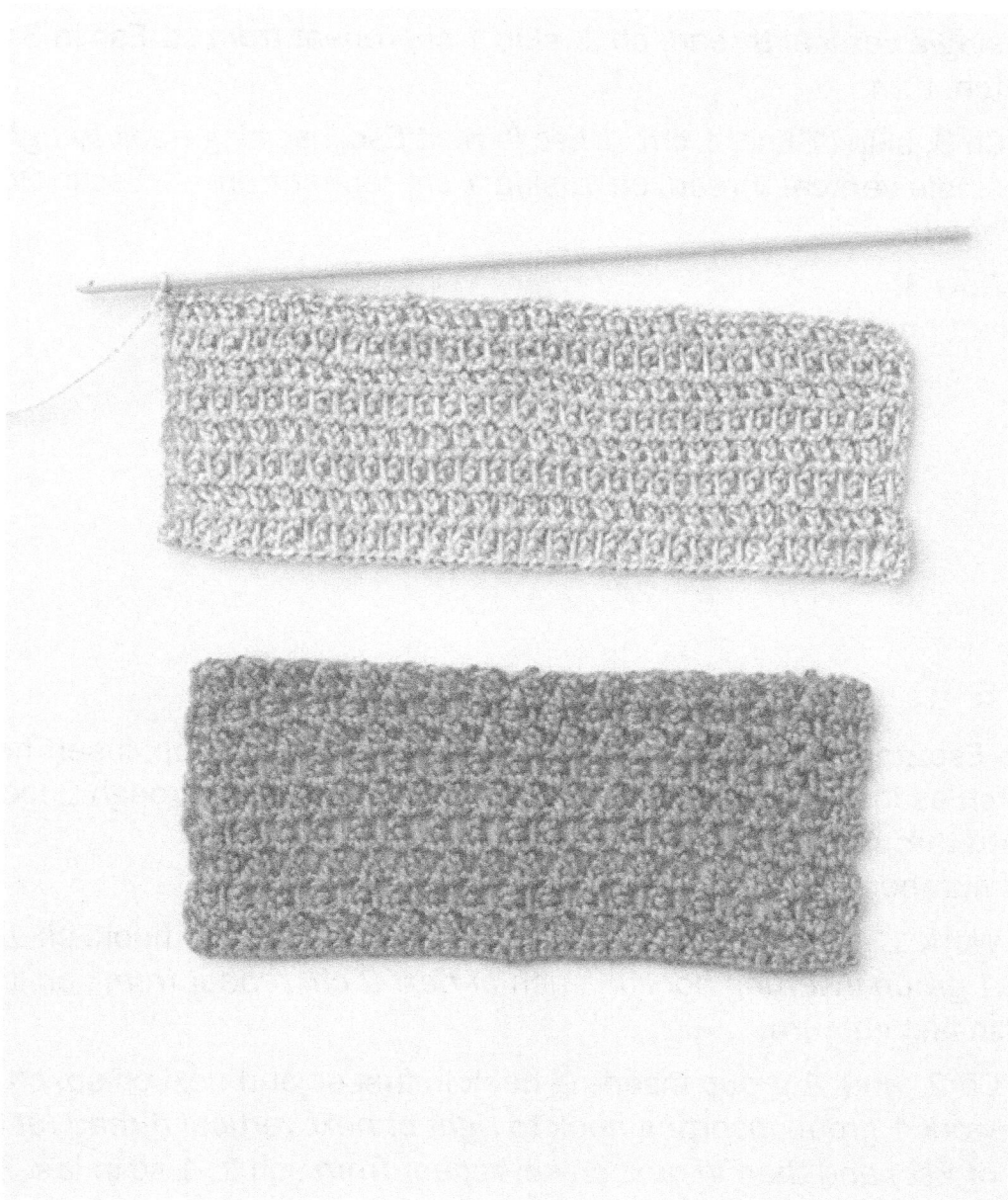

Solid 4 (top) and Solid 5

SOLID 4

Ch: odd number

Row 1: Esc in 5th ch from hook, *ch 1, skip 1 ch, 1 Esc in next ch, repeat from* , turn.

Row 2: Ch 3, skip (1 Esc, 1 ch), *1 Esc in next Esc inserting hook to right of single vertical thread, ch 1, skip 1 ch, repeat from* , 1 Esc in 3rd ch of tch, turn.

Row 3: Ch 3, skip (1 Esc, 1 ch), *1 Esc in next Esc inserting hook to right of single vertical thread, ch 1, skip 1 ch, repeat from* , 1 Esc in 2nd ch of tch.

Repeat Row 3.

See extended single crochet (Esc).

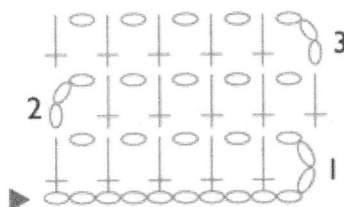

SOLID 5

Group = Esc2tog: Insert hook as instructed, yo, pull up a loop, insert hook in next stitch as instructed, yo, pull up a loop, yo, draw yarn through 2 loops, yo, draw yarn through 2 loops.

Ch: odd number

Row 1: Work 1 group inserting hook in 3rd and 4th ch from hook, *ch 1, work 1 group inserting hook in each of next 2 ch, repeat from* , ch 1, 1 sc in last ch, turn.

Row 2: Ch 2, work 1 group inserting hook in first sc and next ch-sp, *ch 1, work 1 group inserting hook to right of next vertical thread (at center of Esc) and then in next ch-sp, repeat from* , ch 1, 1 sc in last Esc, turn.

Repeat Row 2.

See extended single crochet (Esc).

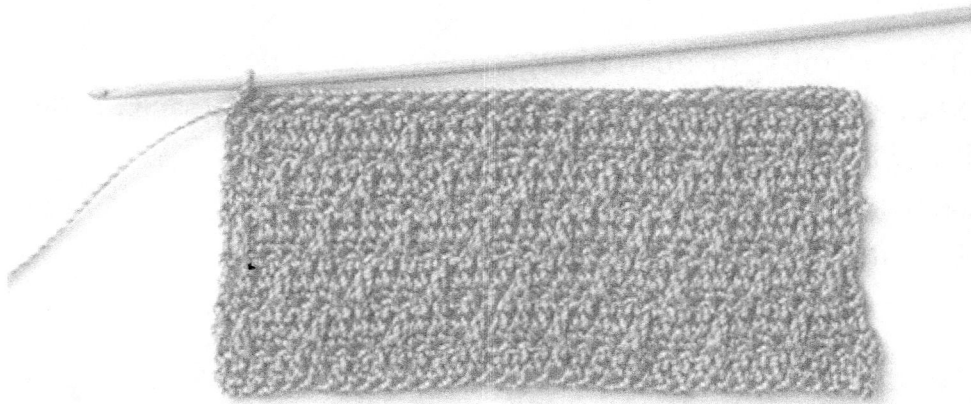

Solid 6 (top) and Solid 7

SOLID 6

Ch: multiple of 4 + 3

Row 1: Dc in 4th ch from hook, 1 dc in each ch, turn.

Row 2: Ch 1, skip first dc, 1 sc in front loop of each dc, 1 sc in 3rd ch of tch,

turn.

Row 3: Ch 3, skip first sc, *1 dc below next sc (work into back loop of dc in Row 1), 1 dc in each of next 3 sc, repeat from* to end with last dc in ch, turn.

Row 4: As Row 2.

Row 5: Ch 3, skip first sc, 1 dc in each of next 2 sc, *1 dc below next sc (work into back loop of dc in Row 3), 1 dc in each of next 3 sc, repeat from* with 1 dc below last sc, 1 dc in tch, turn.

Repeat Rows 2–5.

See working into front and back loops.

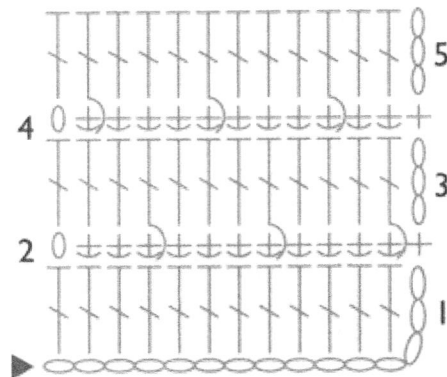

SOLID 7

Ch: multiple of 3

Row 1: Work (2 dc, ch 2, 1 sc) in 3rd ch from hook, *skip 2 ch, (2 dc, ch 2, 1 sc) in next ch, repeat from* , turn.

Row 2: Ch 2, skip first sc, *(2 dc, ch 2, 1 sc) in ch-2 sp, skip (2 dc, 1 sc), repeat from* , skip last 2 dc, turn.

Repeat Row 2.

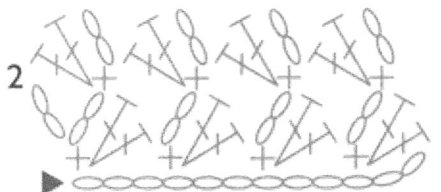

Solid 8 (top) and *Solid 9*

SOLID 8

Ch: multiple of 4 + 1

Row 1: (Dc, ch 1, 1 dc) in 3rd ch from hook, *skip 1 ch, 1 sc in next ch, skip 1 ch, (1 dc, ch 1, 1 dc) in next ch, repeat from* to last 2 ch, skip 1 ch, 1 sc in last ch, turn.

Row 2: Ch 4, skip (first sc, 1 dc), *1 sc in ch-sp, ch 1, skip 1 dc, 1 dc in sc, ch 1, skip 1 dc, repeat from* , 1 sc in last ch-sp, ch 1, skip 1 dc, 1 dc in next ch, turn.

Row 3: Ch 1, skip first dc, *skip 1 ch, (1 dc, ch 1, 1 dc) in sc, skip 1 ch, 1 sc in dc, repeat from* , working last sc in 3rd ch of tch, turn.

Repeat Rows 2 and 3.

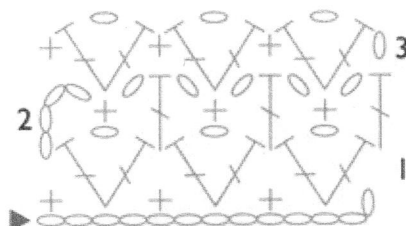

SOLID 9

Group = Work 1 double crochet and 1 half double crochet together: Yo, insert hook in next st, yo, pull up a loop, yo, draw yarn through first 2 loops on hook, yo, insert hook in same st as before, yo, pull up a loop, yo, draw yarn through all 4 loops on hook. Ch: required sts + 3

Row 1: Hdc in 4th ch from hook, work 1 group in each ch, turn.

Row 2: Ch 3, 1 hdc in first group, work 1 group in each group, work 1 group in 1 hdc, turn.

Repeat Row 2.

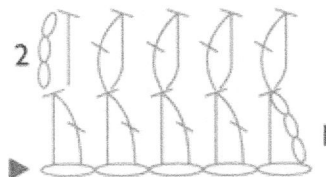

Tip- Work the foundation chain for Solid 9 loosely so that it is easier to work the stitches of the group into it.

Solid 10 (top) and Solid 11

SOLID 10

Ch: multiple of 4 + 3

Row 1: Sc in 2nd ch from hook, 1 sc in each ch, turn.

Row 2: Ch 1, skip first sc, 1 sc in back loop of each sc, 1 sc in ch, turn.

Row 3: Ch 1, skip first sc, 1 sc in back loop of each of next 2 sc, *1 sc in base of sc of Row 2, 1 sc in back loop of each of next 3 sc, repeat from* to end with last sc in ch, turn.

Row 4: As Row 2.

Row 5: Ch 1, skip first sc, *1 sc in base of sc of Row 4, 1 sc in back loop of each of next 3 sc, repeat from* , 1 sc in ch, turn.

Repeat Rows 2–5.

See working into the back loop.

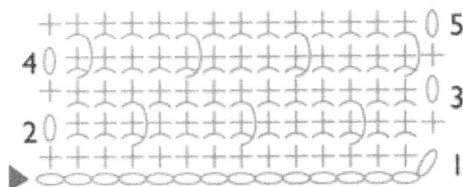

SOLID 11

Ch: multiple of 10 + 5

Row 1: Sc in 2nd ch from hook, 1 sc in each of next 3 ch, *1 dc in each of next 5 ch, 1 sc in each of next 5 ch, repeat from* , turn.

Row 2: Ch 3, skip first sc, 1 dc in each of next 4 sc, *1 sc in each of 5 dc, 1 dc in each of 5 sc, repeat from* with last dc in ch, turn.

Row 3: Ch 1, skip first dc, 1 sc in each of next 4 dc, *1 dc in each of 5 sc, 1 sc in each of 5 dc, repeat from* with last sc in 3rd ch of tch, turn.

Repeat Rows 2 and 3.

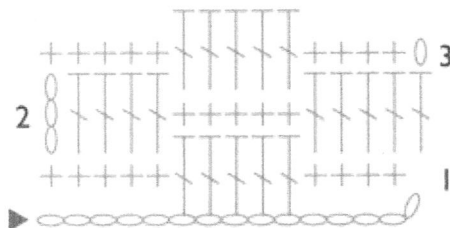

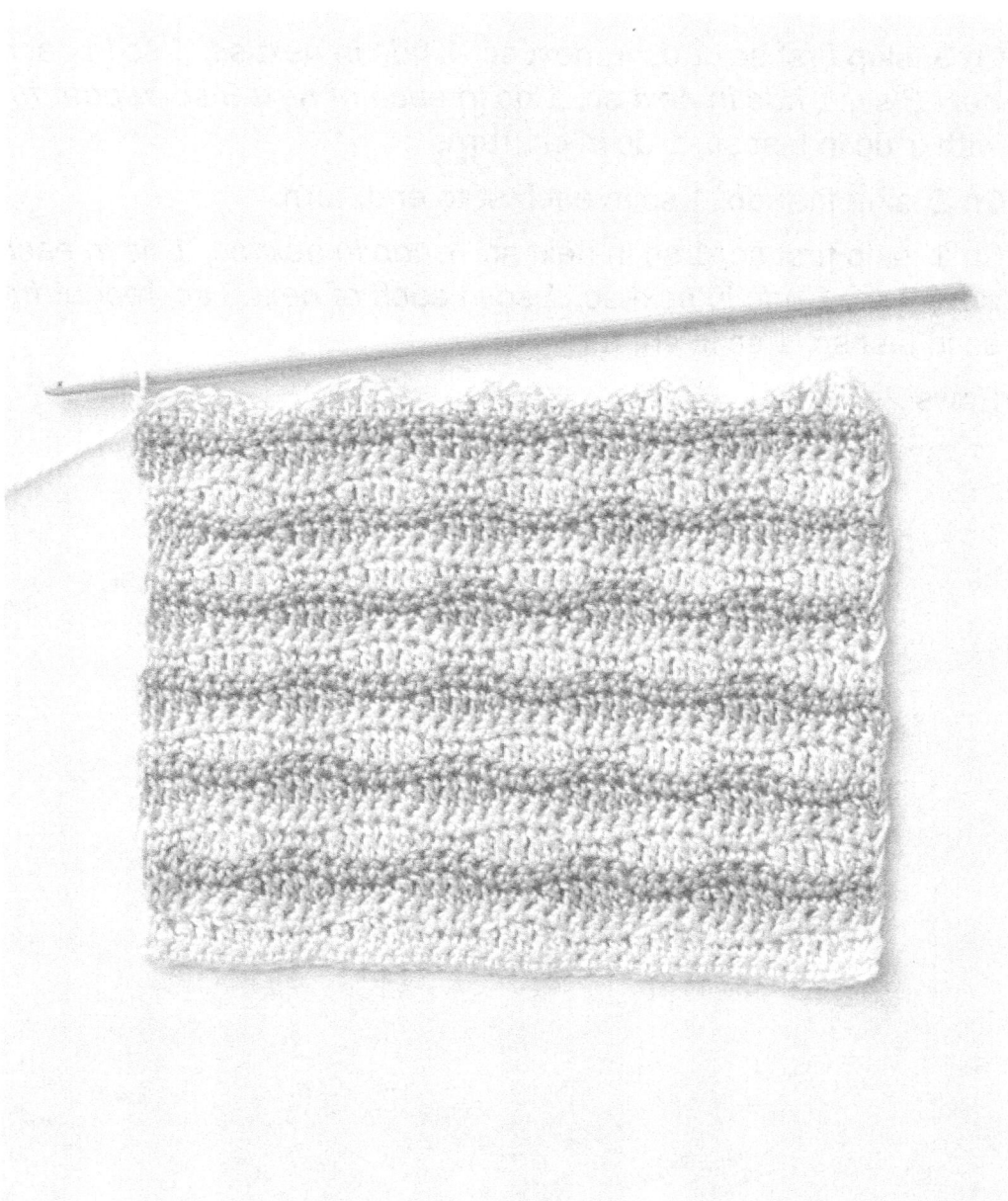

Solid 12

SOLID 12

Ch: multiple of 8 + 1

Row 1: Sc in 2nd ch from hook, *1 hdc in next ch, 1 dc in each of next 3 ch, 1 hdc in next ch, 1 sc in each of next 3 ch, repeat from* , ending with 1 sc in each of last 2 ch, turn.

Row 2: Ch 1, skip first sc, 1 sc in each st to end, turn.

Row 3: Ch 3, skip first sc, 1 dc in next sc, *1 hdc in next sc, 1 sc in each of next 3 sc, 1 hdc in next sc, 1 dc in each of next 3 sc, repeat from* with 1 dc in last sc, 1 dc in ch, turn.

Row 4: Ch 1, skip first dc, 1 sc in each st to end, turn.

Row 5: Ch 1, skip first sc, 1 sc in next sc, *1 hdc in next sc, 1 dc in each of next 3 sc, 1 hdc in next sc, 1 sc in each of next 3 sc, repeat from* , 1 sc in last sc, 1 sc in ch, turn.

Repeat Rows 2–5.

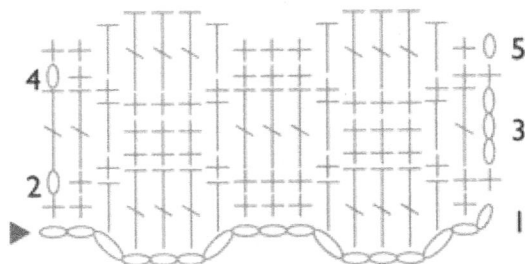

Tip- This pattern is effective when worked in two colors, with two rows worked in each color. See instructions on changing colors frequently.

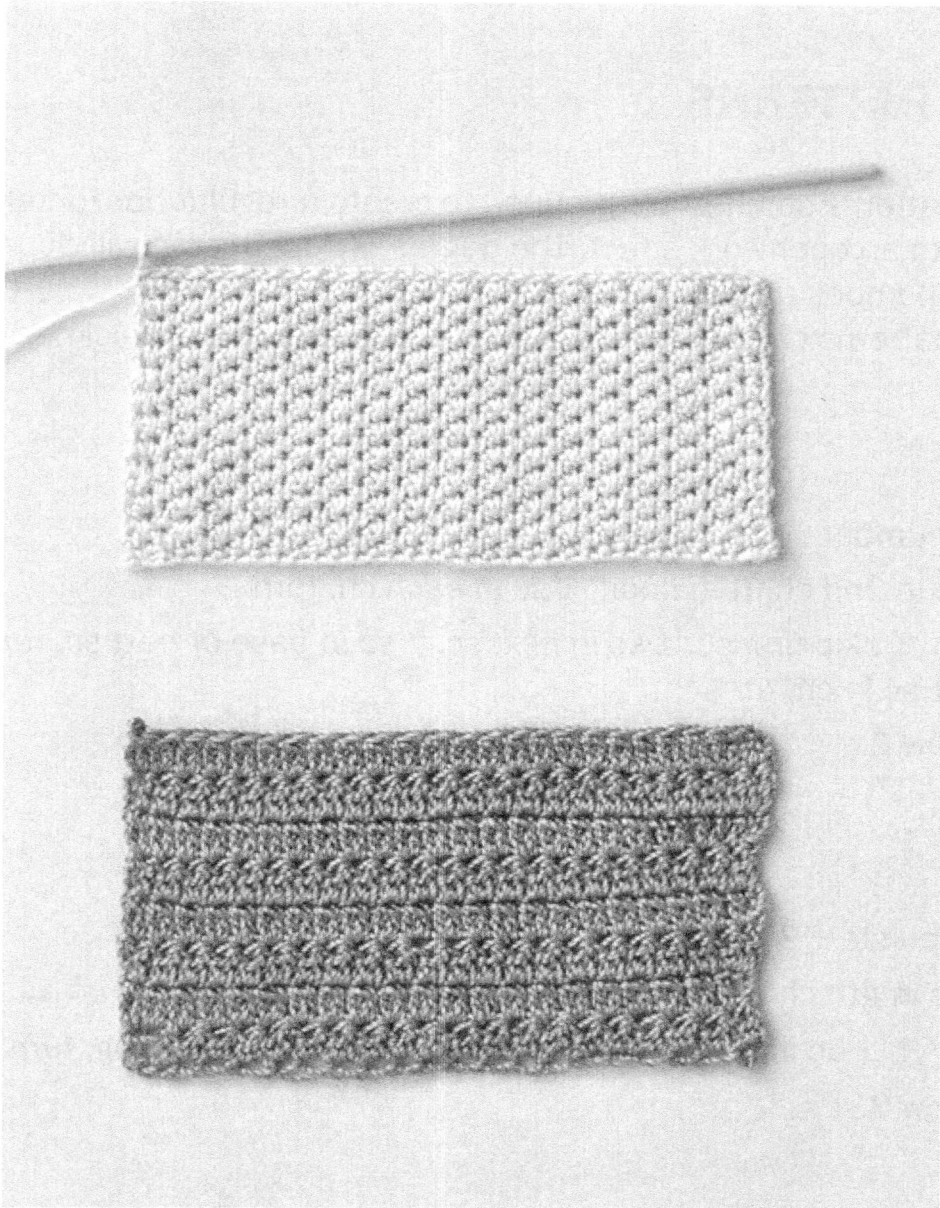

Open 1 (top) and Open 2

OPEN PATTERNS

In these patterns stitches are grouped to create a regular horizontal design, usually with an openwork effect. The degree of "openness" will depend on the yarn and hook used.

These patterns can be worked in cottons or wool, in any thickness.

OPEN 1

Ch: even number

Row 1: Sc in 2nd ch from hook, 1 sc in each ch, turn.

Row 2: Ch 1, skip first sc, *1 sc in next sc, 1 sc in base of next sc, repeat from *, 1 sc in ch, turn.

Repeat Row 2.

OPEN 2

Ch: required sts + **3**

Row 1: Dc in 4th ch from hook, dc2tog in each ch, turn.

Row 2: Ch 3, 1 dc in first dc2tog, dc2tog in top of each dc2tog, turn.

Repeat Row 2.

> **Tip-** Work the Open 2 foundation chain loosely to accommodate the two double crochets to be worked into each chain.

Open 3 (top) and Open 4

OPEN 3

Spike double crochet: Work a double crochet as usual, inserting the hook in the row below, in the space between the two stitches last worked into.
Ch: odd number

Row 1: Hdc2tog over 4th and 5th ch from hook, *1 dc in same ch as last st,* hdc2tog over next 2 ch, repeat from , turn.

Row 2: Ch 3, hdc2tog over hdctog and dc, *1 spike dc, hdc2tog over next hdctog and dc, repeat from* , hdc2tog over last hdctog and 3rd ch of tch, turn.

Row 3: Ch 3, hdc2tog over hdctog and spike dc, *1 spike dc, hdc2tog over next hdctog and spike dc, repeat from* , hdc2tog over last hdctog and 3rd ch of tch, turn.

Repeat Row 3.

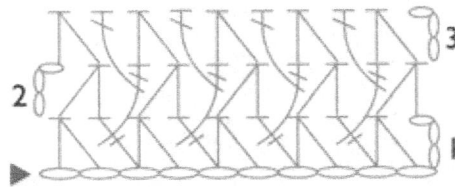

OPEN 4

Ch: multiple of 6 + 3

Row 1: Sc in 2nd ch from hook, 1 sc in next ch, *1 dc in each of next 3 ch, 1 sc in each of next 3 ch, repeat from* , turn.

Row 2: Ch 3, skip first sc, 1 dc in each of 2 sc, *1 sc in front loop of each of 3 dc, 1 dc in each of 3 sc, repeat from* with last dc in ch, turn.

Row 3: Ch 1, skip first dc, 1 sc in back loop of each of 2 dc, *1 dc in each of 3 sc, 1 sc in back loop of each of 3 dc, repeat from* to end with last sc in 3rd ch of tch, turn.

Repeat Rows 2 and 3.

See work into back loops.

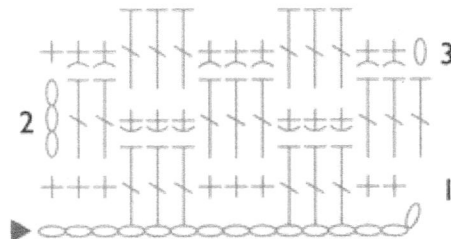

Open 5 (top) and Open 6

OPEN 5

Ch: multiple of 4 + 2

Row 1: (WS) Sc in 2nd ch from hook, 1 sc in each ch, turn.

Row 2: Ch 3, skip first sc, *skip next sc, 1 dc in each of next 3 sc, 1 dc in last* *sc skipped, repeat from , 1 dc in ch, turn.*

Row 3: Ch 1, skip first dc, 1 sc in each dc to end of row, 1 sc in 3rd ch of tch, turn.

Repeat Rows 2 and 3.

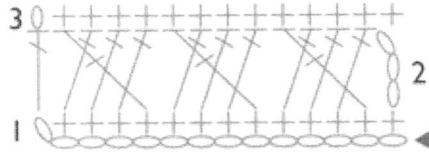

OPEN 6

Ch: required sts + 1

Row 1: Sc2tog inserting hook in 2nd and 3rd ch from hook, *sc2tog inserting hook into same ch as last st and into next ch, repeat from , turn.*

Row 2: Ch 1, sc2tog inserting hook in first and 2nd sc2tog, *sc2tog inserting hook into same place as last st and into next sc2tog, repeat from to end with last st in tch, turn.*

Repeat Row 2.

Tip- Finish this pattern with an odd-numbered row of single crochet, and remember that this is a wrong side row when you are fastening off.

Open 7 (top), Open 8 (center), and Open 9

OPEN 7

Ch: multiple of 6 + 3

Row 1: Dc in 4th ch from hook, 1 dc in next ch, *ch 3, skip 3 ch, 1 dc in each of next 3 ch, repeat from* , ending with 3 ch, skip 3 ch, 1 dc in last ch, turn.

Row 2: Ch 3, skip first dc, 2 dc in first 3 ch-sp, *ch 3, skip 3 dc, 3 dc in next 3 ch-sp, repeat from* , ending ch 3, skip 2 dc, 1 dc in 3rd ch of tch, turn.

Repeat Row 2.

OPEN 8

Bobble = 5 double crochets; small bobble = 2 double crochets Ch: even number

Work 1 bobble in 4th ch from hook, *ch 1, skip 1 ch, work 1 bobble in next ch, repeat from* , turn.

Ch 3, skip first bobble, *work 1 bobble in ch-sp, ch 1, skip next bobble, repeat from* , work small bobble in 3rd ch of tch, turn.

Repeat Row 2.

See a bobble.

OPEN 9

Ch: even number

Row 1: Dc3tog in 4th ch from hook, *ch 1, skip 1 ch, dc3tog in next ch, repeat from* , turn.

Row 2: Ch 3, skip first dctog, *dc3tog in ch-sp, ch 1, skip dctog, repeat from* , dc3tog in 3rd ch of tch, turn.

Repeat Row 2.

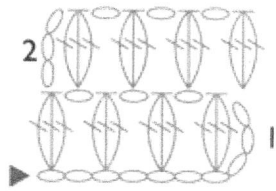

Fan 1 (top) and Fan 2

FAN PATTERNS

Fan patterns are those where multiple stitches are worked into the same place to create a fan, or shell, shape. The number and type of stitches used will vary, but they are consistent within the pattern. Fans can be worked successfully in any yarn.

FAN 1

Ch: multiple of 6 + 1

Row 1: Work 2 dc in 4th ch from hook, skip 2 ch, 1 sc in next ch, *skip 2 ch, 4 dc in next ch, skip 2 ch, 1 sc in next ch, repeat from* , turn.

Row 2: Ch 3, 2 dc in first sc, *1 sc between 2nd and 3rd dc of group (center sp of 4 dc), skip 2 dc, 4 dc in next sc, skip 2 dc, repeat from* , 1 sc in sp between last dc and tch, turn.

Repeat Row 2.

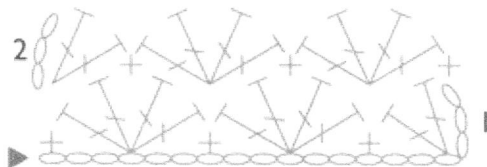

FAN 2

Ch: multiple of 7 + 4

Row 1: Dc in 4th ch from hook, *skip 2 ch, 5 dc in next ch, skip 2 ch, 1 dc in each of next 2 ch, repeat from* , turn.

Row 2: Ch 3, 2 dc in first dc, skip 3 dc, *1 dc in sp between 2nd and 3rd dc of group (either side of central dc of fan), 1 dc in sp between 3rd and 4th dc of 5 dc, skip 3 dc, 5 dc in sp between 2 vertical dc, skip 3 dc, repeat from* , 3 dc in sp between last dc and tch, turn.

Row 3: Ch 3, 1 dc between first 2 dc, *skip 3 dc, 5 dc in sp between 2 vertical* *dc, skip 3 dc, 1 dc in sp between 2nd and 3rd dc of 5 dc, 1 dc in sp between 3rd and 4th dc of 5 dc, repeat from , 1 dc in sp between last dc and ch-3, 1 dc in 3rd ch of tch, turn.*

Repeat Rows 2 and 3.

Fan 3 (top) and Fan 4

FAN 3

Ch: multiple of 10 + 4

Row 1: Dc in 4th ch from hook, 1 dc in each ch to end, turn.

Row 2: Ch 3, skip first dc, *1 dc in each of next 5 dc, skip 2 dc, (dc2tog, ch 1,* dc2tog, ch 1, dc2tog) in next dc, skip 2 dc, repeat from , 1 dc in 3rd ch of tch, turn.

Row 3: Ch 3, skip first dc, *1 dc in dctog, 1 dc in ch-sp, 1 dc in dctog, 1 dc in ch-sp, 1 dc in dctog, 1 dc in each of 5 dc, repeat from , 1 dc in 3rd ch of tch, turn.*

Row 4: Ch 3, skip first dc, *skip next 2 dc, (dc2tog, ch 1, dc2tog, ch 1, dc2tog) in next dc, skip 2 dc, 1 dc in each of next 5 dc, repeat from , 1 dc in 3rd ch of tch, turn.*

Row 5: Ch 3, skip first dc, *1 dc in each of next 5 dc, 1 dc in dctog, 1 dc in ch-sp, 1 dc in dctog, 1 dc in ch-sp, 1 dc in dctog, repeat from , 1 dc in 3rd ch of tch, turn.*

Repeat Rows 2–5.

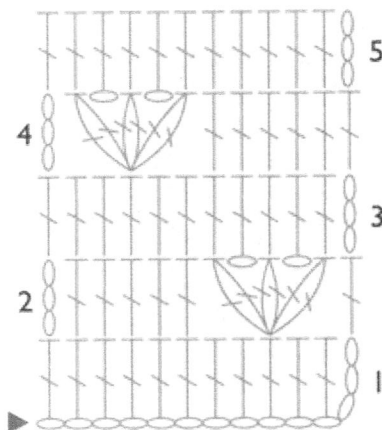

FAN 4

Group = 2 linked double crochets: *Yo, insert hook in next st, yo, pull up a loop, yo, draw yarn through first 2 loops, skip next 3 sts, repeat from to in next st, yo, draw yarn through first 2 loops, yo, draw yarn through all loops on hook.*

Ch: multiple of 6 + 1

Row 1: Work (2 dc, ch 1, 2 dc) in 4th ch from hook, *work 1 group, (2 dc, ch 1, 2 dc) in next ch, repeat from to last 3 ch, work 1 group ending in last ch, turn.*

Row 2: Ch 3, skip (first group, 1 dc), 1 dc in next dc, *(2 dc, ch 1, 2 dc) in ch-sp, work 1 group, repeat from , ending last group in 3rd ch of tch,*

turn.

Repeat Row 2.

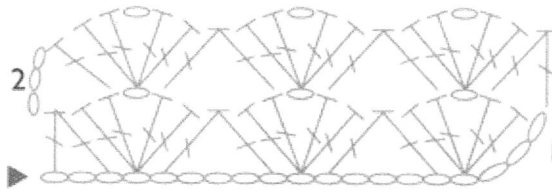

Fan 5 (top) and Fan 6

FAN 5

Ch: multiple of 6 + 1

Row 1: Work 2 dc in 4th ch from hook, skip 2 ch, *1 sc in next ch, skip 2 ch, 5 dc in next ch, skip 2 ch, repeat from* , 1 sc in last ch, turn.

Row 2: Ch 3, 2 dc in front loop of first sc, skip 2 dc, *1 sc in front loop of next dc (center dc of 5 dc), skip 2 dc, 5 dc in front loop of next sc, skip 2 dc, repeat from* , 1 sc in 3rd ch of tch, turn.

Row 3: As Row 2, but work in back loops of sts.

Repeat Rows 2 and 3.

See working in front and back loops.

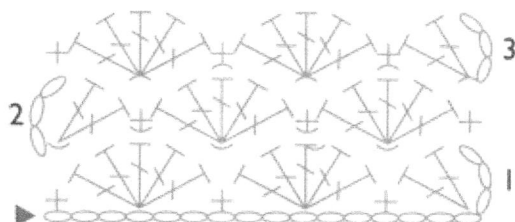

FAN 6

Ch: multiple of 4 + 1

Row 1: Work 3 dc in 5th ch from hook, skip 3 ch, 1 sc in next ch, *ch 3, 3 dc in same ch as last sc, skip 3 ch, 1 sc in next ch, repeat from* , turn.

Row 2: Ch 4, 3 dc in first ch of ch-4, skip (1 sc, 3 dc), 1 sc in ch-3 sp, *ch 3, 3 dc in same ch-sp as last sc, skip (1 sc, 3 dc), 1 sc in next ch-3 sp, repeat from* , working last sc under 4th ch of tch, turn.

Repeat Row 2.

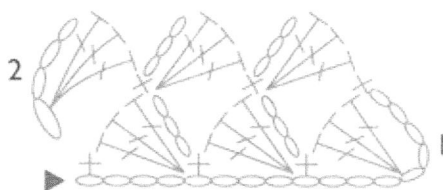

Fan 7 (top) and Fan 8

FAN 7

Ch: multiple of 6 + 2

Row 1: (WS) Work 5 dc in 5th ch from hook, skip 2 ch, 1 sc in next ch, *skip 2 ch, 5 dc in next ch, skip 2 ch, 1 sc in next ch, repeat from* , turn.

Row 2: Ch 5, skip (first sc, 2 dc), *1 sc in next dc (center dc of 5 dc), ch 2, skip 2 dc, 1 dc in sc, ch 2, skip 2 dc, repeat from* , 1 dc in tch, turn.

Row 3: Ch 3, 2 dc in first dc, *skip 2 ch, 1 sc in sc, skip 2 ch, 5 dc in dc, repeat from* , ending 3 dc in 3rd ch of tch, turn.

Row 4: Ch 1, skip first dc, *ch 2, skip 2 dc, 1 dc in sc, ch 2, skip 2 dc, 1 sc in next dc (center dc of 5 dc), repeat from* , 1 sc in 3rd ch of tch, turn.

Row 5: Ch 1, skip first sc, *skip 2 ch, 5 dc in dc, skip 2 ch, 1 sc in sc, repeat from* with last sc in first ch of tch, turn.

Repeat Rows 2–5.

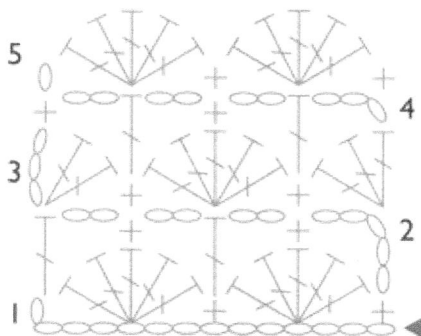

FAN 8

Ch: multiple of 4 + 1

Row 1: (Dc, ch 1) 3 times in 6th ch from hook, 1 dc in same ch, *skip 3 ch, (1 dc, ch 1) 3 times in next ch, 1 dc in same ch, repeat from* to last 3 ch, skip 2 ch, 1 dc in last ch, turn.

Row 2: Ch 3, skip (1 dc, 1 ch, 1 dc), *(1 dc, ch 1) 3 times in next ch-sp, 1 dc in same ch-sp, skip (1 dc, 1 ch, 2 dc, 1 ch, 1 dc), repeat from* to center of last group, skip (1 dc, 1 ch, 1 dc), 1 dc in 5th ch of tch, turn.

Repeat Row 2, ending subsequent rows with 1 dc in 3rd ch of tch, turn.

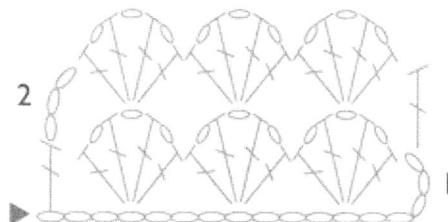

Fan 9 (top) and Fan 10

FAN 9

Ch: multiple of 10 + 2

Row 1: Sc in 2nd ch from hook, *skip 4 ch, 9 tr in next ch, skip 4 ch, 1 sc, repeat from* , turn.

Row 2: Ch 4, 1 tr in first sc, *ch 3, skip 4 tr, 1 sc in center tr of 9 tr, ch 3, skip 4 tr, 2 tr in sc, repeat from* , turn.

Row 3: Ch 1, 1 sc in sp between 2 tr, *skip 3 ch, 9 tr in sc, skip 3 ch, 1 sc in sp between 2 tr, repeat from* , 1 sc in sp between last tr and tch, turn.

Repeat Rows 2 and 3.

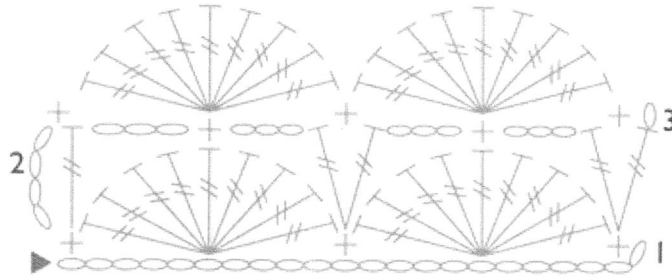

FAN 10

Ch: multiple of 8 + 2

Row 1: (Dc, ch 1) 4 times in 6th ch from hook, 1 dc in same ch, skip 3 ch, 1 sc in next ch, skip 3 ch, *(1 dc, ch 1) 4 times in next ch, 1 dc in same ch, skip 3 ch, 1 sc in next ch, skip 3 ch, repeat from* , turn.

Row 2: Ch 6, skip first sc, *skip (1 dc, 1 ch) twice, 1 sc in center dc of 5 dc, ch 3, skip (1 ch, 1 dc) twice, 1 dc in sc, ch 3, repeat from* , 1 dc in ch after last dc, turn.

Row 3: Ch 1, skip first dc, *skip 3 ch, 1 dc in sc, (ch 1, 1 dc) 4 times in same sc as last dc, skip 3 ch, 1 sc in dc, repeat from* , 1 sc in 3rd ch of tch, turn.

Repeat Rows 2 and 3.

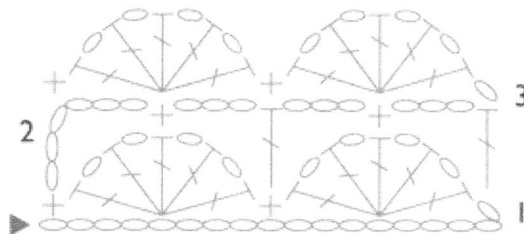

Fan 11 (top) and Fan 12

FAN 11

Ch: multiple of 4 + 1

Row 1: (Dc, ch 2, 1 dc) in 6th ch from hook, *skip 3 ch, (1 dc, ch 2, 1 dc) in next ch, repeat from* to last 3 ch, skip 2 ch, 1 dc in last ch, turn.

Row 2: Ch 3, skip first 2 dc, *4 dc in ch-2 sp, skip 2 dc, repeat from* , skip last dc, 1 dc in ch, turn.

Row 3: Ch 4, 1 dc in sp between first 2 dc, *skip 4 dc, (1 dc, ch 2, 1 dc) in sp before next group of 4 dc, repeat from* , (1 dc, ch 1, 1 dc) in sp before tch, turn.

Row 4: Ch 3, skip first dc, 2 dc in ch-1 sp, *skip 2 dc, 4 dc in ch-2 sp, repeat from* , 3 dc in ch-4 sp, turn.

Row 5: Ch 3, skip first 3 dc, *(1 dc, ch 2, 1 dc) in sp before next group, skip 4 dc, repeat from* , skip last 2 dc, 1 dc in sp between last dc and tch, turn.

Repeat Rows 2–5.

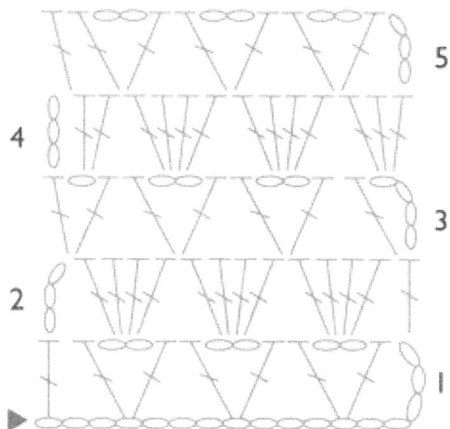

FAN 12

Ch: multiple of 4 + 3

Row 1: Work (2 dc, ch 1, 2 dc) in 5th ch from hook, *skip 3 ch, (2 dc, ch 1, 2 dc) in next ch, repeat from* to last 2 ch, skip 1 ch, 1 dc in last ch, turn.

Row 2: Ch 3, skip first 3 dc, *(2 dc, ch 1, 2 dc) in ch-sp, skip next 4 dc, repeat from* , skip last 2 dc, 1 dc below 3rd ch of tch, turn.

Repeat Row 2.

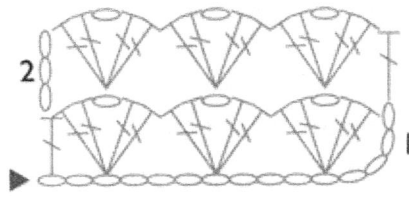

⋮ TRELLIS PATTERNS

In these patterns the stitches are arranged to create a trellis or latticelike design. The effect is open and decorative, although the fabric is not durable. Most yarns work well with these patterns.

USING OLDER PATTERNS

One of the joys of becoming adept at a craft such as crochet is finding old patterns, perhaps ones your grandmother had put away in a cupboard or some you find tucked away among a pile of books from a thrift shop. Some of these patterns are really beautiful, and you may be inspired to try them. Modern crocheters can, however, find old patterns difficult to follow, as they do not give the detailed instructions we are used to.

Crocheters of the nineteenth and early twentieth centuries learned to crochet as children, at school, and from family members. It was natural to them and they did not need to be told to turn the piece at the end of the row, to work turning chains, or even when to skip stitches. All they needed was the outline of the pattern.

So when you use an older pattern, do not despair if it does not seem to be working. Take time to make a swatch and figure out what the pattern is not telling you. Then you can crochet your heirloom piece with confidence.

Trellis 1 (top) and Trellis 2

TRELLIS 1

Ch: odd number

Row 1: Dc in 5th ch from hook, *ch 1, skip 1 ch, 1 dc in next ch, repeat from ,* turn.

Row 2: Ch 4, skip first dc, *1 dc in next ch-sp, ch 1, skip 1 dc, repeat from , 1* dc below 4th ch of tch, turn.

Repeat Row 2.

TRELLIS 2

Ch: multiple of 3 + 2

Row 1: Dc in 8th ch from hook, *ch 2, skip 2 ch, 1 dc in next ch, repeat from* , turn.

Row 2: Ch 5, skip first dc and 2 ch, *1 dc in next dc, ch 2, skip 2 ch, repeat from* , 1 dc in next ch, turn.

Repeat Row 2.

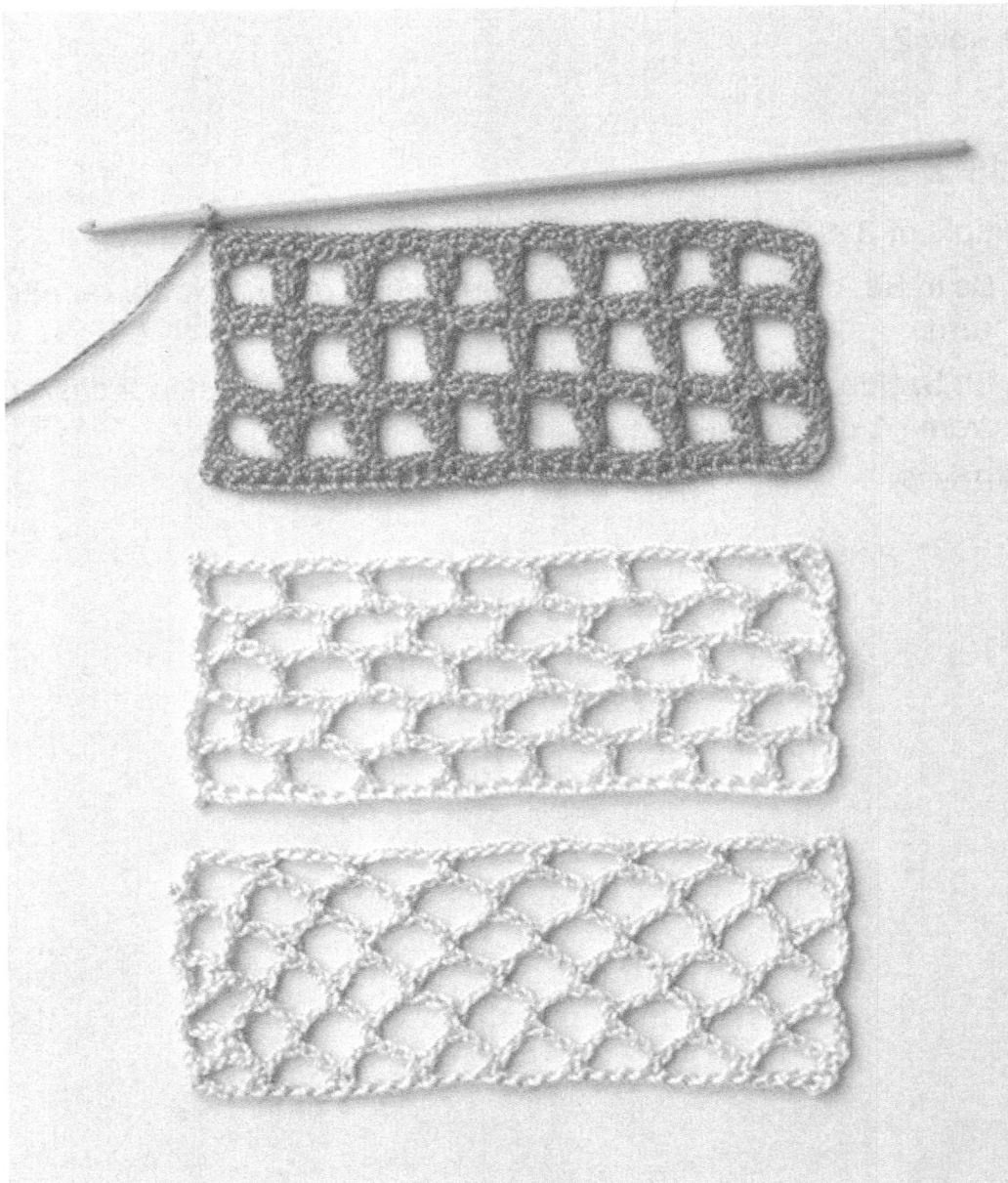

Trellis 3 (top), Trellis 4 (center), and Trellis 5

TRELLIS 3

Ch: multiple of 4 + 2

Row 1: (WS) Sc in 2nd ch from hook, 1 sc in each ch, turn.

Row 2: Ch 9, skip first 4 sc, Sl st in next sc, turn, 1 sc in each of first 3 ch, *ch*

6, *turn, skip next 3 sc of previous row, SI st in next sc, 1 sc in each of first 3 ch, repeat from*, turn.

Row 3: Ch 1, 1 sc in same ch as last sc of Row 2, *1 sc in each of next 3 ch, 1 sc in same ch as top sc of vertical, repeat from*, working last sc in 3rd ch of empty ch-3 at beginning of Row 2, turn.

Repeat Rows 2 and 3.

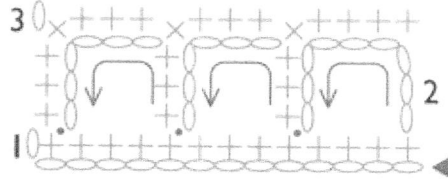

TRELLIS 4

Ch: multiple of 4

Row 1: Dc in 8th ch from hook, *ch 4, skip 3 ch, 1 dc in next ch, repeat from*, turn.

Row 2: Ch 5, 1 dc in first ch-sp, *ch 4, 1 dc in next ch-sp, repeat from*, turn.

Repeat Row 2.

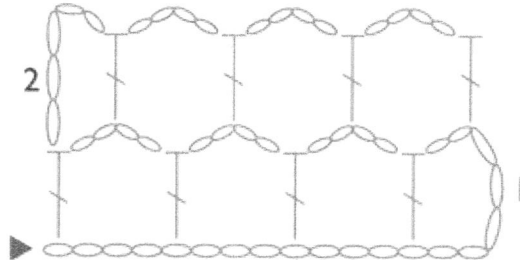

TRELLIS 5

Ch: multiple of 4 + 2

Row 1: Sc in 10th ch from hook, *ch 5, skip 3 ch, 1 sc in next ch, repeat from*, turn.

Row 2: Ch 6, skip (1 sc, 2 ch), *1 sc in next ch, ch 5, skip (2 ch, 1 sc, 2 ch), repeat from*, after last sc ch 2, skip 2 ch, 1 dc in next ch, turn.

Row 3: ch 6, skip (1 dc, 2 ch, 1 sc, 2 ch), 1 sc in next ch, *ch 5, skip (2 ch, 1 *sc, 2 ch), 1 sc in next ch, repeat from , turn.*

Repeat Rows 2 and 3.

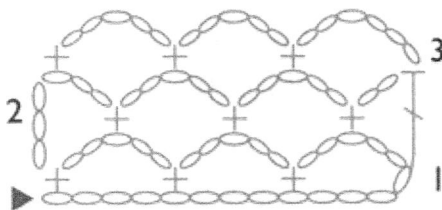

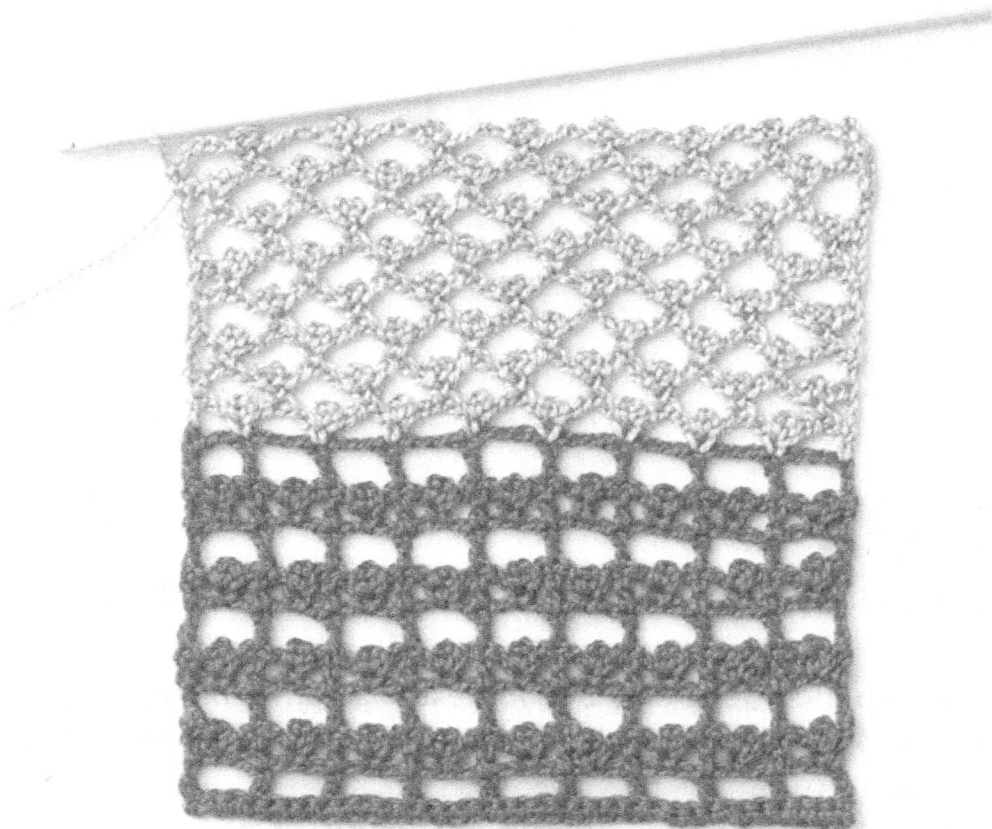

Trellis 6 (top) and Trellis 7

TRELLIS 6

Picot: chain-3 picot
Ch: multiple of 4

Row 1: Sc in 8th ch from hook, work 1 picot, *ch 5, skip 3 ch, 1 sc in next ch, work 1 picot, repeat from* with 1 sc in last ch, turn.

Row 2: Ch 5, skip first sc and 2 ch, *1 sc in next ch, work 1 picot, ch 5, skip (2 ch, 1 sc, picot, 2 ch), repeat from* with 1 sc in 3rd ch of tch, turn.

Row 3: Ch 5, skip first sc and 2 ch, *1 sc in next ch, work 1 picot, ch 5, skip (2 ch, 1 sc, picot, 2 ch), repeat from* with 1 sc in 3rd ch of last tch.

Repeat Row 3.

 See work a picot.

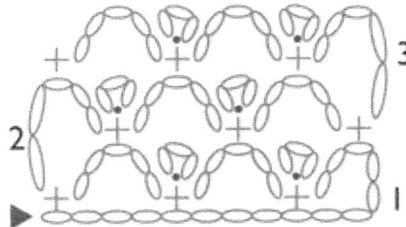

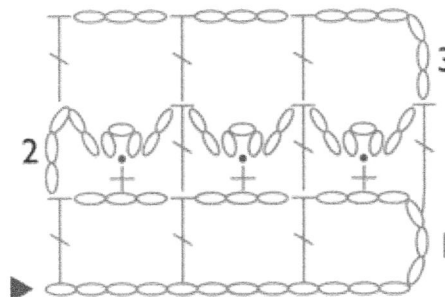

TRELLIS 7

Picot: chain-3 picot
Ch: multiple of 4 + 2

Row 1: Dc in 10th ch from hook, *ch 3, skip 3 ch, 1 dc in next ch, repeat from* , turn.

Row 2: Ch 5, skip (first dc, 1 ch), *1 sc in next ch, work 1 picot, ch 2, skip 1 ch, 1 dc in dc, ch 2, skip 1 ch, repeat from* with last dc in 2nd ch after sc, turn.

Row 3: Ch 6, skip (first dc, 2 ch, picot, 2 ch), *1 dc in dc, ch 3, skip (2 ch, picot, 2 ch), repeat from* with last dc in 2nd ch after sc, turn.

Repeat Rows 2 and 3.

 See work a picot.

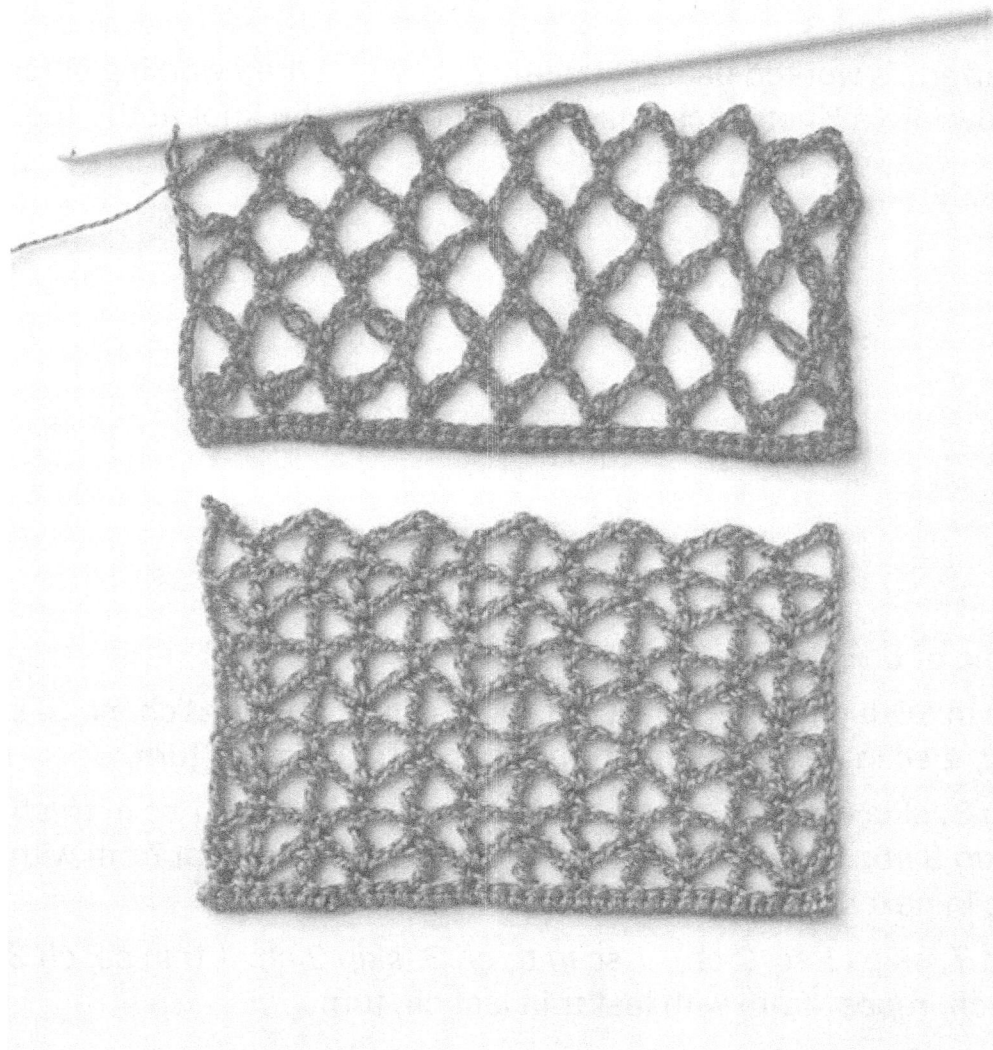

Trellis 8 (top) and Trellis 9

TRELLIS 8

Ch: multiple of 4 + 2

Row 1: Sc in 2nd ch from hook, *2 KS, skip 3 ch, 1 sc in next ch, repeat from* to end, turn.

Row 2: Ch 5, 1 KS, skip (first sc, 1 KS), *1 sc in next KS, 2 KS, skip (1 sc, 1 KS), repeat from* with 1 sc in last KS, 1 KS, 1 dtr in sc, turn.

Row 3: Ch 1, 1 sc in first KS, *2 KS, skip (1 sc, 1 KS), 1 sc in next KS, repeat from* , working last sc in 5th ch of tch, turn.

Repeat Rows 2 and 3.

This pattern is worked using Knot stitches (KS): When working stitches of the next row into a Knot stitch, insert the hook into the knot at the top, not the loop.

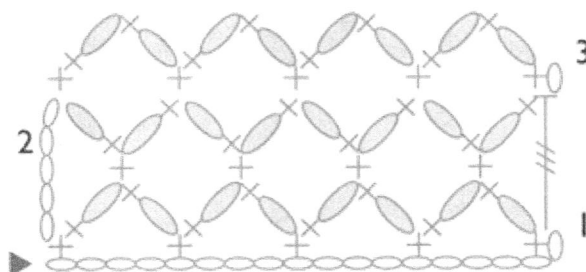

TRELLIS 9

Ch: multiple of 6 + 1

Row 1: Sc in 10th ch from hook, *ch 3, skip 2 ch, 1 tr in next ch, ch 3, skip 2 ch, 1 sc in next ch, repeat from* with 1 tr in last ch, turn.

Row 2: Ch 3, skip (first tr, 3 ch), 1 tr in sc, ch 2, skip 3 ch, 1 sc in tr, *ch 2, skip 3 ch, 1 tr in sc, ch 2, skip 3 ch, 1 sc in tr, repeat from* with last sc in next ch, turn.

Row 3: Ch 7, skip (1 sc, 2 ch), *1 sc in tr, ch 3, skip 2 ch, 1 tr in sc, ch 3, skip 2 ch, repeat from* with last tr in last ch, turn.

Repeat Rows 2 and 3.

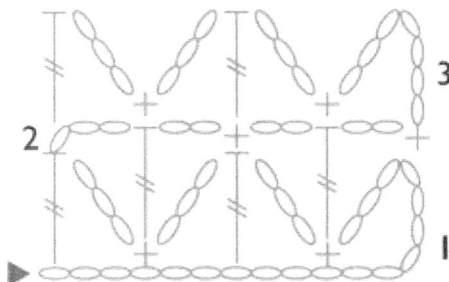

Tip- When worked in fine thread, Knot stitches make an open, lacy stitch, producing a cobweblike fabric.

*Trellis 10 **(top)**, Trellis 11 **(center)**, and Trellis 12*

TRELLIS 10

Ch: multiple of 4 + 3

Row 1: KS 1, skip 6 ch, 1 dc in next ch, *1 KS, skip 3 ch, 1 dc in next ch, repeat from* , turn.

Row 2: Ch 3, 1 KS, skip (first dc, 1 KS), 1 dc in dc, *1 KS, skip 1 KS, 1 dc in dc, repeat from* with last dc in last ch of tch, turn.

Repeat Row 2.

See Knot stitch (KS).

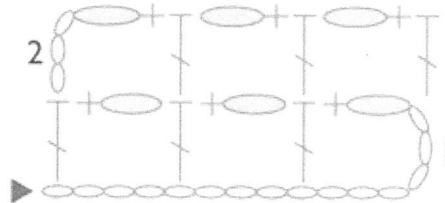

TRELLIS 11

Ch: multiple of 4 + 2

Row 1: Dc in 10th ch from hook, *ch 3, skip 3 ch, 1 dc in next ch, repeat from* to end, turn.

Row 2: Ch 4, skip (first dc, 3 ch), 1 sc in dc, *ch 3, skip 3 ch, 1 sc in dc, repeat from* with last sc in 4th ch, turn.

Row 3: Ch 6, skip (1 sc, 3 ch), *1 dc in next sc, ch 3, skip 3 ch, repeat from* with last dc in last ch, turn.

Repeat Rows 2 and 3.

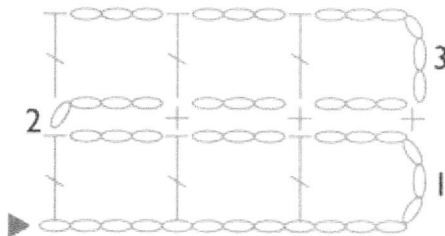

TRELLIS 12

Ch: multiple of 6 + 1

Row 1: (Sc, ch 3, 1 sc) in 13th ch from hook, *ch 5, skip 5 ch, (1 sc, ch 3, 1 sc) in next ch, repeat from* , ending with ch 5, skip 5 ch, 1 Esc in last ch, turn.

Row 2: Ch 7, skip first Esc, *skip 5 ch, (1 sc, ch 3, 1 sc) in ch-3 loop, ch 5, *repeat from* , ending with ch 5, skip 5 ch, 1 Esc in last ch, turn.

Repeat Row 2.

See extended single crochet (Esc).

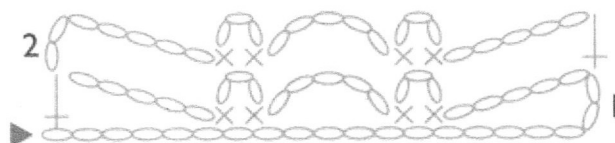

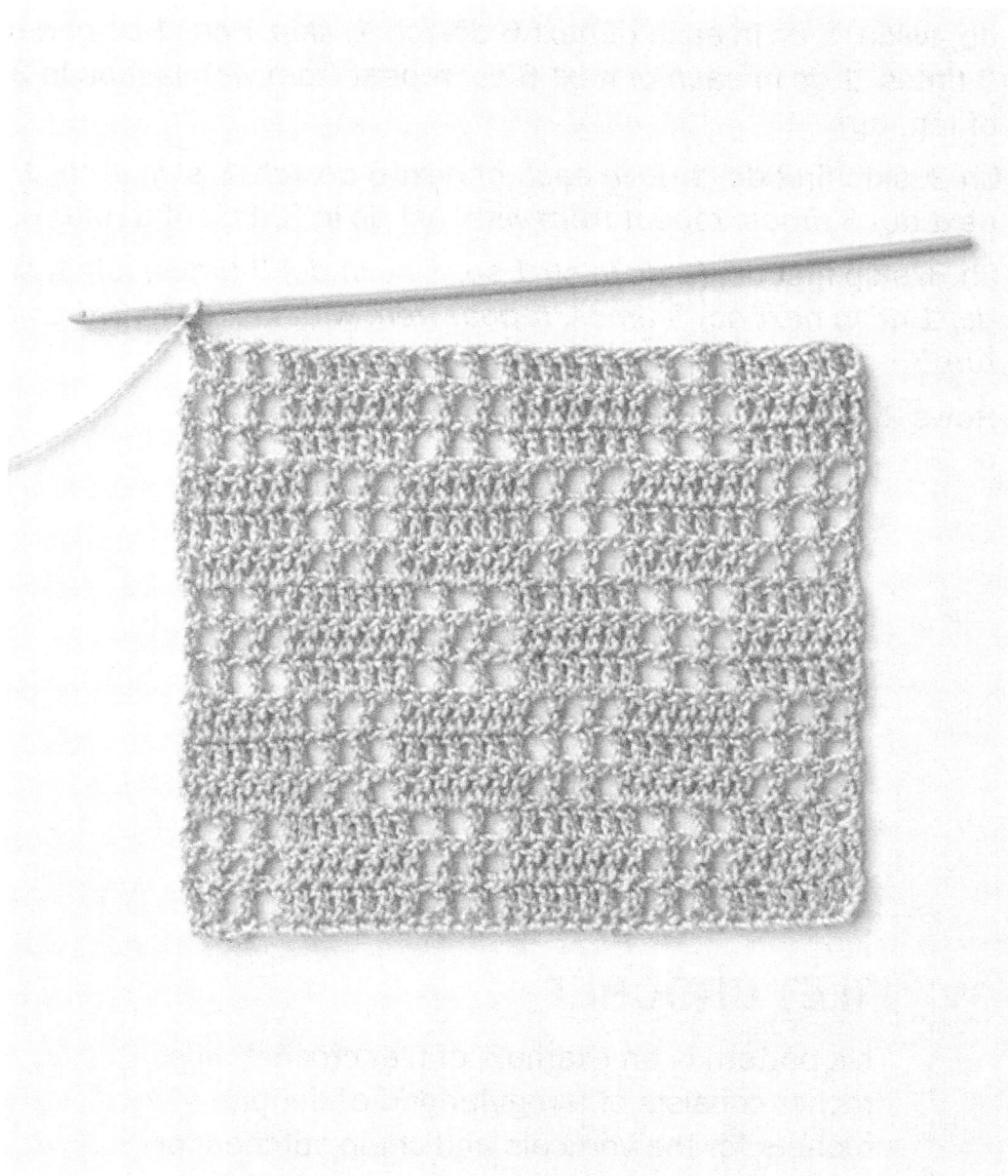

Trellis 13

TRELLIS 13

Ch: multiple of 12 + 3

Row 1: Dc in 4th ch from hook, 1 dc in each of next 5 ch, (ch 1, skip 1 ch, 1 dc in next ch) 3 times, *1 dc in each of next 6 ch, (ch 1, skip 1 ch, 1 dc in next ch) 3 times, repeat from* , turn.

Row 2: Ch 4, skip (first dc, 1 ch), 1 dc in next dc, (ch 1, skip 1 ch, 1 dc in next dc) twice, 1 dc in each of next 6 dc, *(ch 1, skip 1 ch, 1 dc in next dc) 3 times, 1 dc in each of next 6 dc, repeat from* with last dc in 3rd ch of tch, turn.

Row 3: Ch 3, skip first dc, *1 dc in each of next 6 dc, (ch 1, skip 1 ch, 1 dc in next dc) 3 times, repeat from* with last dc in 3rd ch of tch, turn.

Row 4: Ch 3, skip first dc, *(1 dc in ch-1 sp, 1 dc in dc) 3 times, (ch 1, skip 1 dc, 1 dc in next dc) 3 times, repeat from* with last dc in 3rd ch of tch, turn.

Repeat Rows 2–4.

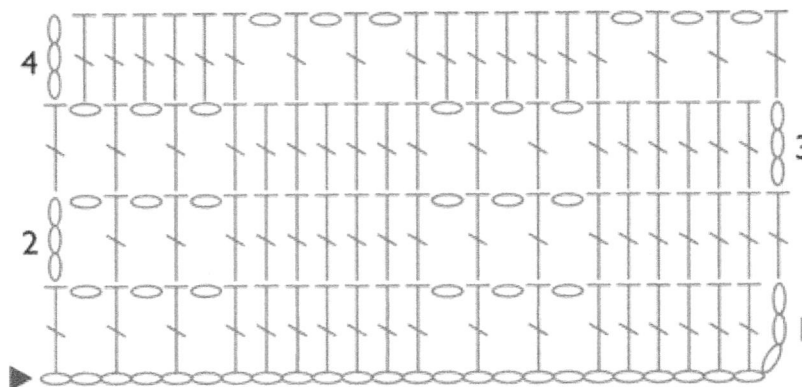

FILET CROCHET

This pattern is an example of filet crochet. Filet crochet consists of a regular grid of double crochets for the verticals and chain stitches for the horizontals. Designs are produced by filling in some of the squares with double crochets. Although the pattern chart can be indicated by symbols, it is traditionally presented as a squared chart, with the double crochets indicated by vertical lines and the chains by horizontal ones. Extremely fine hooks and yarns can be used to create intricate designs, but simpler designs in thicker threads–such as this one-can also be effective.

Trellis 14 (top) and Trellis 15

TRELLIS 14

Ch: multiple of 5

Row 1: Sl st in 4th ch from hook to make a picot, ch 2, skip 11 ch from hook and picot, 1 dc in next ch, *ch 7, Sl st in 4th ch from hook, ch 2, skip 4 ch, 1 dc in next ch, repeat from* , turn.

Row 2: Ch 10, Sl st in 4th ch from hook, ch 2, skip (first dc, 2 ch, 1 picot, 1 ch), 1 dc in next ch, *ch 7, Sl st in 4th ch from hook, ch 2, skip (2 ch, 1 dc, 2 ch, 1 picot, 1 ch), 1 dc in next ch, repeat from* , turn.

Repeat Row 2.

See work a picot.

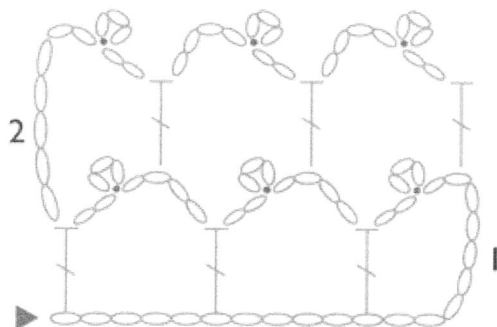

TRELLIS 15

Group: (Yo, insert hook as indicated, yo, pull up a loop) 4 times in same place, yo, draw yarn through first 8 loops on hook, yo, draw yarn through remaining 2 loops on hook Ch: even number

Work 1 group in 4th ch from hook, ch 1, *skip 1 ch, work 1 group in next ch, ch 1, repeat from* replacing last group with 1 dc in last ch, turn.

Ch 3, skip first dc, work 1 group in first ch-sp, *ch 1, skip 1 group, work 1 group in next ch-sp, repeat from* , replacing last group with 1 dc in 3rd ch of tch, turn.

Repeat Row 2.

Arch 1

ARCH PATTERNS

These patterns incorporate arched designs that are worked into loops of chains. They tend to be open and intricate and are best worked in firm cottons.

ARCH 1

Ch: multiple of 6 + 1

Row 1: Sc in 2nd ch from hook, *ch 3, skip 3 ch, 1 sc in each of next 3 ch, repeat from* , ending with 2 sc, turn.

Row 2: Ch 1, skip first sc, *skip 1 sc, 5 dc in ch-3 sp, skip 1 sc, 1 sc in next sc, repeat from* with last sc in tch, turn.

Row 3: Ch 3, skip (1 sc, 1 dc), *1 sc in each of next 3 dc, ch 3, skip (1 dc, 1 sc, 1 dc), repeat from* to last 3 sc, ch 2, skip 1 dc, 1 sc in tch, turn.

Row 4: Ch 3, skip first sc, 2 dc in ch-2 sp, *skip 1 sc, 1 sc in next sc (the center sc of 3 sc), skip 1 sc, 5 dc in ch-3 sp, repeat from* to last sc, skip 1 sc, 3 dc below tch, turn.

Row 5: Ch 1, skip first dc, 1 sc in next dc, *ch 3, skip (1 dc, 1 sc, 1 dc), 1 sc in each of next 3 dc (the center 3 dc of 5 dc), repeat from* , ending with 1 sc in last dc, 1 sc in 3rd ch of tch, turn.

Repeat Rows 2–5.

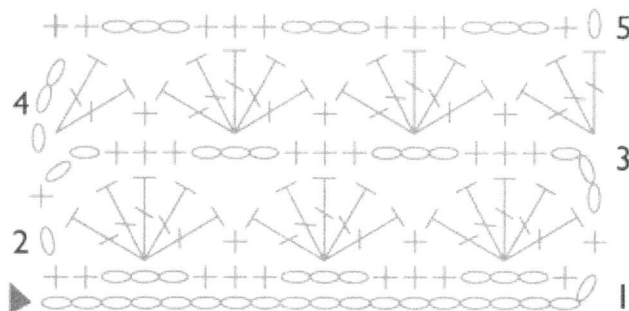

Arch 2 (top) and Arch 3

ARCH 2

Ch: multiple of 12 + 7

Row 1: (WS) Sc in 11th ch from hook, *ch 5, skip 3 ch, 1 sc in next ch, repeat from* , turn.

Row 2: Ch 5, skip first sc, 1 sc in ch-5 sp, *skip 1 sc, 7 dc in next ch-5 sp, skip 1 sc, 1 sc in next ch-5 sp, ch 5, skip 1 sc, 1 sc in next ch-5 sp, repeat from* to sc in last ch-sp, ch 2, 1 dc in 6th ch from last sc of previous row, turn.

Row 3: Ch 6, skip (1 dc, 2 ch, 1 sc, 1 dc), *1 sc in next dc (the 2nd dc of 7 dc), ch 5, skip 3 dc, 1 sc in next dc (the 6th dc of 7 dc), ch 5, skip (1 dc, 1 sc), 1 sc in ch-5 sp, ch 5, skip (1 sc, 1 dc), repeat from* , ending with 1 sc, turn.

Repeat Rows 2 and 3.

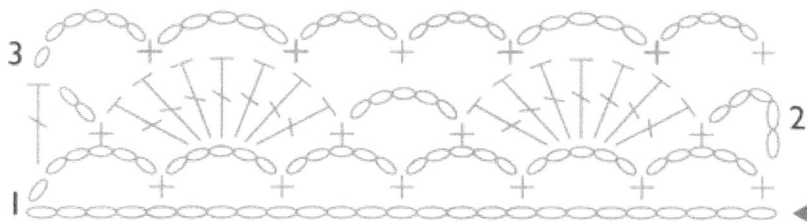

ARCH 3

Ch: multiple of 4

Row 1: (Sc, ch 3, 1 sc) in 4th ch from hook, 1 sc in next ch, *ch 2, skip 2 ch, (1 sc, ch 3, 1 sc) in next ch, 1 sc in next ch, repeat from* to last 3 ch, ch 2, skip 2 ch, 1 sc in last ch, turn.

Row 2: Ch 3, skip first sc, *(1 dc, ch 3, 1 sc in back loop of dc, 1 dc) in ch-2 sp, ch 2, skip 1 group, repeat from* , 1 dc below tch, turn.

Row 3: Ch 3, skip first dc, *(1 dc, ch 3, 1 sc in back loop of dc, 1 dc) in ch-2 sp, ch 2, skip 1 group, repeat from* , 1 dc in tch, turn.

Repeat Row 3.

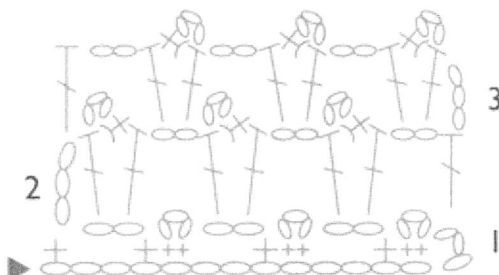

Arch 4

ARCH 4

Ch: multiple of 8 + 2

Row 1: Sc in 3rd ch from hook, 1 sc in next ch, *ch 5, skip 3 ch, 1 sc in each of next 5 ch, repeat from* , ending with 1 sc in each of last 3 ch, turn.

Row 2: Ch 2, skip first 2 sc, *1 sc in next sc, 9 tr in ch-5 sp, 1 sc in next sc, ch 2, skip 3 sc, repeat from* to last 2 sc, 1 sc in next sc, ch 1, skip 1 sc, 1 sc in tch, turn.

Row 3: Ch 8, skip (first sc, 1 ch, 1 sc, 3 tr), *1 sc in each of next 3 tr (center tr), ch 3, skip (3 tr, 1 sc), 1 dtr in ch-2 sp, ch 3, skip (1 sc, 3 tr), repeat from* ending with 1 dtr, turn.

Row 4: Ch 4, skip first dtr, *1 sc in ch-3 sp, 1 sc in each of 3 sc, 1 sc in ch-3 sp, ch 5, skip 1 dtr, repeat from* , ending with ch 3, 1 sc in 5th ch of tch, turn.

Row 5: Ch 4, skip first sc, 4 tr in ch-3 sp, *1 sc in next sc, ch 2, skip 3 sc, 1 sc in next sc, 9 tr in ch-5 sp, repeat from* , ending with 5 tr in ch-4 sp, turn.

Row 6: Ch 1, skip first tr, 1 sc in next tr, *ch 3, skip (3 tr, 1 sc), 1 dtr in ch-2 sp, ch 3, skip (1 sc, 3 tr), 1 sc in each of next 3 tr, repeat from* with 1 sc in last tr, 1 sc in 4th ch of tch, turn.

Row 7: Ch 1, skip first sc, 1 sc in next sc, *1 sc in ch-3 sp, ch 5, skip 1 dtr, 1 sc in next ch-3 sp, 1 sc in each of 3 sc, repeat from* with 1 sc in last sc, 1 sc in last ch, turn.

Repeat Rows 2–7.

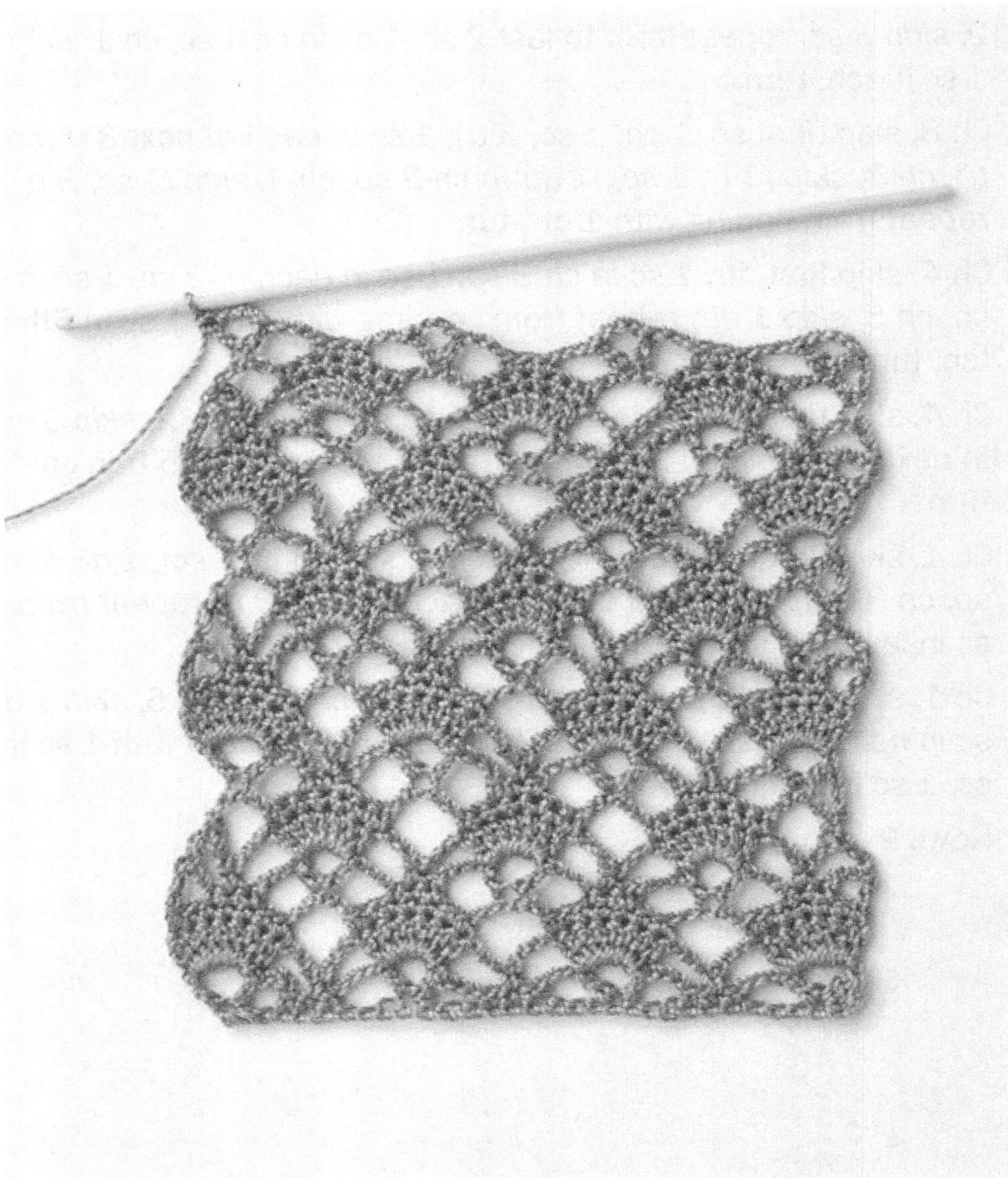

Arch 5

ARCH 5

Ch: multiple of 10 + 4

Row 1: (Dc, ch 3, 1 dc) in 4th ch from hook, *ch 3, skip 3 ch, 1 sc in each of next 3 ch, ch 3, skip 3 ch, (1 dc, ch 3, 1 dc) in next ch, repeat from ,* turn.

Row 2: Ch 3, skip first dc, *7 dc in ch-3 sp, ch 3, skip (1 dc, 3 ch, 1 sc), 1 sc in next sc, ch 3, skip (1 sc, 3 ch, 1 dc), repeat from* with 7 dc in last ch-3 sp, turn.

Row 3: Ch 1, skip first dc, 1 sc in each of next 6 dc, *ch 5, skip (3 ch, 1 sc, 3 ch), 1 sc in each of next 7 dc, repeat from* , turn.

Row 4: Ch 6, skip first 2 sc, *1 sc in each of next 3 sc (center 3 sc), ch 3, skip (2 sc, 2 ch), (1 dc, ch 3, 1 dc) in next ch, ch 3, skip (2 ch, 2 sc), repeat from* , ending with 3 sc, ch 3, skip 1 sc, 1 dc in last st, turn.

Row 5: Ch 6, skip (first dc, 3 ch, 1 sc), *1 sc in next sc, ch 3, skip (1 sc, 3 ch, 1 dc), 7 dc in next ch-3 sp, ch 3, skip (1 dc, 3 ch, 1 sc), repeat from* , ending with ch 3, 1 dc in 3rd ch of tch, turn.

Row 6: Ch 5, skip (first dc, 3 ch, 1 sc, 3 ch), *1 sc in each of next 7 dc, ch 5, skip (3 ch, 1 sc, 3 ch), repeat from* , ending with 1 sc in 3rd ch of tch, turn.

Row 7: Ch 3, skip (first sc, 2 ch), *(1 dc, ch 3, 1 dc) in next ch, ch 3, skip (2 ch, 2 sc), 1 sc in each of next 3 sc, ch 3, skip (2 sc, 2 ch), repeat from* , ending with (1 dc, ch 3, 1 dc) in 3rd ch of tch, turn.

Repeat Rows 2–7.

Arch 6

ARCH 6

Ch: multiple of 8 + 7

Row 1: Sc in 11th ch from hook, ch 3, skip 3 ch, 1 dc in next ch, *ch 3, skip 3 ch, 1 sc in next ch, ch 3, skip 3 ch, 1 dc in next ch, repeat from ,* turn.

Row 2: Ch 4, skip first dc, *skip 1 ch, 1 sc in next ch, ch 3, skip (1 ch, 1 sc, 1 ch), 1 sc in next ch, ch 1, skip 1 ch, 1 dc in dc, ch 1, repeat from* , working last dc in 4th ch from last sc of Row 1, turn.

Row 3: Ch 3, skip first dc, *skip (1 ch, 1 sc), 7 dc in ch-3 sp, skip (1 sc, 1 ch), 1 dc in dc, repeat from* , working last dc in 2nd ch of tch, turn.

Row 4: Ch 6, skip first 4 dc, 1 sc in next dc (center dc of 7 dc), ch 3, skip 3 dc, 1 dc in next dc, *ch 3, skip 3 dc, 1 sc in next dc (center dc of 7 dc), ch 3, skip 3 dc, 1 dc in next dc, repeat from* with last dc in 3rd ch of tch, turn.

Repeat Rows 2–4.

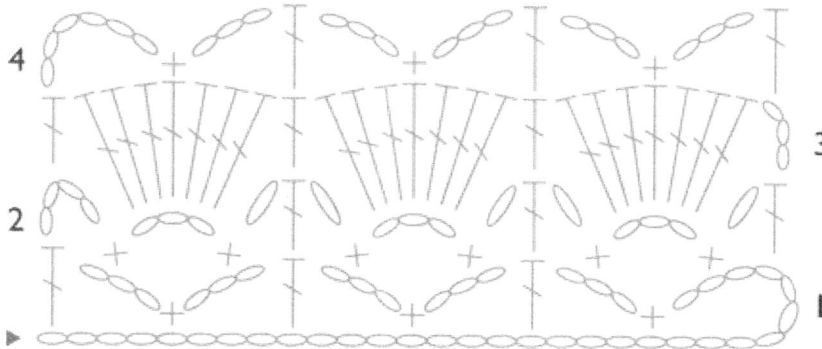

Arch 7 (top) and Arch 8

ARCH 7

Ch: multiple of 12 + 3

Row 1: Work CL of 3 dc over 4th, 5th, and 6th ch from hook, *ch 1, (1 tr in next ch, ch 1) twice, (1 tr, ch 1, 1 tr) in next ch, (ch 1, 1 tr in next ch) twice, ch 1, work CL of 7 dc over next 7 ch, repeat from* with CL of 4 dc over last 4 ch, turn.

Row 2: Ch 3, skip first CL, 1 dc in ch-1 sp, *(1 dc in tr, 1 dc in ch-1 sp) 5 times, 1 dc in next tr, work CL of 2 dc in next 2 ch-sps (skip CL), repeat from* with CL of 2 dc over last ch-sp and last CL, turn.

Row 3: Ch 3, skip CL, work CL of 3 dc over next 3 dc, *ch 1, (1 tr in next dc, ch 1) twice, (1 tr, ch 1, 1 tr) in next dc, (ch 1, 1 tr in next dc) twice, ch 1, work CL of 7 dc over next 7 sts, repeat from* with CL of 4 dc over last 4 tr, turn.

Repeat Rows 2 and 3.

See work a cluster (CL).

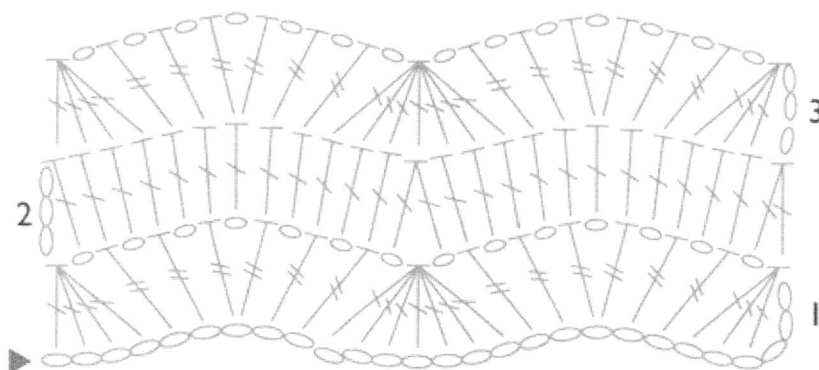

ARCH 8

Ch: multiple of 4

Row 1: Sc in 4th ch from hook, *ch 3, 1 sc in next ch, ch 3, skip 2 ch, 1 sc in next ch, repeat from* , turn.

Row 2: Ch 3, skip first sc, *(1 sc, ch 3, 1 sc) in ch-3 sp, ch 3, skip (1 sc, 3 ch, 1 sc), repeat from* with last sc below tch, turn.

Repeat Row 2.

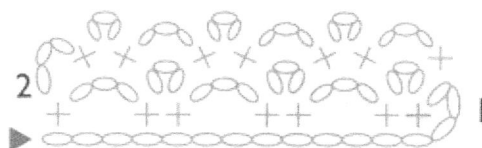

Arch 9

ARCH 9

Ch: multiple of 7 + 3

Row 1: Hdc in 3rd ch from hook, *ch 3, skip 2 ch, 1 sc in next ch, ch 3, skip 2 ch, 1 hdc in each of next 2 ch, repeat from , turn.*

Row 2: Ch 2, skip first hdc, 1 hdc in next hdc, *ch 3, skip 3 ch, (1 sc, ch 3, 1 sc) in sc, ch 3, skip 3 ch, 1 hdc in each of 2 hdc, repeat from* with last hdc in 2nd ch of tch, turn.

Row 3: Ch 1, skip first hdc, 1 sc in next hdc, *1 sc in ch-3 sp, ch 5, skip (1 sc, 3 ch, 1 sc), 1 sc in next ch-3 sp, 1 sc in each of 2 hdc, repeat from* with last sc in 2nd ch of tch, turn.

Row 4: Ch 1, skip first sc, 1 sc in next sc, *skip 1 sc, 7 sc in ch-5 sp, skip 1 sc, 1 sc in each of next 2 sc, repeat from* with last sc in tch, turn.

Row 5: Ch 2, skip first sc, 1 hdc in next sc, *ch 3, skip 3 sc, 1 sc in next sc (center sc of 7 sc), ch 3, skip 3 sc, 1 hdc in each of next 2 sc, repeat from* with last hdc in tch, turn.

Repeat Rows 2–5.

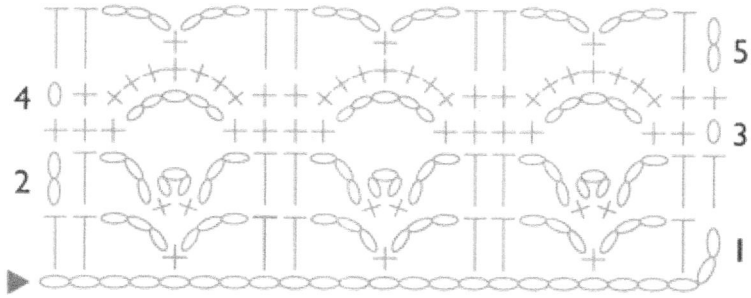

Arch 10

ARCH 10

Picot: chain-3 picot

Ch: multiple of 8 + 1

Row 1: Skip first ch, *1 sc in each of next 4 ch, work 1 picot, 1 sc in each of next 4 ch, turn, ch 9, Sl st in first sc of 8 sc, turn, (7 sc, 3 picot, 7 sc)* *in ch-9 sp, return to foundation row, repeat from , turn.*

Row 2: Ch 9, skip (first 7 sc, 1 picot), *1 sc in center of next picot, ch 8, skip (1 picot, 14 sc, 1 picot), repeat from* , ending with ch 4, skip (1 picot, 7 sc), 1 dtr in first ch of foundation row, turn.

Row 3: Ch 1, skip 1 dtr, 1 sc in each of first 4 ch, turn, ch 5, 1 dc in ch-1 at beginning of row, turn, (work 2 picot, 7 sc) in ch-5 sp, *return to previous row, skip 1 sc, 1 sc in each of next 4 ch, 1 picot, 1 sc in each of next 4 ch, turn, ch 9, Sl st in first sc of 8 sc, turn, (7 sc, 3 picot, 7 sc) in ch-9 sp, repeat from* , ending with skip 1 sc, 1 sc in each of first 4 ch of ch-9, turn, ch 8, Sl st in first sc of 4 sc just made, turn, (7 sc, 2 picot) in ch-8 sp, turn.

Row 4: Ch 1, 1 sc in center of first picot, *ch 8, skip (1 picot, 14 sc, 1 picot), 1 sc in center of next picot, repeat from* , turn.

Row 5: Ch 1, skip first sc, *1 sc in each of next 4 ch, 1 picot, 1 sc in each of next 4 ch, turn, ch 9, Sl st in first sc of 8 st, turn, (7 sc, 3 picot, 7 sc) in ch-9 sp, return to foundation row, skip sc, repeat from* , turn.

Repeat Rows 2–5.

⊘ See work a picot.

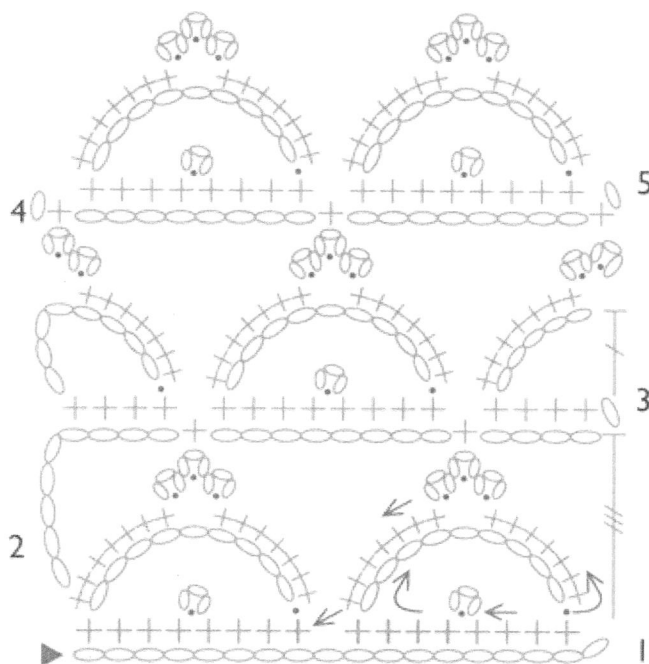

Arch 11

ARCH 11

Ch: multiple of 8 + 6

Row 1: Sc in 10th ch from hook, *ch 4, skip 3 ch, 1 sc in next ch, repeat from*, turn.

Row 2: Ch 3, skip first sc, *4 dc in ch-4 sp, ch 2, skip 1 sc, 1 sc in next ch-4 sp, ch 2, skip 1 sc, repeat from* , ending with 4 dc in ch-4 sp, ch 2, skip 1 sc, 1 sc in next ch-4 sp, ch 2, 1 dc in last ch, turn.

Row 3: Ch 1, skip first dc, *1 sc in ch-2 sp, ch 4, skip 1 sc, 1 sc in next ch-2 sp, ch 4, skip 4 dc, repeat from* with last sc in 3rd ch of tch, turn.

Row 4: Ch 5, skip first sc, *1 sc in ch-4 sp, ch 2, skip 1 sc, 4 dc in next ch-4 sp, ch 2, skip 1 sc, repeat from* , ending with 4 dc in last ch-4 sp, skip 1 sc, 1 dc in tch, turn.

Row 5: Ch 5, skip 5 dc, *1 sc in ch-2 sp, ch 4, skip 1 sc, 1 sc in next ch-2 sp, ch 4, skip 4 dc, 1 sc in ch-2 sp, ch 4, skip 1 sc, 1 sc in next ch-2 sp, repeat from* with last sc in 3rd ch of tch, turn.

Repeat Rows 2–5.

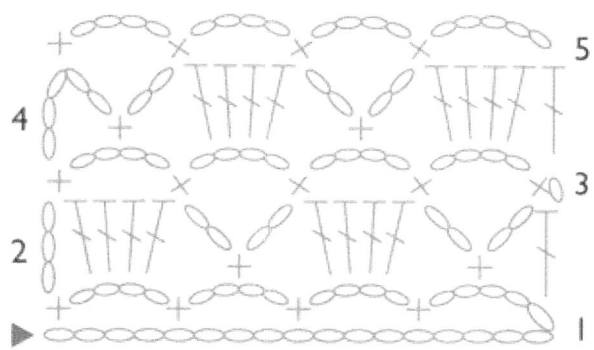

Lace 1

LACY PATTERNS

Although worked in rows, these patterns have an irregular, lacy appearance. They are usually intricate and most look best when worked in strong cottons.

LACE 1

Picot: chain-3 picot. Insert hook downward through the 3 front loops of the treble crochet just worked.
Ch: multiple of 4 + 3

Row 1: Tr in 5th ch from hook, *ch 3, tr2tog, inserting hook first in same ch as previous tr then in 4th ch (skip 3 ch), work 1 picot, repeat from* working last tr in last ch as previous tr, then in last ch (skipping only 1 ch) and finishing with 1 picot, turn.

Row 2: Ch 3, skip (1 picot, 1 ch), 1 tr in next ch (center ch of ch-3), *ch 3, tr2tog inserting hook first in same ch as previous tr then in 2nd ch of next ch-3, work 1 picot, repeat from* , ending with last tr in last tr and finishing with 1 picot, turn.

Repeat Row 2.

See work a picot. See working into front loops.

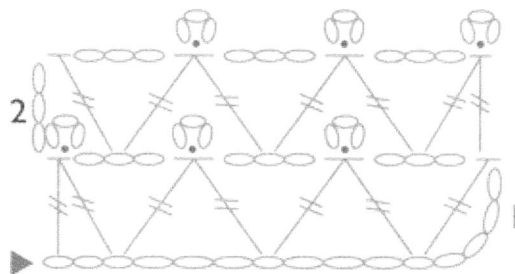

IRISH CROCHET

Irish crochet was inspired by the Venetian laces popular in the nineteenth century. It was introduced into Ireland by nuns trained in France and is the most intricate form of crochet. Irish crochet consists of a number of individual motifs, often flowers or leaves, laid out on a board and joined together by a network of crocheted mesh. It is usually worked in fine cotton for a traditional delicate, lacy look.

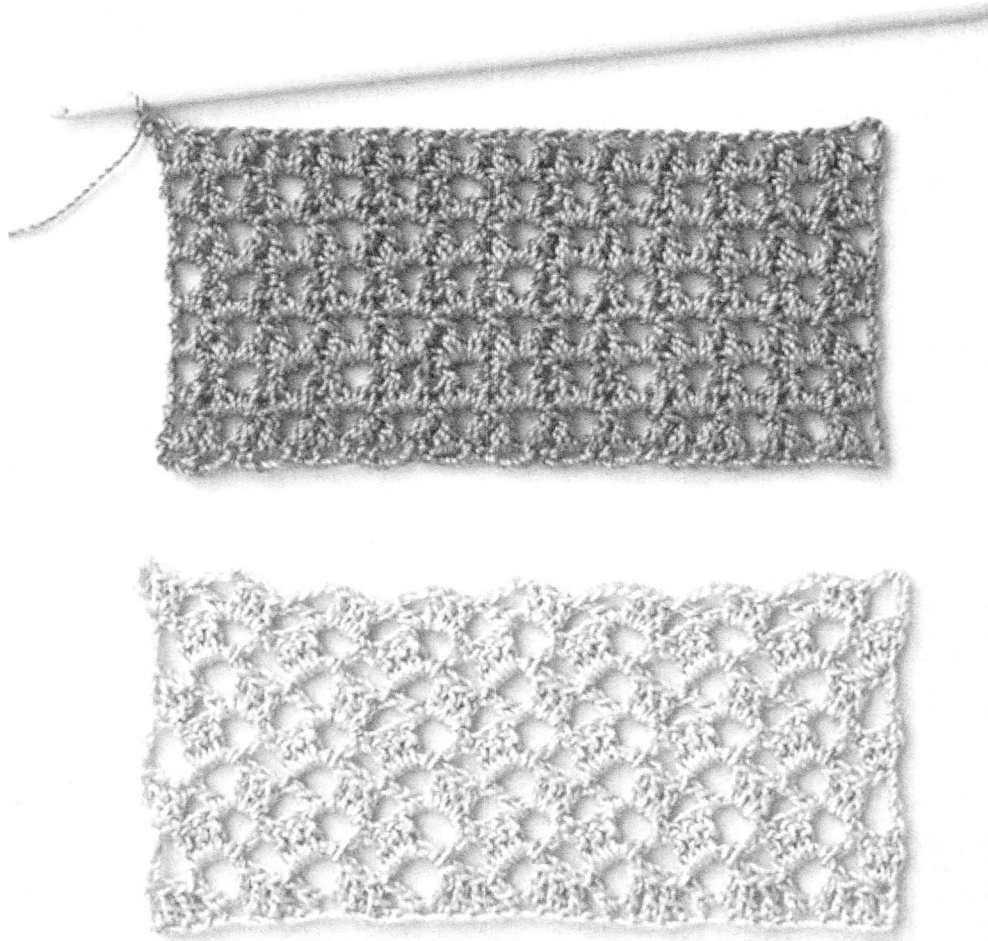

Lace 2 (top) and Lace 3

LACE 2

Group: *(Yo, insert hook in first position, yo, pull up a loop) twice in same place, yo, draw yarn through first 4 loops on hook, repeat from* in second position, yo, draw yarn through all 3 loops on hook.
Ch: multiple of 3 + 2

Row 1: Work 1 group inserting hook in 5th and 7th ch from hook, *ch 2, work 1 group inserting hook in next ch and next but one (skip 1 ch), repeat from* to last ch, ch 1, 1 dc in last ch, turn.

Row 2: Ch 4, skip first dc, work 1 group inserting hook in first and 2nd ch-sps (skip group), *ch 2, work 1 group inserting hook in same ch-sp as last group and in next ch-sp (skip group), repeat from* with (last leg, ch 1, 1 dc) below tch, turn.

Repeat Row 2.

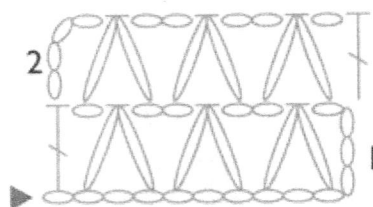

LACE 3

Ch: multiple of 4 + 2

Row 1: Dc in 4th ch from hook, 1 dc in next ch, *(1 dc, ch 3, 1 dc) in next ch, skip 1 ch, 1 dc in each of next 2 ch, repeat from* , 1 dc in last ch, turn.

Row 2: Ch 5, skip first 4 dc, *(3 dc, ch 3, 1 dc) in ch-3 sp, skip next 4 dc, repeat from* , skip last 3 dc, 3 dc in 3rd ch of tch, turn.

Row 3: Ch 5, skip first 4 dc, *(3 dc, ch 3, 1 dc) in ch-3 sp, skip next 4 dc, repeat from* , skip last 3 dc, 3 dc in 5th ch of tch, turn.

Repeat Row 3.

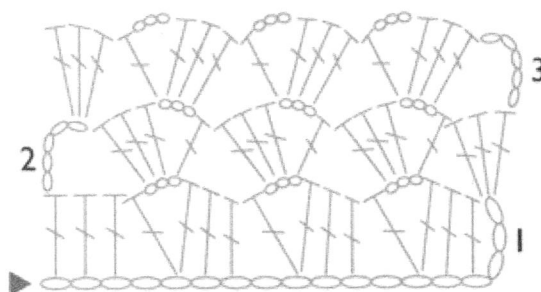

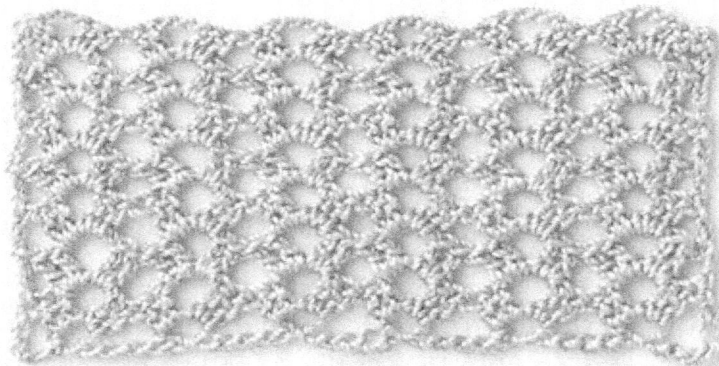

Lace 4 (top) and Lace 5

LACE 4

Popcorn (pc) = 5 double crochets: For a right side (RS) row, reinsert the hook under the back loop of the first treble crochet; for a wrong side (WS) row, reinsert the hook under the front loop of the first treble crochet.
Ch: multiple of 4 + 3

Row 1: (RS) Pc in 5th ch from hook, skip 1 ch, 1 dc in next ch, *skip 1 ch, 1 pc in next ch, skip 1 ch, 1 dc in next ch, repeat from* , turn.

Row 2: (WS) Ch 3, skip first dc, *1 dc in pc, 1 pc in dc, repeat from* with 1 dc in last pc, 1 dc in last ch, turn.

Row 3: (RS) Ch 3, skip first dc, *1 pc in next dc, 1 dc in pc, repeat from* with 1 pc in last dc, 1 dc in 3rd ch of tch, turn.

Repeat Rows 2 and 3.

See work a popcorn (pc). **See** working into front and back loops.

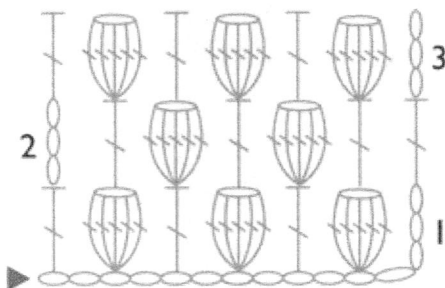

LACE 5

Ch: multiple of 6 + 4

Row 1: Work (2 dc, ch 3, 2 dc) in 6th ch from hook, *skip 5 ch, (2 dc, ch 3, 2 dc) in next ch, repeat from* to last 4 ch, skip 3 ch, 1 dc in last ch, turn.

Row 2: Ch 3, skip first 3 dc, *(2 dc, ch 3, 2 dc) in ch-3 sp, skip next 4 dc, repeat from* , ending skip last 2 dc, 1 dc in next ch, turn.

Repeat Row 2.

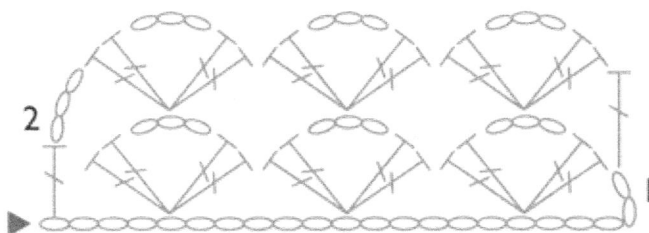

Lace 6

LACE 6

Ch: multiple of 10 + 2

Row 1: Sc in 3rd ch from hook, *ch 3, skip 2 ch, 1 sc in each of next 3 ch, repeat from* with 1 sc in each of last 2 ch, turn.

Row 2: Ch 1, skip first sc, 1 sc in next sc, 1 sc in ch-3 sp, *ch 3, skip 1 sc, 1 dc in next sc (center sc of 3 sc), ch 3, skip 1 sc, 1 sc in ch-3 sp, 1 sc in each of next 3 sc, 1 sc in ch-3 sp, repeat from* with 1 sc in last ch-3 sp, 1 sc in last sc, 1 sc in next ch, turn.

Row 3: Ch 1, skip first sc, 1 sc in next sc, *ch 3, skip 1 sc, 1 sc in ch-3 sp, 1 sc in dc, 1 sc in ch-3 sp, ch 3, skip 1 sc, 1 sc in each of next 3 sc (center 3 sc of 5 sc), repeat from* with 1 sc in last sc, 1 sc in ch, turn.

Row 4: Ch 6, skip first 2 sc, *1 sc in ch-3 sp, 1 sc in each of 3 sc, 1 sc in ch-3 sp, ch 3, skip 1 sc, 1 dc in next sc (center sc of 3 sc), ch 3, skip 1 sc, repeat from* , ending with 1 dc in last ch, turn.

Row 5: Ch 1, skip first dc, *1 sc in ch-3 sp, ch 3, skip 1 sc, 1 sc in each of next 3 sc (center 3 sc of 5 sc), ch 3, skip 1 sc, 1 sc in ch-3 sp, 1 sc in dc, repeat from* , ending with 1 sc below ch-6, 1 sc in 3rd ch of these ch-6, turn.

Repeat Rows 2–5.

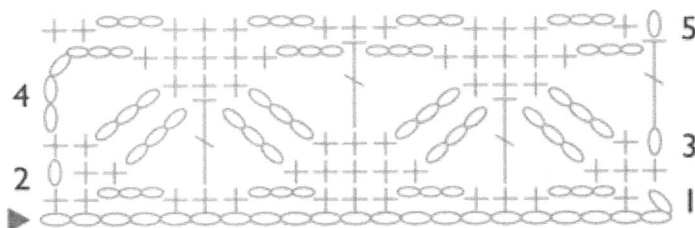

Lace 7

LACE 7

Ch: multiple of 14 + 6

Row 1: Dc in 10th ch from hook, (ch 1, skip 2 ch, 1 dc in next ch) twice, ch 4, skip 3 ch, 1 sc in next ch, ch 4, skip 3 ch, *1 dc in next ch, (ch 1, skip 2 ch, 1 dc in next ch) twice, ch 4, skip 3 ch, 1 sc in next ch, ch 4, skip*

3 ch, repeat from , ending with 1 sc in last ch, turn.

Row 2: Ch 5, skip 1 sc, *skip 4 ch, (1 dc, ch 2, 1 dc) in next dc, skip 1 ch, 1 dc in next dc, skip 1 ch, (1 dc, ch 2, 1 dc) in next dc, ch 2, skip 4 ch, 1 dc in sc, ch 2, repeat from* , ending with 1 dc in 5th ch after last dc of previous row, turn.

Row 3: Ch 5, skip 1 dc, *skip 2 ch, 1 hdc in dc, ch 2, skip 2 ch, 1 sc in dc, Sl st in next dc, 1 sc in next dc, ch 2, skip 2 ch, 1 hdc in dc, ch 2, 1 dc in dc, ch 2, repeat from* , ending with 1 dc in 3rd ch of ch-5, turn.

Row 4: Ch 5, skip first dc, *skip 2 ch, 1 hdc in hdc, ch 2, skip 2 ch, 1 sc in sc, ch 1, skip Sl st, 1 sc in sc, ch 2, skip 2 ch, 1 hdc in hdc, ch 2, skip 2 ch, 1 dc in dc, ch 2, repeat from* , ending with 1 dc in 3rd ch of ch-5, turn.

Row 5: Ch 7, skip first dc, *skip 2 ch, dc2tog inserting hook in next hdc and following sc, ch 1, 1 dc in ch-1 sp, ch 1, dc2tog inserting hook in next sc and following hdc, ch 4, skip 2 ch, 1 dc in dc, ch 4, repeat from* , ending with 1 dc in 3rd ch of ch-5, turn.

Row 6: ch 4, skip first dc, *skip 4 ch, 1 dc in dc2tog, ch 2, skip 1 ch, 1 dc in dc, ch 2, skip 1 ch, 1 dc in dc2tog, ch 3, skip 4 ch, 1 sc in dc, ch 3, repeat from* , ending with 1 sc in 3rd ch of ch-7, turn.

Row 7: ch 5, skip first sc, *skip 3 ch, 1 dc in next dc, (ch 1, skip 2 ch, 1 dc in dc) twice, ch 4, skip 3 ch, 1 sc in sc, ch 4, repeat from* , ending with 1 sc in last ch, turn.

Repeat Rows 2–7.

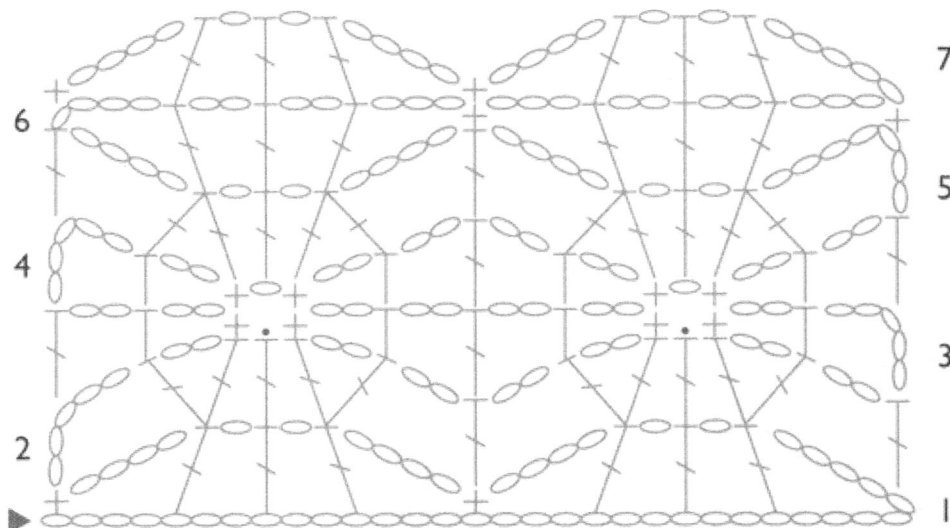

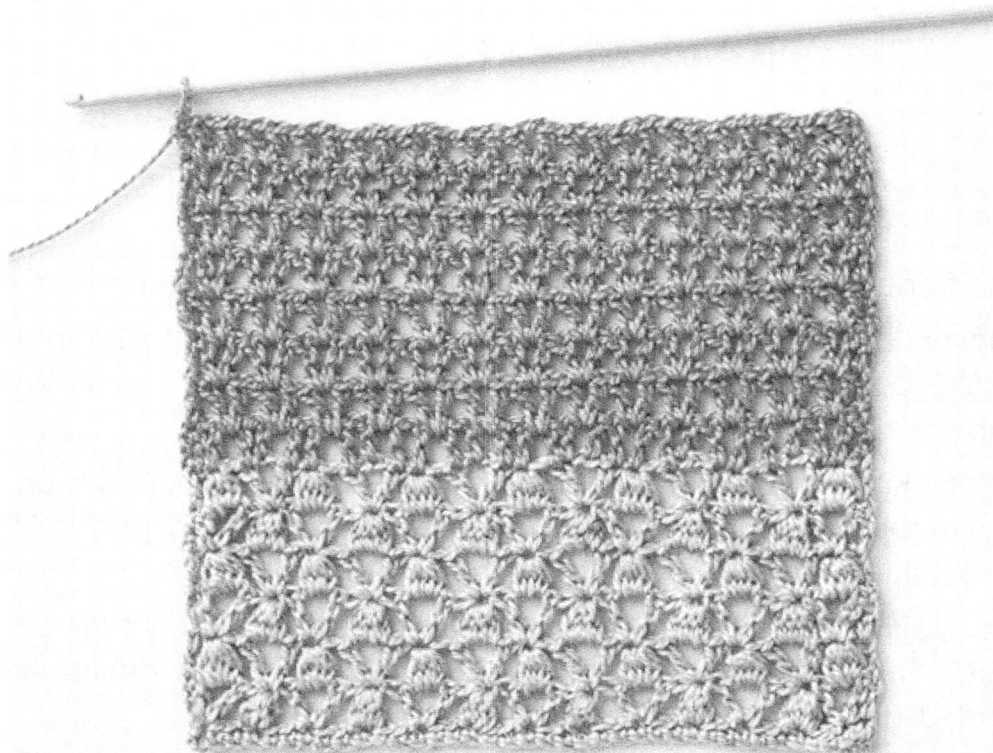

Lace 8 (top) and Lace 9

LACE 8

Ch: multiple of 3

Row 1: Dc in 4th ch from hook, ch 1, 1 dc in next ch, *skip 1 ch, 1 dc in next ch, ch 1, 1 dc in next ch, repeat from* , 1 dc in last ch, turn.

Row 2: Ch 3, skip first 2 dc, *(1 dc, ch 1, 1 dc) in ch-1 sp, skip 2 dc, repeat from* , skip last dc, 1 dc in 3rd ch of tch, turn.

Repeat Row 2.

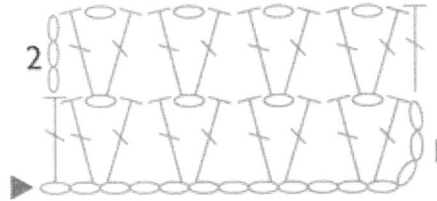

LACE 9

Puff = 4 half double crochets with chain stitch to close Ch: multiple of 6 + 5

Row 1: (Dc, ch 2, 1 dc) in 4th ch from hook, *skip 2 ch, work 1 puff in next ch, skip 2 ch, (1 dc, ch 2, 1 dc) in next ch, repeat from* , 1 dc in last ch, turn.

Row 2: Ch 3, skip first 2 dc, *work 1 puff in ch-2 sp, skip 1 dc, (1 dc, ch 2, 1 dc) in top of next puff, skip 1 dc, repeat from* , work 1 puff in last ch-2 sp, skip 1 dc, 1 dc in 3rd ch of tch, turn.

Row 3: Ch 3, skip first dc, *(1 dc, ch 2, 1 dc) in top of next puff, skip 1 dc, 1 puff in ch-2 sp, skip 1 dc, repeat from* , (1 dc, ch 2, 1 dc) in top of last puff, 1 dc in 3rd ch of tch, turn.

Repeat Rows 2 and 3.

See work a puff.

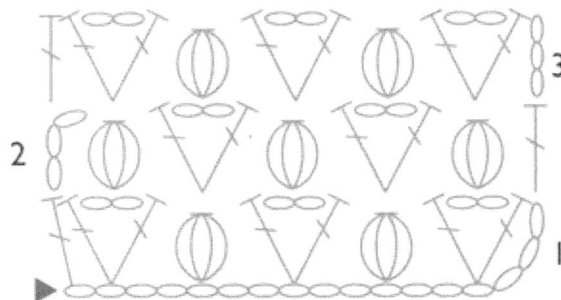

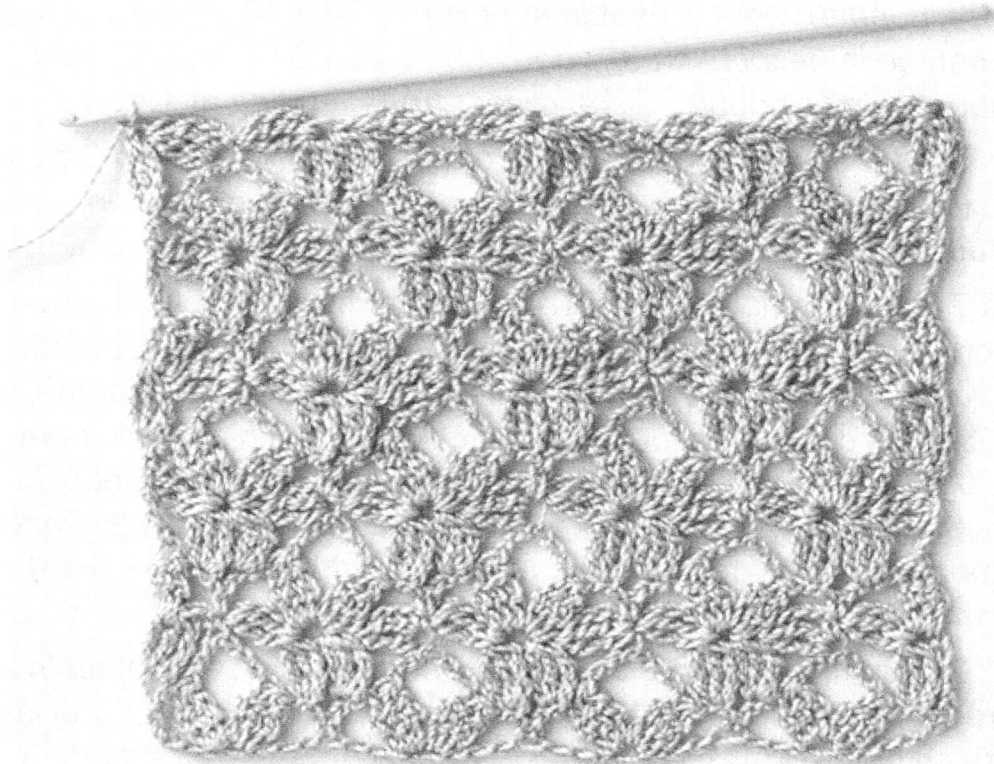

Lace 10

LACE 10

Bobble = 3 treble crochets;
small bobble = 2 treble crochets
Ch: multiple of 8 + 4

Row 1: Work 1 bobble in 8th ch from hook, ch 7, work 1 bobble in same ch as last bobble, ch 3, skip 3 ch, 1 sc in next ch, *ch 3, skip 3 ch, (work 1 bobble, ch 7, 1 bobble) in next ch, ch 3, skip 3 ch, 1 sc in next ch, repeat from* , turn.

Row 2: Ch 5, skip (sc, 2 ch), work 1 bobble in next ch, ch 3, work 1 small bobble in top of bobble just made, skip (1 bobble, 3 ch), *1 sc in next ch (4th ch of ch-7), ch 3, work 1 small bobble in sc just made, skip (3 ch, 1 bobble), work 1 bobble in next ch†, skip (2 ch, 1 sc, 2 ch), work 1 bobble in next ch, ch 3, work 1 small bobble in top of bobble just made, skip (1 bobble, 3 ch), repeat from* , ending at †, turn.

Row 3: Ch 3, work 1 small bobble in top of first group, *ch 3, skip 3 ch, 1 sc in next sc, ch 3, skip 3 ch, (work 1 bobble, ch 7, 1 bobble) in top of next group, repeat from* , ending with 1 bobble in top of last group, turn.

Row 4: Ch 7, work 1 small bobble in 4th ch from hook, skip (3 ch, 1 bobble), work 1 bobble in next ch, skip (2 ch, 1 sc, 2 ch), work 1 bobble in next ch, ch 3, work 1 small bobble in top of bobble just made, skip (1 bobble, 3 ch), *1 sc in next ch (4th ch of ch-7), ch 3, work 1 small bobble in last sc made, skip (3 ch, 1 bobble), work 1 bobble in next ch, skip (2 ch, 1 sc, 2 ch), work 1 bobble in next ch, ch 3, work 1 small bobble in top of bobble just made, skip (1 bobble, 3 ch), repeat from* , ending with 1 tr in 3rd ch of ch-3, turn.

Row 5: Ch 3, skip first tr, *skip 3 ch, (work 1 bobble, ch 7, 1 bobble) in next group, ch 3, skip 3 ch, 1 sc in next sc, repeat from* , working last sc in 4th ch of ch-7, turn.

Repeat Rows 2–5.

⬤ See work a bobble.

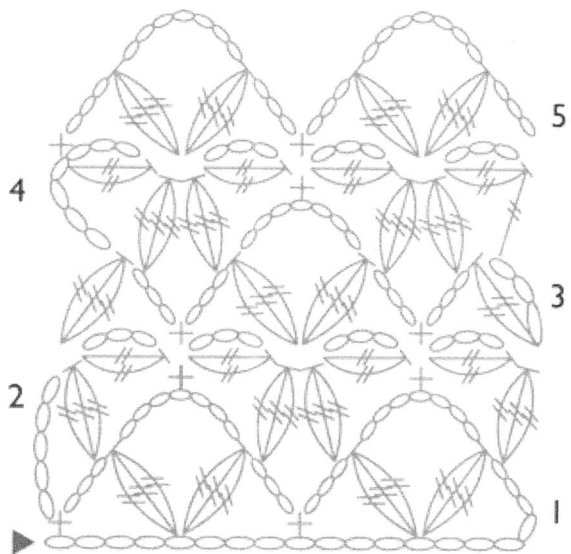

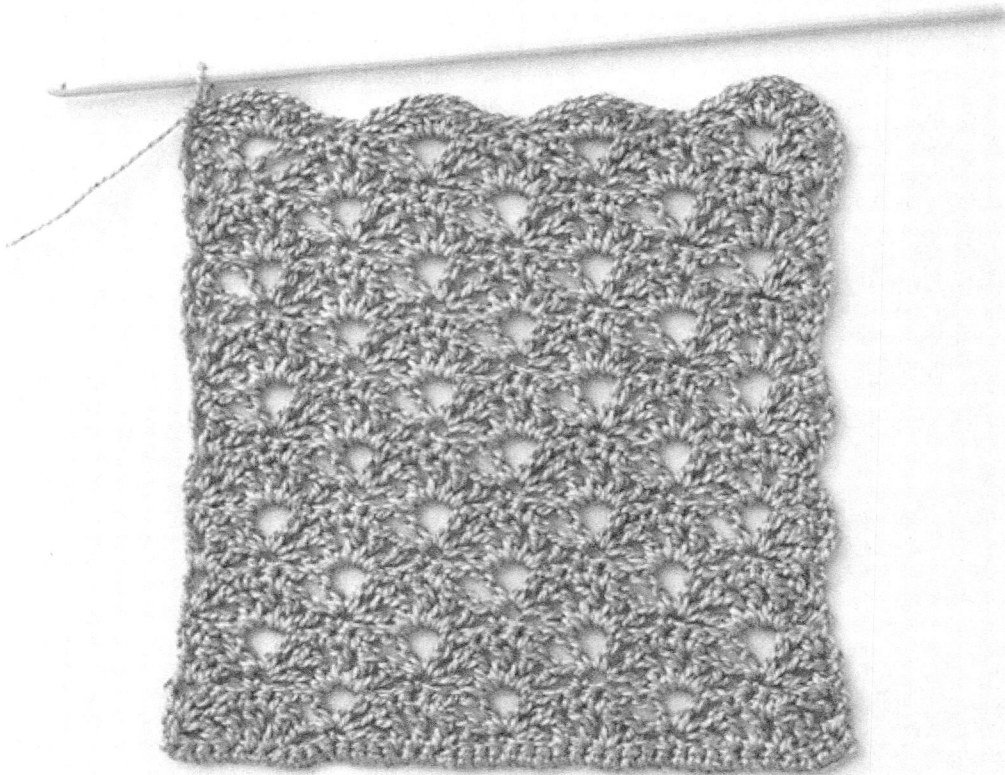

Lace 11

LACE 11

Ch: multiple of 10 + 2

Row 1: (Dc, ch 1, 1 dc) in 6th ch from hook, ch 1, 1 dc in next ch, ch 1, (1 dc, ch 1, 1 dc) in next ch, skip 3 ch, 1 sc in next ch, *skip 3 ch, (1 dc, ch 1, 1 dc) in next ch, ch 1, 1 dc in next ch, ch 1, (1 dc, ch 1, 1 dc) in* *next ch, skip 3 ch, 1 sc in next ch, repeat from , turn.*

Row 2: Ch 4, 1 dc in first sc, *ch 1, skip (1 dc, 1 ch, 1 dc), 1 sc in ch-1 sp, 1 sc in dc, 1 sc in ch-1 sp, ch 1, skip (1 dc, 1 ch, 1 dc), (1 dc, ch 3, 1 dc) in next sc, repeat from* , ending with (1 dc, ch 1, 1 dc) in next ch, turn.

Row 3: Ch 4, skip first dc, (1 dc, ch 1, 1 dc) in first ch-1 sp, *skip (1 dc, 1 ch, 1 sc), 1 sc in next sc, skip (1 sc, 1 ch, 1 dc), 1 dc in next ch-3 sp, (ch 1, 1 dc) 4 times in same ch-3 sp, repeat from* , ending with 1 dc under tch, (ch 1, 1 dc) twice in same ch-4 sp, turn.

Row 4: Ch 1, skip first dc, 1 sc in ch-1 sp, *ch 1, skip (1 dc, 1 ch, 1 dc), (1 dc, ch 3, 1 dc) in next sc, ch 1, skip (1 dc, 1 ch, 1 dc), 1 sc in ch-1 sp, 1 sc in dc, 1 sc in ch-1 sp, repeat from* , ending with 1 sc in ch-4 sp, 1 sc in 3rd ch of ch-4, turn.

Row 5: Ch 1, skip first sc, *skip (1 sc, 1 ch, 1 dc), 1 dc in next ch-3 sp, (ch 1, 1 dc) 4 times in same ch-3 sp, skip (1 dc, 1 ch, 1 sc), 1 sc in next sc, repeat from* with last sc in last ch, turn.

Repeat Rows 2–5.

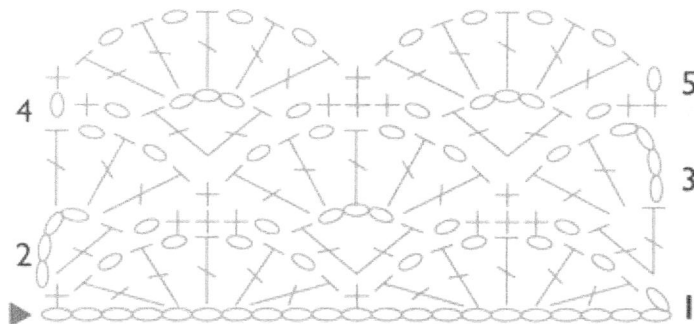

⋮ TEXTURED PATTERNS

Crochet lends itself to textured effects, and in these patterns a raised texture is particularly evident. The design will be clearest when worked in sturdy cottons, but a "woollier" result can also be effective.

Textured 1

TEXTURED 1

Ch: required sts + 2

Row 1: (WS) Esc in 3rd ch from hook, 1 Esc in each ch, turn.

Row 2: Ch 1, 1 sc in front loop of first Esc, *ch 6, 1 sc in front loop of next*

Esc, repeat from , ending with 1 sc in front loop of last Esc, turn.

Row 3: Ch 1, 1 Esc in back loop of each Esc two rows below, turn.

Repeat Rows 2 and 3.

See extended single crochet (Esc). See working into the front and back loops.

Tip- Work the foundation chain for this pattern loosely, as you will be placing an extended single crochet in each chain.

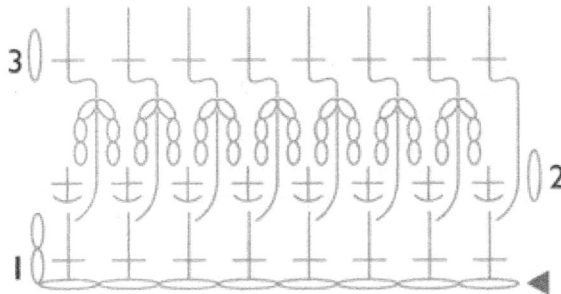

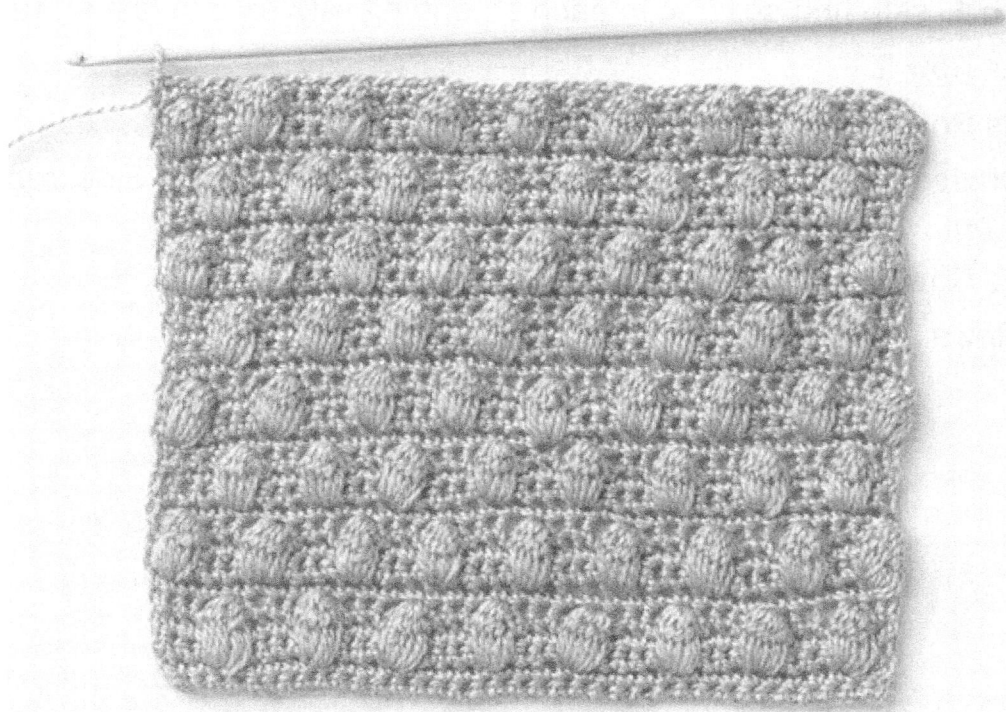

Textured 2

TEXTURED 2

Pineapple stitch (ps): Insert hook, yo, pull up a loop, (yo, insert hook into the stitch 2 rows below, yo, pull up a loop, yo, draw yarn through first 2 loops on hook) 6 times, yo, draw yarn through all 8 loops on hook. Ch: multiple of 4 + 3

Row 1: Sc in 2nd ch from hook, 1 sc in each ch, turn.

Row 2: Ch 1, skip first sc, 1 sc in each sc, ending with last sc in last st, turn.

Row 3: As Row 2.

Row 4: Ch 1, skip first sc, 1 sc in each of next 2 sc, *1 ps in next sc, 1 sc in each of next 3 sc, repeat from* , ending with I sc in last st, turn.

Row 5: Ch 1, skip first sc, 1 sc in each st, ending with 1 sc in last st, turn.

Row 6: As Row 2.

Row 7: As Row 2.

Row 8: Ch 1, skip first sc, *1 ps in next sc, 1 sc in each of next 3 sc, repeat from* , ending with 1 ps in last sc, 1 sc in last st, turn.

Row 9: As Row 5.

Repeat Rows 2–9.

Tip- When working into the stitch two rows below, be careful not to pull the yarn too tightly. Keep a consistent tension so that the threads lie neatly and symmetrically across the fabric.

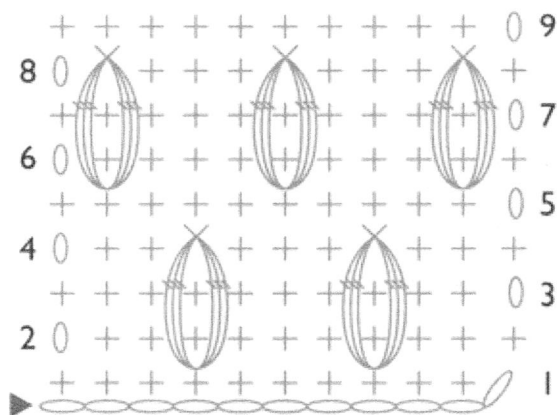

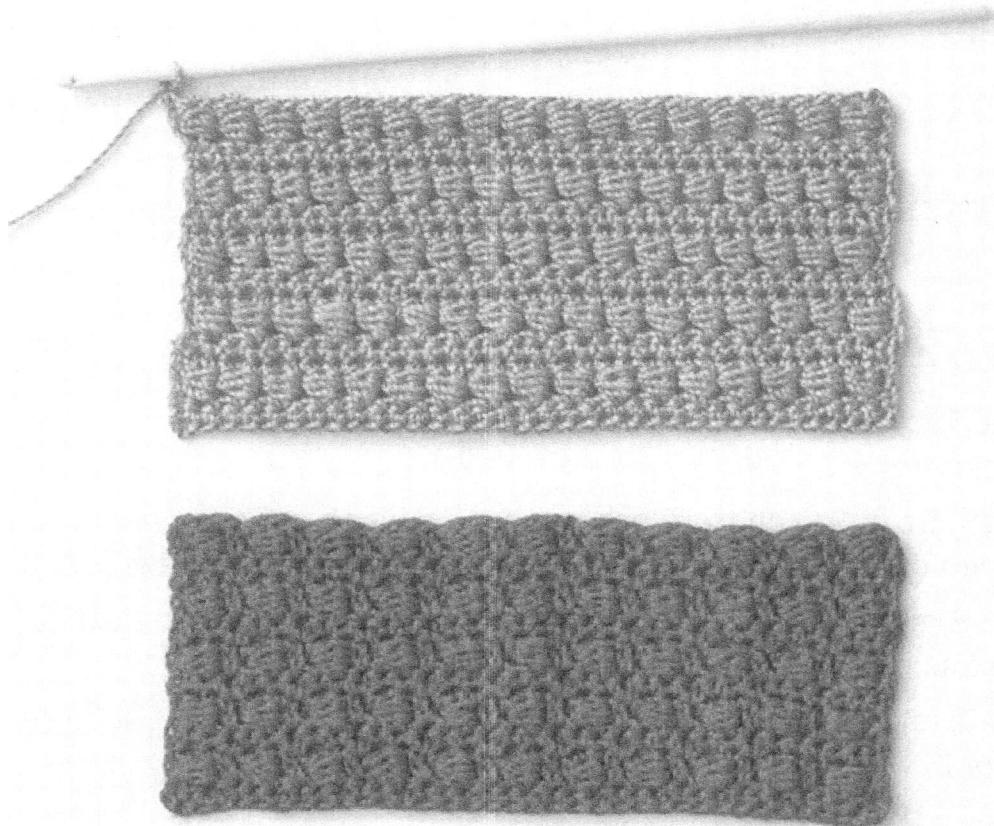

Textured 3 (top) and Textured 4

TEXTURED 3

Group: (Yo, insert hook around post of previous dc from right to left, yo, pull up a loop) 3 times in same place, yo, draw yarn through first 6 loops on hook, yo, draw yarn through both loops on hook.
Ch: even number

Row 1: (WS) Sc in 2nd ch from hook, 1 sc in each ch, turn.

Row 2: Ch 3, skip first sc, *1 dc in next sc, work 1 group, skip 1 sc, repeat from* , ending with 1 dc in last st, turn.

Row 3: Ch 1, skip first dc, *1 sc in group, 1 sc in dc, repeat from* , ending with 1 sc in 3rd ch of tch, turn.

Repeat Rows 2 and 3.

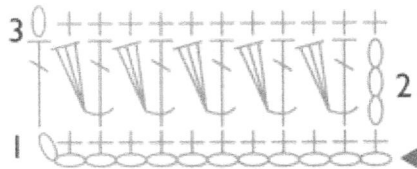

TEXTURED 4

Group: see Textured 3

Ch: multiple of 3 + 2

Row 1: (WS) Sc in 3rd ch from hook, 1 sc in next ch, *1 Esc in next ch, 1 sc in each of next 2 ch, repeat from* , ending with 1 Esc in last ch, turn.

Row 2: Ch 2, skip first Esc, *1 dc in next sc, work 1 group, skip next sc, 1 Esc in Esc, repeat from* , with last Esc in last st, turn.

Row 3: Ch 2, skip first Esc, *1 sc in group, 1 sc in dc, 1 Esc in Esc, repeat from* , with last Esc in last st, turn.

Repeat Rows 2 and 3.

See extended single crochet (Esc).

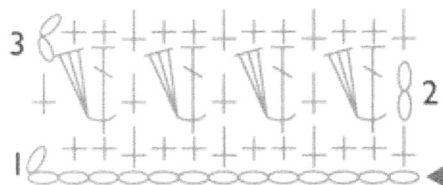

> **Tip-** When working around the post of a double crochet, insert the hook from right to left (see this page).

Textured 5

TEXTURED 5

Bullion stitch (bullion st): yo 7 times Ch: multiple of 6 + 5

Row 1: (WS) Sc in 2nd ch from hook, 1 sc in each ch, turn.

Row 2: Ch 3, skip first sc, 1 dc in each of next 4 sc, *work 1 bullion st in next* *sc, 1 dc in each of next 5 sc, repeat from* to end, with last dc in last st, turn.

Row 3: Ch 1, skip first dc, 1 sc in each st, ending with last sc in 3rd ch of tch, turn.

Row 4: Ch 3, skip first sc, 1 dc in next sc, *work 1 bullion st in next sc, 1 dc in each of next 5 sc, repeat from* , ending with 1 dc in last sc, 1 dc in last st, turn.

Row 5: Ch 1, skip first dc, 1 sc in each st, ending with 1 sc in last dc, 1 sc in 3rd ch of tch, turn.

Repeat Rows 2–5.

⬤ See bullion stitch.

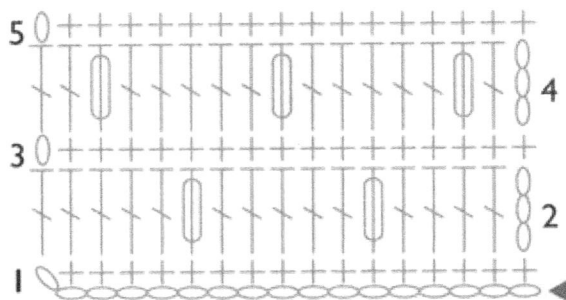

Tip- Most crochet stitches and patterns have a "right side" and a "wrong side," even when both sides look very similar. When you are finishing a piece, make sure all the yarn tails are taken to the wrong side. Also, when you are joining motifs or assembling pattern pieces, check carefully that all the right sides match.

Textured 6 *(top)* *and* *Textured 7*

TEXTURED 6

Puff = 4 half double crochets
Ch: multiple of 4 + 3

Row 1: Sc in 2nd ch from hook, 1 sc in each ch, turn.

Row 2: Ch 1, skip first sc, 1 sc in each of next 2 sc, *work 1 puff in next sc, 1 sc in each of next 3 sc, repeat from* , 1 sc in last ch, turn.

Row 3: Ch 1, skip first sc, 1 sc in each st to end, 1 sc in last st, turn.

Row 4: Ch 1, skip first sc, *work 1 puff in next sc, 1 sc in each of next 3 sc, repeat from* , 1 sc in last st, turn.

Row 5: As Row 3.

Repeat Rows 2–5.

See a puff.

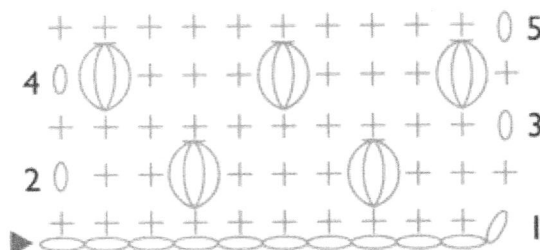

TEXTURED 7

Bobble = 5 double crochets
Ch: multiple of 4 + 1

Row 1: Sc in 2nd ch from hook, 1 sc in each ch, turn.

Row 2: Ch 1, skip first sc, 1 sc in next sc, *work 1 bobble, 1 sc in each of next 3 sc, repeat from* , ending with 1 sc in last sc, 1 sc in last ch, turn.

Row 3: Ch 1, skip first sc, 1 sc in each st, turn.

Row 4: As Row 3.

Row 5: As Row 3.

Repeat Rows 2–5.

See a bobble.

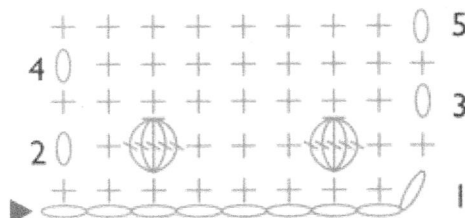

Textured 8

TEXTURED 8

Ch: multiple of 6 + 1

Row 1: Dc in 4th ch from hook, 1 dc in each ch, turn.

Row 2: Ch 2, skip first dc, *1 FPdc around each of next 3 dc, 1 BPdc around* each of following 3 dc, repeat from , ending with 1 FPdc around each of last 3 dc, 1 dc in 3rd ch of tch, turn.

Row 3: Ch 2, skip first dc, *1 BPdc around each of 3 FPdc, 1 FPdc around each of 3 BPdc, repeat from* , ending with 1 BPdc around each of last 3 FPdc, 1 dc in 2nd ch of tch, turn.

Row 4: Ch 2, skip first dc, *1 BPdc around each of 3 BPdc, 1 FPdc around each of 3 FPdc, repeat from* , ending with 1 BPdc around each of last 3 BPdc, 1 dc in 2nd ch of tch, turn.

Row 5: Ch 2, skip first dc, *1FPdc around each of 3 BPdc, 1 BPdc around each of 3 FPdc, repeat from* , ending with 1 FPdc around each of last 3 BPdc, 1 dc in 2nd ch of tch, turn.

Row 6: Ch 2, skip first dc, *1 FPdc around each of 3 FPdc, 1 BPdc around each of 3 BPdc, repeat from* , ending with 1 FPdc around each of last 3 FPdc, 1 dc in 2nd ch of tch, turn.

Repeat Rows 3–6.

See front post double crochet (FPdc) **and** back post double crochet (BPdc).

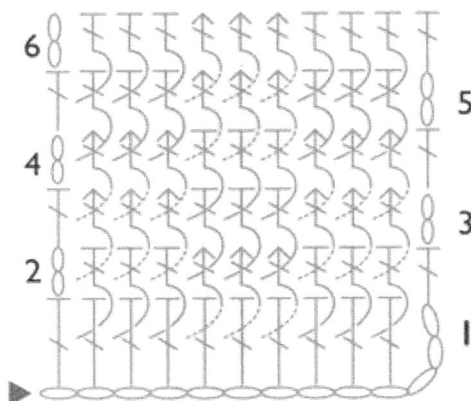

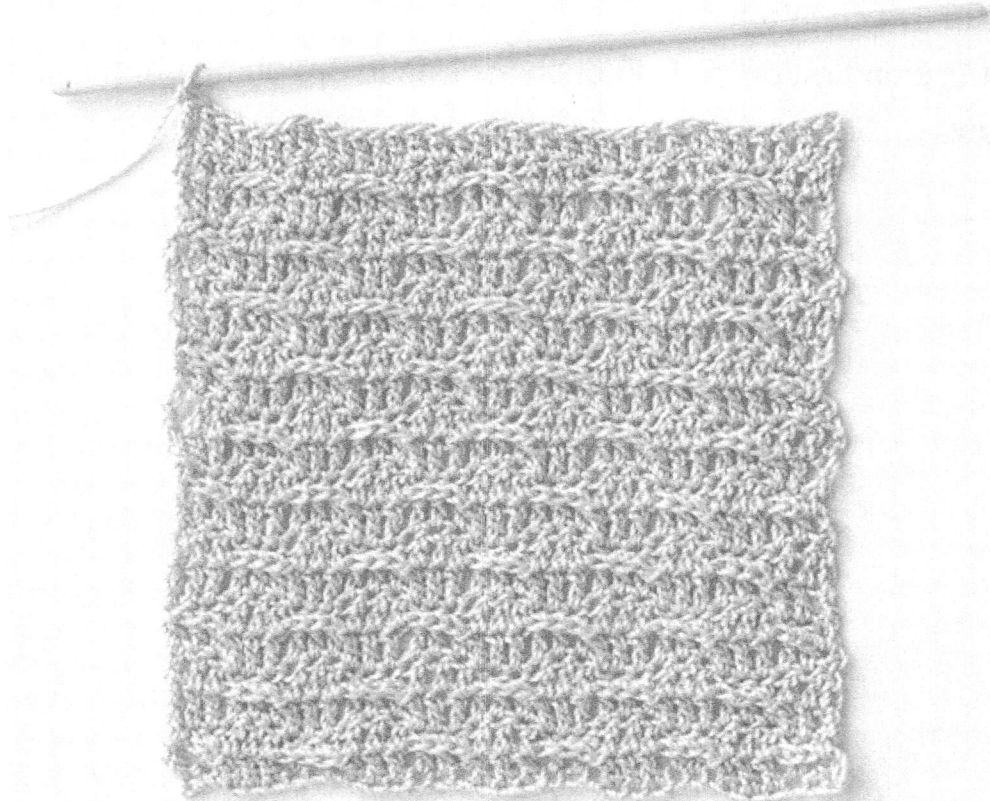

Textured 9

TEXTURED 9

Front post single crochet (FPsc): Insert hook as for front post double crochet and work a single crochet as usual. Ch: multiple of 6 + 5

Row 1: (WS) Dc in 4th ch from hook, 1 dc in each ch, turn.

Row 2: Ch 1, 1 FPsc around each of first 3 dc, *1 dc in each of next 3 dc, 1 FPsc around each of following 3 dc, repeat from* , turn.

Row 3: Ch 3, skip first FPsc, 1 dc in each st, turn.

Row 4: Ch 3, skip first dc, 1 dc in each of next 2 dc, *1 FPsc around each of next 3 dc, 1 dc in each of following 3 dc, repeat from* , working last dc in 3rd ch of tch, turn.

Row 5: Ch 3, skip first dc, 1 dc in each st, 1 dc in 3rd ch of tch, turn.

Repeat Rows 2–5.

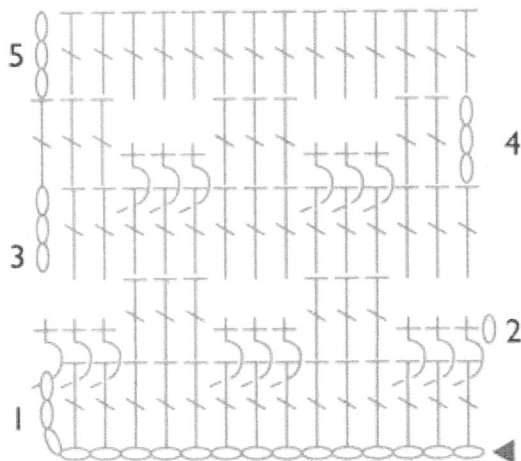

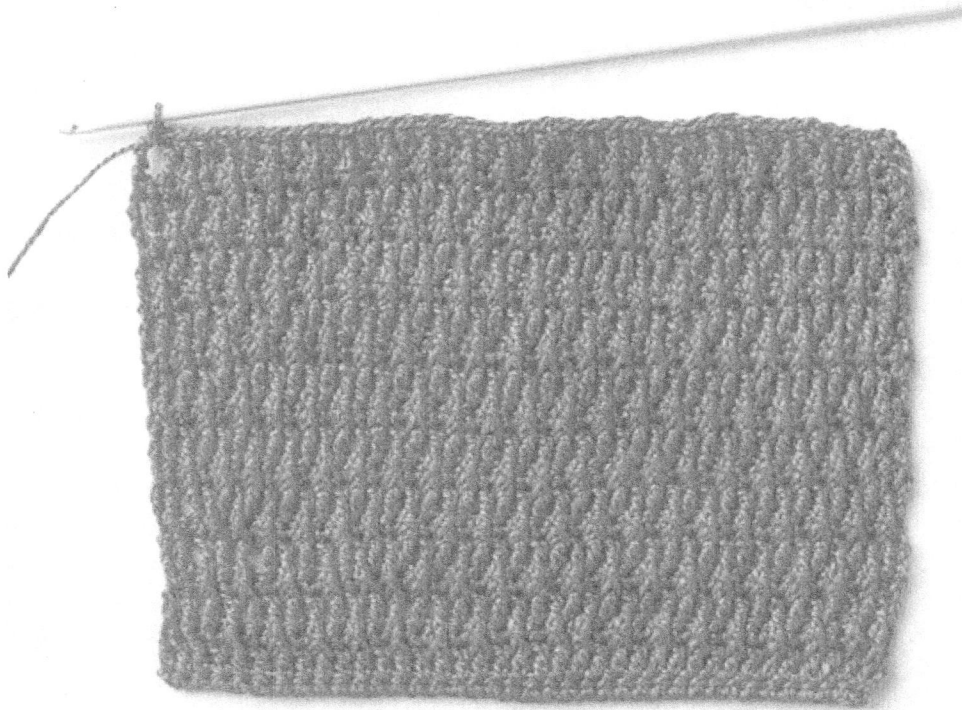

Textured 10

TEXTURED 10

Front post treble crochet (FPtr): Insert hook as for front post double crochet and work a treble crochet as usual. Ch: odd number

Dc in 4th ch from hook, 1 dc in each ch, turn.

Ch 1, skip first st, 1 sc in each st, ending with 1 sc in 3rd ch of tch, turn.

Ch 3, skip first sc, *1 FPtr around dc below next sc, skip this sc, 1 dc in next sc, repeat from* , ending with 1 dc in tch, turn.

As Row 2.

Ch 3, skip first sc, *1 dc in next sc, 1 FPtr around dc below next sc, skip this sc, repeat from* , ending with 1 FPtr around dc below tch, turn.

Repeat Rows 2–5.

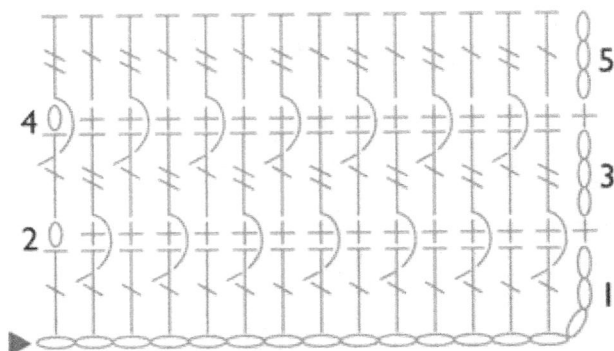

Tip- Textured patterns such as the one on the facing page are well suited to use for sweaters and vests. Working to the correct gauge is particularly important when you are making garments and other fitted pieces. Always do a gauge swatch to check your tension before you begin work, and use a smaller or larger hook if necessary.

Textured 11

TEXTURED 11

Ch: multiple of 4 + 1

Row 1: (WS) Dc in 4th ch from hook, 1 dc in each ch, turn.

Row 2: Ch 3, skip first dc, *1 FPtr around next dc, 1 dc in each of next 3 dc,* *repeat from* , ending with 1 FPtr around last dc, 1 dc in 3rd ch of tch, turn.

Row 3: Ch 2, skip first dc, *1 BPdc around FPtr, 1 FPdc around each of next 3 dc, repeat from* , ending with 1 BPdc around last FPtr, 1 FPdc around tch, turn.

Row 4: Ch 3, skip first FPdc, 1 dc in each of next 2 sts, *1 FPtr around next FPdc (center FPdc of 3 FPdc), 1 dc in each of next 3 sts, repeat from* , with last dc in 2nd ch of tch, turn.

Row 5: Ch 2, skip first dc, 1 FPdc around each of next 2 dc, *1 BPdc around FPtr, 1 FPdc around each of 3 dc, repeat from* , with last FPdc around tch, turn.

Row 6: Ch 3, skip first FPdc, *1 FPtr around next FPdc (center FPdc of 3 FPdc), 1 dc in each of next 3 sts, repeat from* , ending with 1 FPtr around last FPdc, 1 dc in 2nd ch of tch, turn.

Repeat Rows 3–6.

See a front post double (FPdc) and a back post double crochet (BPdc). See a front post treble crochet (FPtr).

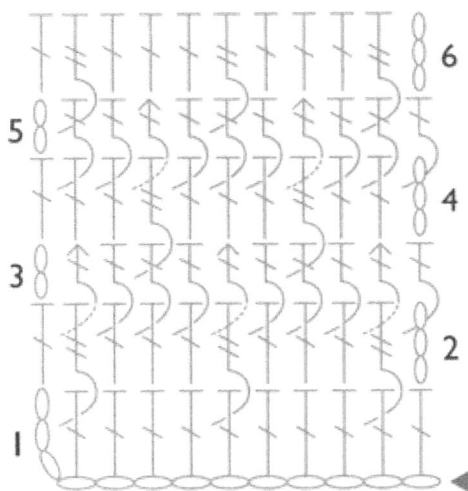

Textured 12

TEXTURED 12

This pattern is produced by adding an overlaid chain to a fabric of open double crochet rows. It is usually worked in three colors: A, B, and C. Work the foundation chain in A.

Ch: multiple of 8 + 3

Row 1: Dc in 4th ch from hook, 1 dc in next ch, *ch 1, skip 1 ch, 1 dc in next ch, ch 1, skip 1 ch, 1 dc in each of next 5 ch, repeat from* , ending with 1 dc in each of last 3 ch, turn.

Row 2: Ch 3, skip first dc, 1 dc in each of next 2 dc, *ch 1, skip 1 ch, 1 dc in next dc, ch 1, skip 1 ch, 1 dc in each of next 5 dc, repeat from* , ending with 1 dc in each of last 2 dc, 1 dc in 3rd ch of tch, turn.

Row 3: As Row 2 and change to B at the end of the row.

Row 4: As Row 2 and change to C at the end of the row.

Row 5: As Row 2 and change to A at the end of the row.

Row 6: As Row 2.

Repeat Rows 2–6 as required, making three rows of A, one row of B, and one row of C.

Overlaid chain Starting at the bottom right-hand corner, work vertically over the chain-spaces as follows, using doubled yarn.

Join B to foundation ch, 1 och in first ch-sp, *lengthen loop on hook to match next row, 1 och in next ch-sp, repeat from* to top of work, fasten off.

Join C to foundation ch of next ch-sps and work to the top as in Step 1.

Repeat Steps 1–2 across the work, filling all the ch-sps.

See change yarns. See an overlaid chain (och).

> **Tip-** An overlaid chain can be used to add vertical stripes to any fabric with a regular, open pattern.

Textured 13 (top) and Textured 14

TEXTURED 13

Bobble = 5 double crochets

Ch: multiple of 3 + 1

Row 1: Sc in 2nd ch from hook, 1 sc in each ch, turn.

Row 2: Ch 1, 1 sc in each of first 2 sc, *work 1 bobble in next sc, 1 sc in each of next 2 sc, repeat from* , work 1 bobble in last sc, turn.

Row 3: Ch 1, *1 sc in bobble, 1 sc in each of next 2 sc, repeat from* to end, turn.

Row 4: Ch 1, work 1 bobble in first sc, *1 sc in each of next 2 sc, work 1 bobble in next sc, repeat from* , 1 sc in each of last 2 sc, turn.

Row 5: Ch 1, 1 sc in first sc, 1 sc in next sc, *1 sc in bobble, 1 sc in each of next 2 sc, repeat from* , 1 sc in last bobble, turn.

Repeat Rows 2–5.

See a bobble.

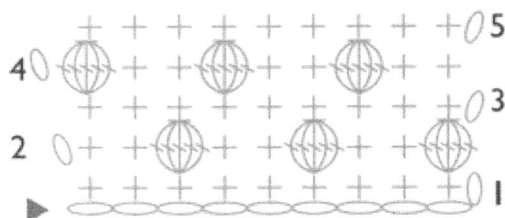

TEXTURED 14

Popcorn (pc) = 5 double crochets
Ch: multiple of 6 + 1

Row 1: (WS) Sc in 2nd ch from hook, *ch 1, skip 1 ch, 2 sc in next ch, ch 1, skip 1 ch, 1 sc in each of next 3 ch, repeat from* , ending with 1 sc in each of last 2 ch, turn.

Row 2: Ch 3, skip first sc, 1 dc in next sc, *skip 1 ch, 1 pc in next sc, ch 1, 1 pc in next sc, skip 1 ch, 1 dc in each of next 3 sc, repeat from* , ending with 1 dc in last sc, 1 dc in last ch, turn.

Row 3: Ch 1, skip first dc, 1 sc in next dc, *ch 1, skip 1 pc, 2 sc in ch-1 sp, ch 1, skip 1 pc, 1 sc in each of next 3 dc, repeat from* , ending with 1 sc in last dc, 1 sc in 3rd ch of tch, turn.

Repeat Rows 2 and 3.

See a popcorn (pc).

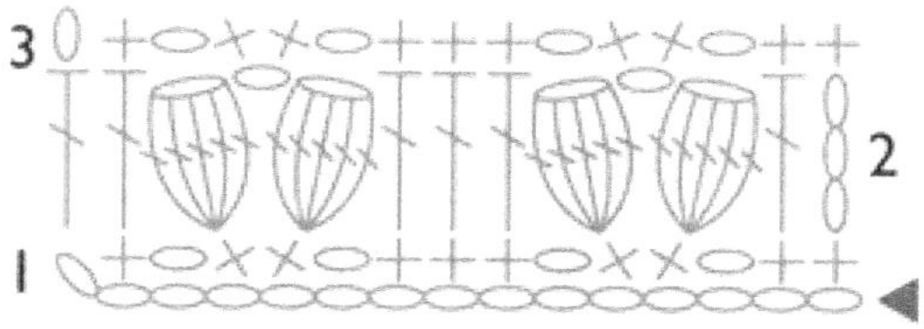
3
2
1

Textured 15 (top) and Textured 16

TEXTURED 15

Ch: multiple of 8 + 1

Row 1: (WS) Skip 4 ch, *9 dc in next ch, skip 3 ch, 1 sc, skip 3 ch, repeat from *, 1 sc in ch, turn.

Row 2: Ch 3, skip first sc, CL of 4 dc over next 4 dc, *ch 4, 1 sc in next dc (the center dc of 9 dc), ch 3, CL of 9 dc over (4 dc, 1 sc, 4 dc), repeat from* , CL of 5 dc over last 4 dc and 1 ch.

Row 3: Ch 4, 4 dc in top of 5-dc CL, *skip 3 ch, 1 sc in sc, skip 4 ch, 9 dc in top of 9-dc CL, repeat from* , 5 dc in top of 4-dc CL, turn.

Row 4: Ch 4, skip first dc, *CL of 9 dc over (4 dc, 1 sc, 4 dc), ch 4, 1 sc in next dc (the center dc of 9 dc), ch 3, repeat from* , 1 sc in 4th ch of tch, turn.

Row 5: Ch 1, skip first sc, *skip 4 ch, 9 dc in top of 9-dc CL, skip 3 ch, 1 sc in sc, repeat from* with sc in first ch of tch, turn.

Repeat Rows 2–5.

See work a cluster (CL).

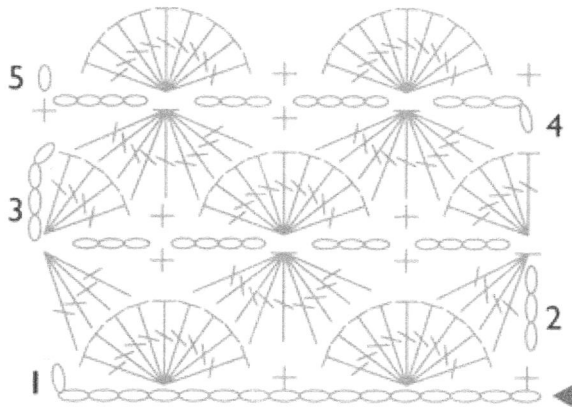

TEXTURED 16

Ch: multiple of 3 + 3

Row 1: Work 2 dc in 3rd ch from hook, *skip 2 ch, (1 sc, 2 dc) in next ch, repeat from* to last 3 ch, skip 2 ch, 1 sc in last ch, turn.

Row 2: Ch 2, 2 dc in first sc, *skip 2 dc, (1 sc, 2 dc) in next sc, repeat from* , skip 2 dc, 1 sc in last ch, turn.

Repeat Row 2.

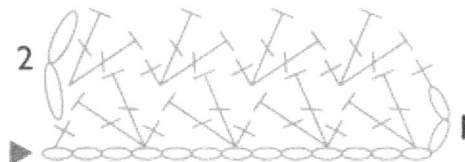

Textured 17

TEXTURED 17

Ch: multiple of 8 + 1

Row 1: Work (3 dc, ch 1, 3 dc) in 5th ch from hook, skip 3 ch, 1 sc in next ch, *skip 3 ch, (3 dc, ch 1, 3 dc) in next ch, skip 3 ch, 1 sc in next ch, repeat from* , turn.

Row 2: Ch 3, skip first sc, CL of 3 dc over next 3 dc, *ch 7, skip ch, CL of 6 dc over next 6 dc (leaving sc between dc groups unworked), repeat from* , CL of 3 dc over last 3 dc, 1 dc in ch, turn.

Row 3: Ch 3, skip first dc, 3 dc in top of 3-dc CL, *1 sc in ch-1 sp between dc of Row 1, (3 dc, ch 1, 3 dc) in top of 6-dc CL, repeat from* , 3 dc in top of 3-dc CL, 1 dc in 3rd ch of tch, turn.

Row 4: Ch 4, skip first dc, *CL of 6 dc over next 6 dc (leaving sc between dc groups unworked), ch 7, skip 1 ch, repeat from* , ch 3, 1 sc in 3rd ch of tch, turn.

Row 5: Ch 1, skip sc and 3 ch, *(3 dc, ch 1, 3 dc) in top of 6-dc CL, 1 sc in ch-1 sp between dc of Row 3, repeat from* , 1 sc in first ch of tch, turn.

Repeat Rows 2–5.

See work a cluster (CL).

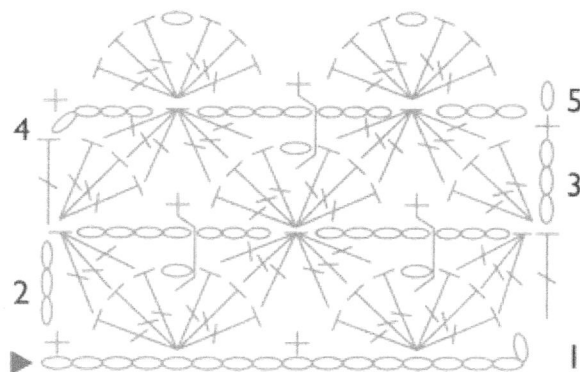

Tip- This pattern can be worked in two or more colors, using one color for the foundation chain and Row 1, another for Rows 2 and 3, another for Rows 4 and 5, and so on.

Medallion 1

: MEDALLIONS

Medallions are worked in rounds, with the number of stitches in each round increasing so that the medallion lies flat (see this page and the box). They can be circles, squares, or other geometric shapes. Square medallions are worked with some of the additional stitches grouped together at the four corners so that they form a corner. Medallions can be worked in any yarn, although the more intricate ones are best worked in finer cottons.

MEDALLION 1

Ch: ch 4, Sl st into first ch to make a ring

Ch 5, (3 dc into ring, ch 2) 3 times, 2 dc into ring, Sl st in 3rd ch of ch-5.

Sl st into 4th ch of ch-5, ch 6, 2 dc in ch-sp, *1 dc in each of 3 dc, (2 dc, ch 4, 2 dc) in next ch-sp, repeat from* twice, 1 dc in each of 2 dc, 1 dc in 3rd ch of ch-5 at beg of previous rnd, 1 dc in next ch-sp, Sl st in 3rd ch of ch-6 at beg of this rnd.

Sl st in 4th ch of ch-6, ch 6, 2 dc in ch-sp, *1 dc in each dc to next corner, (2 dc, ch 4, 2 dc) in ch-sp, repeat from* twice, 1 dc in each dc of 4th group, 1 dc in 3rd ch of ch-6 at beg of previous rnd, 1 dc in next ch-sp, Sl st in 3rd ch of ch-6 at beg of this rnd.

Repeat Round 3 as required (4 dc are added to each group in each round).

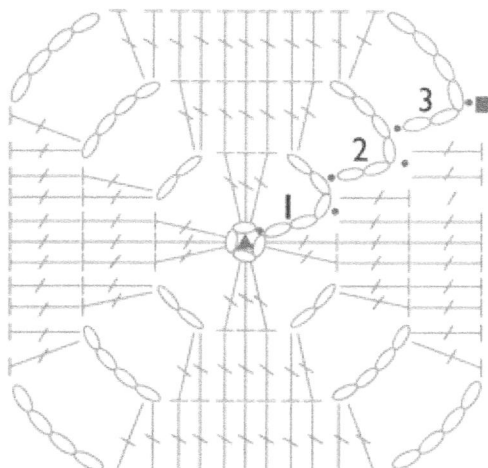

Medallion 2

MEDALLION 2

Known as the granny square, this medallion is usually worked in many colors, with the yarn changed for each round.

Ch: ch 6, Sl st into first ch to make a ring

Ch 3, 2 dc into ring, ch 2, (3 dc into ring, ch 2) 3 times, Sl st in 3rd ch of ch-3.

Fasten off.

Join yarn in next ch-2 sp, ch 3, (2 dc, ch 2, 3 dc) in same ch-sp, *ch 1, (3 dc, ch 2, 3 dc) in next ch-2 sp, ch 1, repeat from* twice, Sl st in 3rd ch of rnd. Fasten off.

Join yarn in next ch-2 sp, ch 3, (2 dc, ch 2, 3 dc) in same ch-sp, *ch 1, 3 dc in ch-1 sp, ch 1, (3 dc, ch 2, 3 dc) in ch-2 sp, repeat from* twice, ch 1, 3 dc in ch-1 sp, ch 1, Sl st in 3rd ch of rnd. Fasten off.

Repeat Round 3 as required, working 3 dc in each ch-1 sp (an extra group of 3 dc is added on each side in each round).

See chain for height.

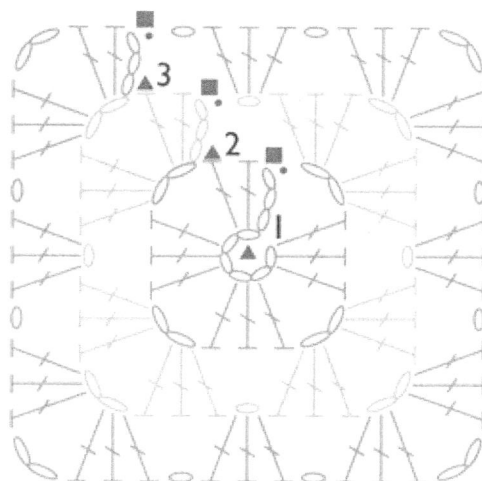

Tip- Many medallions can be worked very successfully using several colors, either to pick out a central design or to show the concentric pattern of the rounds.

Traditionally, rugs were worked in many colors to use up whatever ends of wool were available, but a subtler and more modern effect can be achieved by restricting yourself to, say, three colors, or even three shades of one color. See for instructions on working in several colors.

Medallion 3

MEDALLION 3

Cluster (CL) = 3 treble crochets

Ch: ch 5, Sl st in first ch to make a ring

Work 12 sc into ring, Sl st in first sc.

Ch 11, Sl st in next sc, repeat from 11 times.

Sl st in each of first 6 ch of first loop, ch 4, 1 sc in 6th ch of next loop, ch 4, (work 1 CL, ch 4, 1 CL) in next loop, *ch 4, (1 sc in 6th ch of next loop, ch 4) twice, (work 1 CL, ch 4, 1 CL) in next loop, repeat from* twice, ch 4, 1 sc in same ch as 6th Sl st.

Sl st in each of next 2 ch, ch 3, dc2tog in same ch-4 sp, ch 4, 1 sc in next ch-4 sp, ch 4, (work 1 CL, ch 4, 1 CL) in ch-4 sp at corner, *ch 4, 1 sc in next ch-4 sp, ch 4, 1 CL in next ch-4 sp, ch 4, 1 sc in next ch-4 sp, ch 4, (work 1 CL, ch 4, 1 CL) in ch-4 sp at corner, repeat from* twice, ch 4, 1 sc in next ch-4 sp, ch 4, Sl st in 3rd ch of rnd. Fasten off.

See work a cluster (CL).

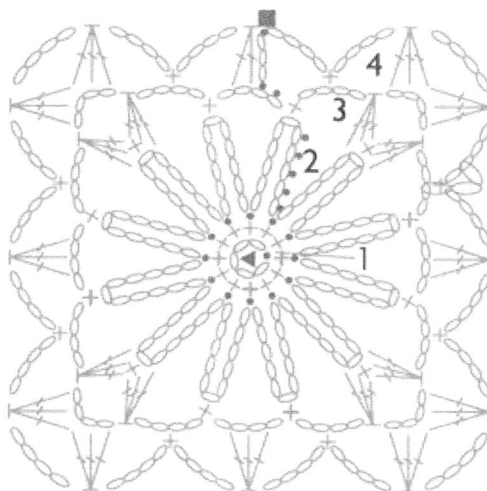

WORKING IN ROUNDS

When working a round, the number of stitches in each round should increase by the number of stitches in the first round, as shown in the table below. If you are working without a pattern, a good guide is to increase one stitch in each stitch in the second round, one in every second stitch in the third round, one in every third stitch in the fourth round and so on.

ROUND	STITCHES

Round 1	6	8	10	12
Round 2	12	16	20	24
Round 3	18	24	30	36
Round 4	24	32	40	48

Medallion 4

MEDALLION 4

This square is normally worked in two colors, A and B. Begin with yarn A.

Ch: ch 8, Sl st in first ch to make a ring

Ch 6, (1 dc into ring, ch 3) 7 times, Sl st in 3rd ch of rnd. Fasten off.

Join yarn B to next ch, ch 3, 3 dc in same ch-sp, ch 3, (4 dc in next ch-3 sp, ch 3) 7 times, Sl st in 3rd ch of rnd. Fasten off.

Join yarn A to first ch of last ch-3 worked, ch 3, 5 dc in same ch-3 sp, ch 1, 6 dc in next ch-3 sp, ch 3, (6 dc in next ch-3 sp, ch 1, 6 dc in next ch-3 sp, ch 3) 3 times, Sl st in 3rd ch of rnd. Fasten off.

Join yarn B to next ch-1 sp, ch 3, *1 sc between 3rd and 4th dc of next group, ch 3, (2 dc, ch 3, 2 dc) in next ch-3 sp, ch 3, 1 sc between 3rd and 4th dc of next group, ch 3, 1 sc in next ch-1 sp, repeat from* , replacing last sc with Sl st in first ch of rnd. Fasten off.

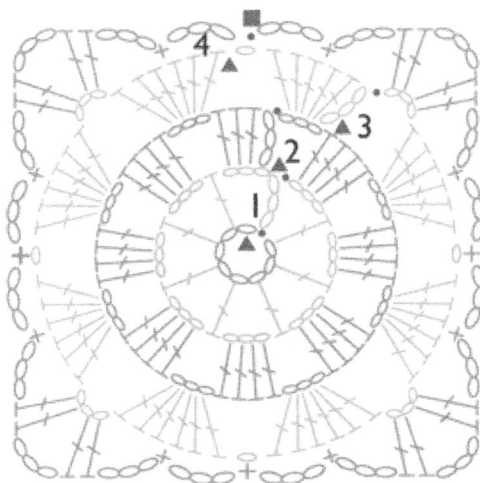

JOINING MEDALLIONS

Medallions can be joined in many ways. Squares can be joined directly to each other using one of the methods given. Using one or more rows of single crochet, perhaps in a contrasting color, can be effective.

Shapes such as stars and diamonds can also be joined using filling motifs, or for a more open effect they can be linked only at the points using picots or several single crochet stitches.

Medallion 5

MEDALLION 5

Large picot: chain-5 picot; small picot: chain-3 picot Ch: ch 6, Sl st in first ch to make a ring

Ch 4, (1 dc into ring, ch 1) 11 times, Sl st in 3rd ch of ch-4.

Sl st in next ch, ch 2, hdc3tog under same ch, ch 2, hdc4tog in next ch-1 sp, ch 3, *1 tr in next dc, ch 3, (hdc4tog in next ch-1 sp, ch 2) twice, hdc4tog in next ch-1 sp, ch 3, repeat from* twice, 1 tr in next dc, ch 3, hdc4tog in next ch-1 sp, ch 2, Sl st in top of hdc3tog.

Ch 1, *1 sc in top of group, work large picot, ch 2, skip (2 ch, 1 group), 5 dc in next ch-3 sp, ch 1, 1 tr in tr, work small picot, ch 1, 5 dc in next ch-3 sp, ch 2, skip (1 group, 2 ch), repeat from* 3 times, Sl st in first sc in rnd. Fasten off.

◔ See work a picot.
See work stitches together.

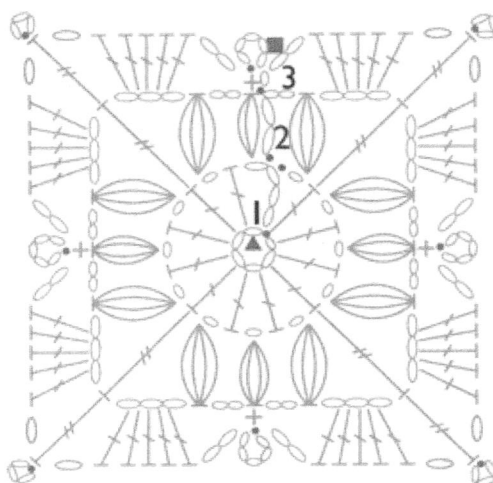

Tip- Since you don't turn your work when working in rounds, the front and back may look very different. When you are joining medallions, be careful that the fronts are all faceup.

Medallion 6

MEDALLION 6

Large picot: chain-5 picot;
small picot: chain-3 picot

Round 1: Yarn loop, Sl st into yarn loop, ch 6, (1 sc into wrap, ch 5) 3 times,
Sl st in first ch of ch-6.

Round 2: Ch 1, 7 sc in first ch-loop, (1 sc in next sc, work large picot, 7 sc in next ch-loop) 3 times, Sl st in ch-1, ch 2, 1 dc in same ch as last Sl st.

Round 3: *Ch 4, skip 1 sc, 1 tr in each of next 5 sc, skip 1 sc, ch 4, Sl st in next picot, repeat from* twice, ch 4, skip 1 sc, 1 tr in each of next 5 sc, skip 1 sc, ch 1, 1 dc in dc of Round 2.

Round 4: Ch 3, work tog (1 dc under dc of Round 3, 1 tr under [2 ch, 1 dc] of Round 2, 2 dc in next ch-4 sp), ch 5, *work tog (1 tr in first tr of 5 tr, 1 dc in each of next 2 tr), ch 5, work tog (1 dc in same tr as last dc, 1 dc in next tr, 1 tr in next tr), ch 5, work tog (2 dc in next ch-4 sp, 1 tr in picot of Round 2, 2 dc in next ch-4 sp), ch 5, repeat from* twice, work tog (1 tr in first tr, 1 dc in each of next 2 tr), ch 5, work tog (1 dc in same tr as last dc, 1 dc in next tr, 1 tr in next tr), ch 5, Sl st in first ch of rnd.

Round 5: Ch 1, 6 sc in first ch-5 sp, *(4 sc, small picot, 3 sc) in corner ch-5 sp, 6 sc in next ch-5 sp, (1 sc, small picot) in top of next group, 6 sc in next ch-5 sp, repeat from* twice, (4 sc, small picot, 3 sc) in corner ch-5 sp, 6 sc in next ch-5 sp, (Sl st, small picot) in ch-1. Fasten off.

See a yarn loop. See work a picot. work stitches together.

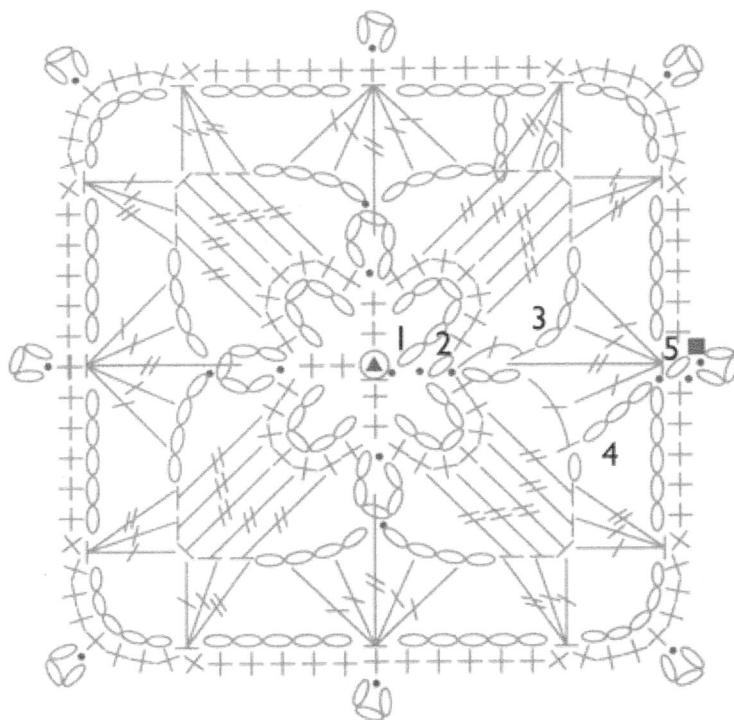

Medallion 7

MEDALLION 7

This square is normally worked in several colors, but Rounds 1 and 2 should be the same color to bring out the flower design in the center.

Cluster (CL) = 6 double treble crochets Ch: ch 8, Sl st in first ch to make a ring

Ch 7, (6 tr into ring, ch 3) 3 times, 5 tr into ring, Sl st in 4th ch of ch-7.

Sl st in each of next 2 ch, (ch 5, work CL over next 6 tr, ch 5, Sl st in 2nd ch of ch-3) 4 times, working last Sl st in same place as 2nd Sl st at beginning of rnd. Fasten off.

Join yarn with Sl st in top of next CL, *(3 tr, ch 1, 3 tr, ch 2, 3 tr, ch 1, 3 tr) in next ch-3 sp of Round 1, Sl st in top of next group, repeat from* 3 times, with last Sl st in same sp as first Sl st of rnd. Fasten off (if changing yarn).

Join yarn to same place, ch 4, 5 tr in same Sl st, *skip (3 tr, 1 ch, 3 tr), (6 tr, ch 2, 6 tr) in corner ch-2 sp, skip (3 tr, 1 ch, 3 tr), 6 tr in next Sl st, repeat from* twice, skip (3 tr, 1 ch, 3 tr), (6 tr, ch 2, 6 tr) in corner ch-2 sp, skip (3 tr, 1 ch, 3 tr), Sl st in 4th ch of rnd. Fasten off (if changing yarn).

Join yarn to same place, ch 1, 1 sc in each of 5 tr, *1 dc in ch-1 sp of Round 3, 1 sc in each of 6 tr, 3 sc in corner ch-2 sp, 1 sc in each of 6 tr, 1 dc in ch-1 sp of Round 3, 1 sc in each of 6 tr, repeat from* twice, 1 dc in ch-1 sp of Round 3, 1 sc in each of 6 tr, 3 sc in corner ch-2 sp, 1 sc in each of 6 tr, 1 dc in ch-1 sp of Round 3, Sl st in first ch of round.

Ch 3, 1 dc in each st of Round 5 with (1 dc, 1 tr, 1 dc) in center sc of 3 dc at corners, Sl st in 3rd ch of rnd. Fasten off.

See a cluster (CL).

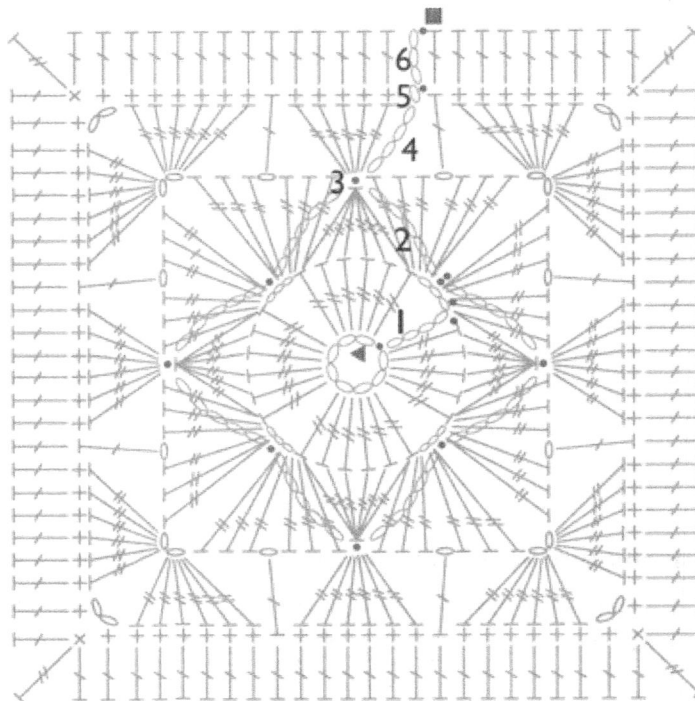

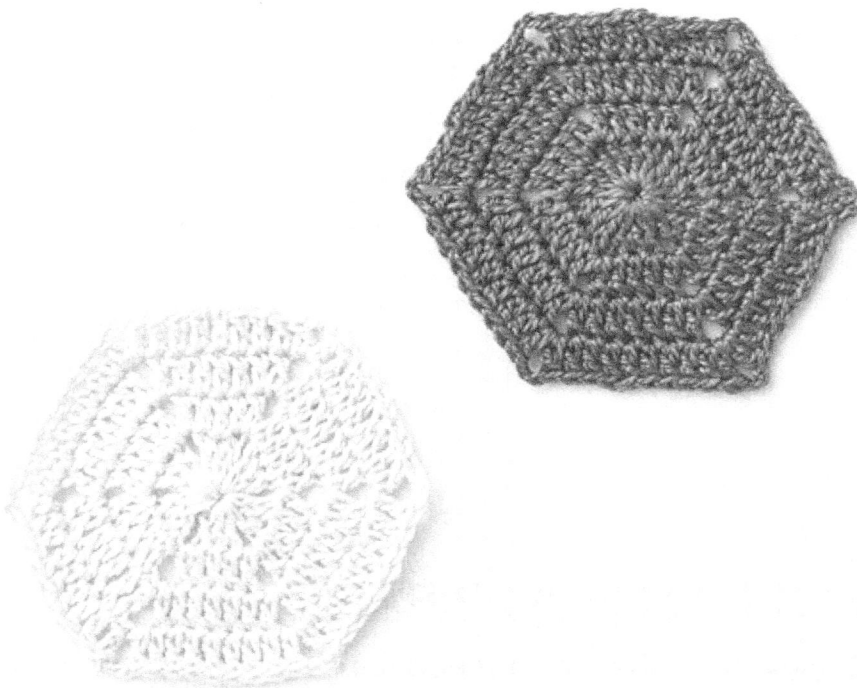

Medallion 8

MEDALLION 8

Ch: ch 4, Sl st in first ch to make a ring

Ch 5, (3 dc into ring, ch 2) 5 times, 2 dc into ring, Sl st in 3rd ch of ch-5.

Sl st in next ch, ch 5, 1 dc under next ch, *1 dc in each of 3 dc, (1 dc, ch 2, 1* dc) in ch-2 sp, repeat from 4 times, 1 dc in each of next 2 dc, 1 dc in 3rd ch of ch-5 of Round 1, Sl st in 3rd ch of ch-5 of this rnd.

Sl st in next ch, ch 5, 1 dc under next ch, *1 dc in each dc, (1 dc, ch 2, 1 dc) in ch-2 sp, repeat from* 4 times, 1 dc in each dc, 1 dc in 3rd ch of ch-5 of previous rnd, Sl st in 3rd ch of ch-5 of this rnd.

Repeat Round 3 as required (an extra 2 dc are added on each side in every round).

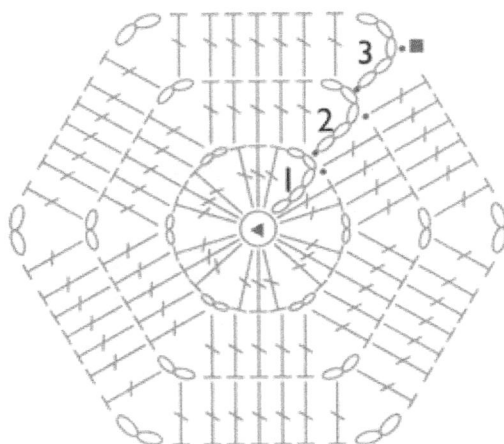

WORKING IN A SPIRAL

Circles and other plain medallions can also be worked in a spiral by omitting the slip stitch at the end of the round and working the first stitch of the new round into the first stitch of the previous round (see Medallion 10). The method only works well, however, when you are using small stitches, such as single crochet, in a tight pattern.

Working in a spiral means you do not have a visible seam in your work. This is particularly useful when making three-dimensional items.

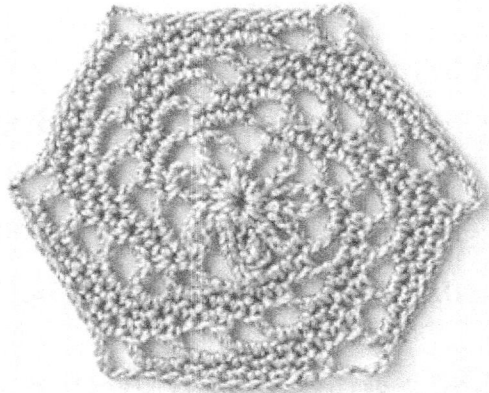

Medallion 9 (top) and Medallion 10

MEDALLION 9

Ch: ch 6, Sl st in first ch to make a ring

Ch 8, (5 dc into ring, ch 5) twice, 4 dc into ring, Sl st in 3rd ch of ch-8.

Sl st in each of next 2 ch, ch 8, 2 dc in ch-loop of previous rnd, *1 dc in each* dc of group, (2 dc, ch 5, 2 dc) in ch-5 sp, repeat from once, 1 dc in each dc, 2 dc in ch-loop of previous rnd, Sl st in 3rd ch of ch-8.

Repeat Round 2 as required (4 dc are added on each side in every round).

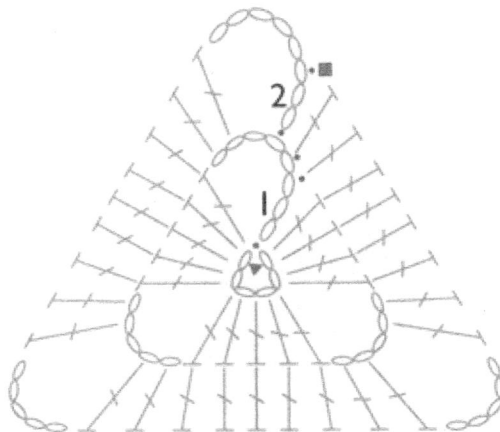

MEDALLION 10

Ch: ch 4, Sl st in first ch to make a ring

Ch 7, 1 sc into ring, (ch 6, 1 sc into ring) 5 times, Sl st in first ch of rnd.

Sl st in next 3 ch, *ch 4, 1 sc in next ch-loop, repeat from* 5 times.

Ch 4, 2 sc in next ch-4 sp, 1 sc in next sc, repeat from 5 times.

Ch 4, 2 sc in next ch-4 sp, 1 sc in each of next 2 sc, skip 1 sc, repeat from 5 times.

Ch 4, 2 sc in next ch-4 sp, 1 sc in each of next 3 sc, skip 1 sc, repeat from 5 times.

Continue rounds as required, adding 1 sc on each side in every round.

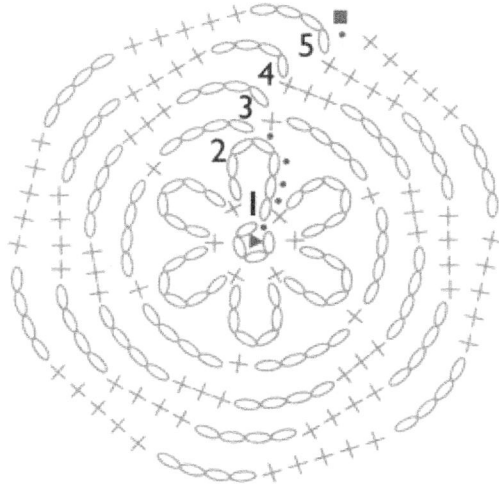

5
4
3
2
1

Shape 1

SHAPES

These shapes can be incorporated into crocheted fabric as an accent or as a repeated motif, joined together by picots or single crochet stitches. Cotton yarns that are not too thick will give the best definition to the shapes.

SHAPE 1

Scale pattern

Row 1: Yarn loop, ch 3, (1 dc, ch 3, 2 dc) into loop, turn.

Row 2: Ch 3, skip first dc, 1 dc in back loop of next dc, (2 dc, ch 3, 2 dc) in ch-3 sp, 1 dc in back loop of next dc, 1 dc in back loop of 3rd ch of tch, turn.

Row 3: Ch 3, skip first dc, 1 dc in back loop of each dc, (2 dc, ch 3, 2 dc) in ch-3 sp, 1 dc in back loop of each dc, with last dc in back loop of 3rd ch of tch, turn.

Repeat Row 3 as required (4 dc are added in each row).

st row: Ch 3, 1 dc in back loop of each dc, 6 dc in ch-3 sp, 1 dc in back loop of each dc, with last dc in back loop of 3rd ch of tch. Fasten off.

See a yarn loop. See working into the back loop.

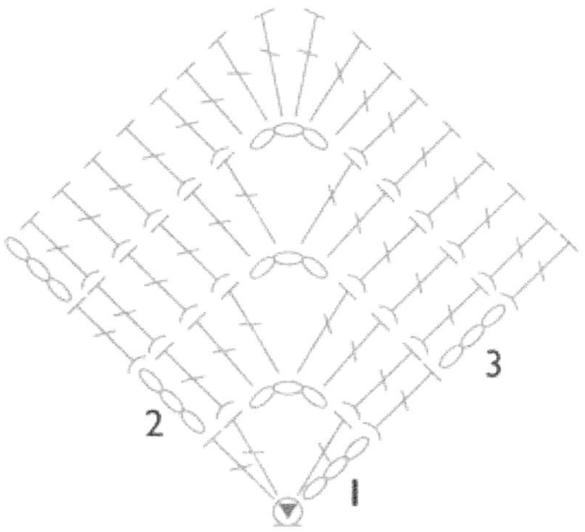

Tip- This scale pattern can be worked in several colors.

Shape 2 (left) and Shape 3

SHAPE 2

Flower pattern

Ch: ch 7, Sl st in first ch to make a ring

Ch 1, 14 sc into ring, Sl st in ch-1.

Ch 4, *(tr4tog, inserting hook twice in next sc and twice in following sc)*, ch 3, *1 sc in next sc, ch 3, repeat from* 4 times omitting last sc, Sl st in first ch of rnd. Fasten off.

See work stitches together.

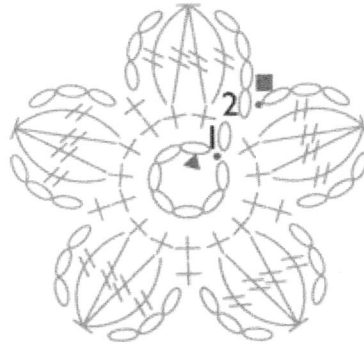

SHAPE 3

Flower pattern

Ch: ch 4, Sl st in first ch to make a ring

Ch 5, (1 dc into ring, ch 2) 5 times, Sl st in 3rd ch of ch-5.

Ch 5, *dtr3tog in ch-2 sp, ch 5, 1 sc around post of next dc, ch 4, repeat from* 4 times, dtr3tog, ch 5, 1 sc around first ch-2 of Round 1, Sl st in first ch of rnd. Fasten off.

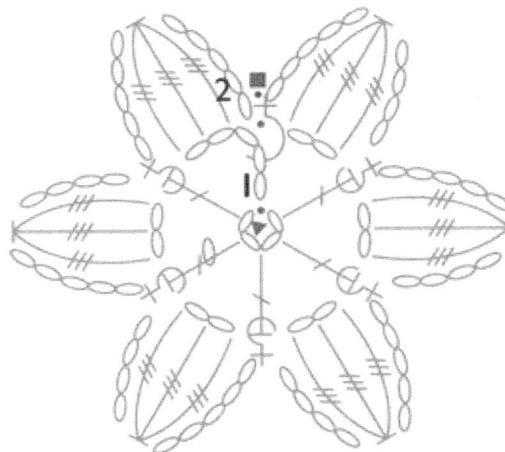

Tips- For these flower shapes, different colors

may be used in each round.

When working around the post of a double crochet, insert the hook from right to left (see this page).

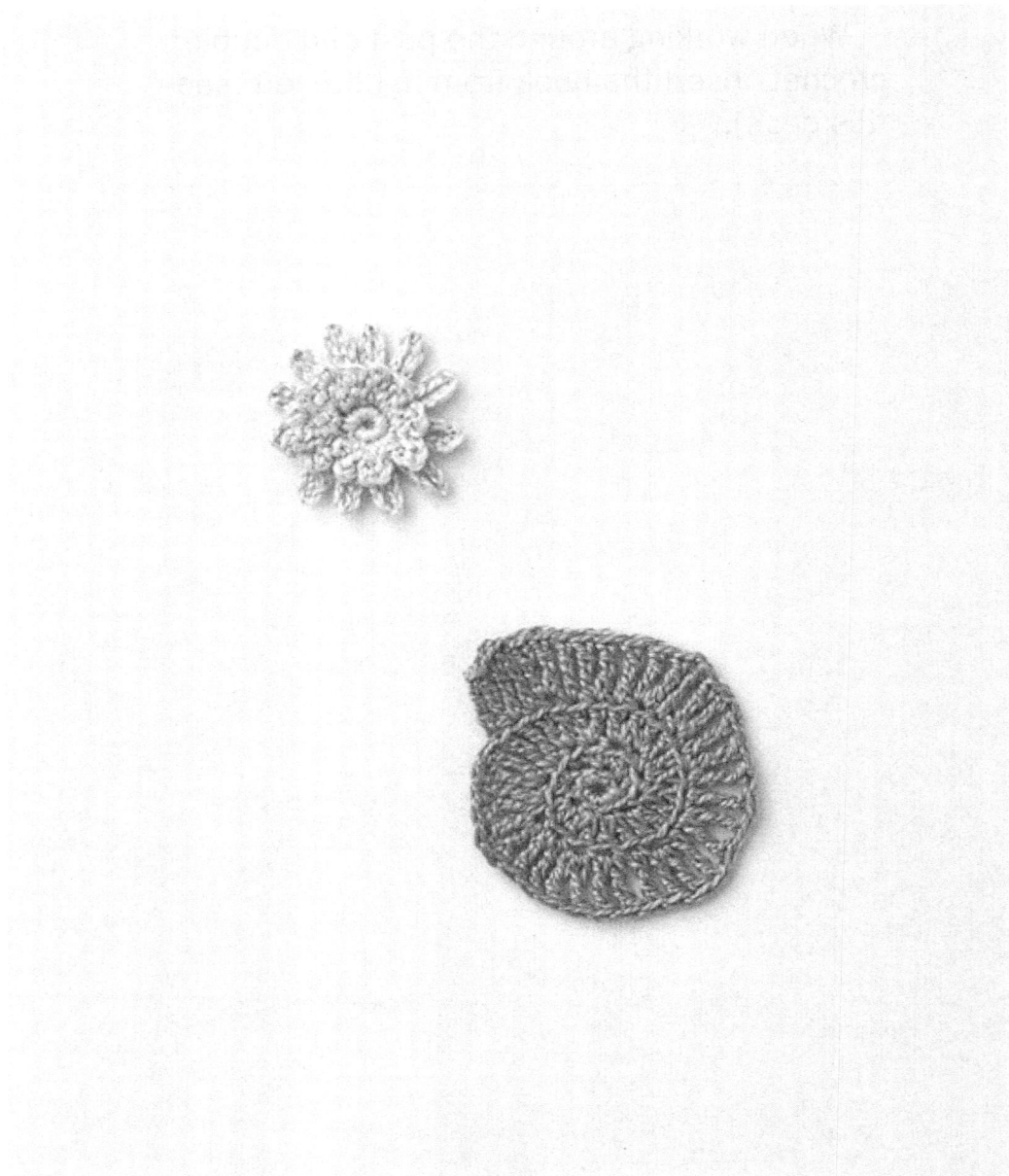

Shape 4 (top) and Shape 5

SHAPE 4

Flower with raised petals

Ch: Ch 4, Sl st in first ch to make a ring

Ch 1, 11 sc into ring, Sl st in ch-1.

(Sc, ch 4, 1 sc) in front loop of ch-1, (1 sc, ch 4, 1 sc) in front loop of each sc, Sl st in first sc of rnd.

(Sl st, ch 7, 1 sc) in back loop of ch-1 of Round 1, (1 sc, ch 7, 1 sc) in back loop of each sc of Round 1, Sl st in first Sl st of rnd. Fasten off.

See working into front and back loops.

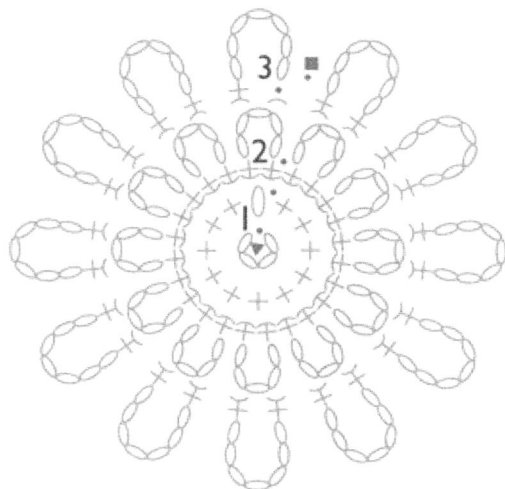

SHAPE 5

Shell pattern

Ch: ch 4, Sl st in first ch to make a ring

Work 8 sc into ring.

Work 2 hdc in back loop of first sc, 2 hdc in back loop of each of next 4 sc, 2 dc in back loop of each of next 3 sc.

Work 2dc in back loop of each of next 6 hdc, 2 tr in back loop of each of next 4 hdc, 2 tr in back loop of each of next 3 dc, 1 tr in back loop of next dc, 2 tr in back loop of next dc, 1 tr in back loop of next dc.

(Tr 2 in back loop of next dc, 1 tr in back loop of next dc) 6 times, 2 tr in back loop of next tr, 1 tr in back loop of next tr. Fasten off.

See working into front and back loops.

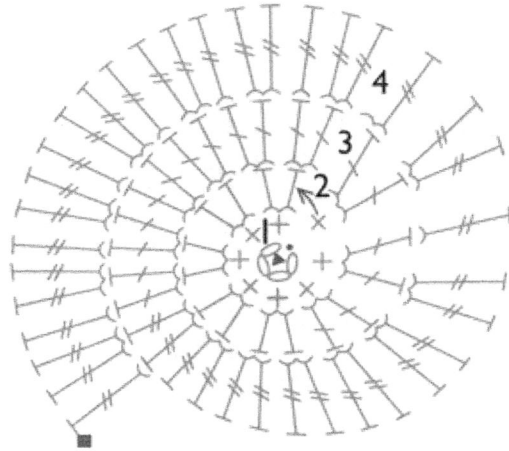

4

3

2

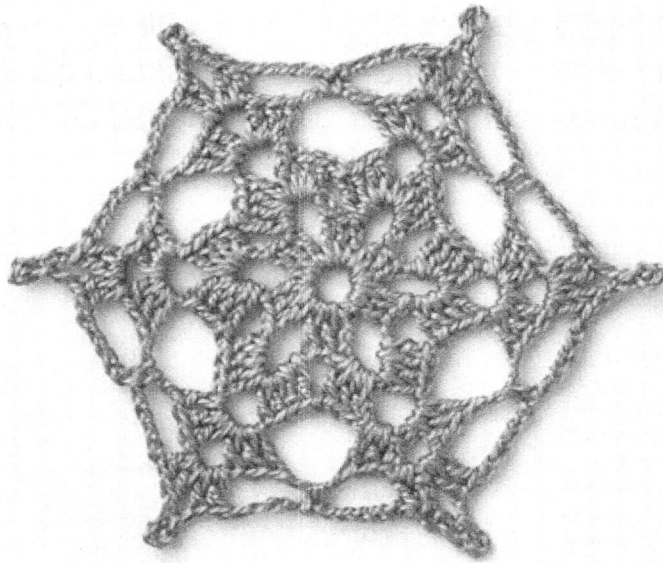

Shape 6

SHAPE 6

Snowflake pattern

Ch: ch 9, Sl st in first ch to make a ring

Ch 8, 3 dc into ring, (ch 5, 3 dc into ring) 4 times, ch 5, 2 dc into ring, Sl st in

3rd ch of ch-8.

Sl st in each of next 2 ch, ch 7, 4 dc in same ch-loop, *ch 1, skip 3 dc, (4 dc, ch 4, 4 dc) in ch-5 loop, repeat from* 4 times, ch 1, skip 2 dc, 3 dc in loop, Sl st in 3rd ch of ch-7.

Sl st in each of next 2 ch, ch 6, 3 dc in same ch-loop, ch 3, skip (4 dc, ch 1, 4 dc), *(3 dc, ch 3, 3 dc) in ch-4 loop, ch 3, skip (4 dc, 1 ch, 4 dc), repeat from* 4 times, 2 dc in ch-loop, Sl st in 3rd ch of ch-6.

Sl st in each of next 2 ch, ch 8, Sl st in 4th ch from hook, ch 1, 2 dc in same ch-loop, ch 5, skip 3 dc, 1 sc in ch-3 loop, *ch 5, skip 3 dc, (2 dc, ch 5, Sl st in 4th ch from hook, ch 1, 2 dc) in ch-3 loop, ch 5, skip 3 dc, 1 sc in next ch-3 loop, repeat from* 4 times, ch 5, skip 2 dc, 1 dc in next ch-loop, Sl st in 3rd ch of ch-8. Fasten off.

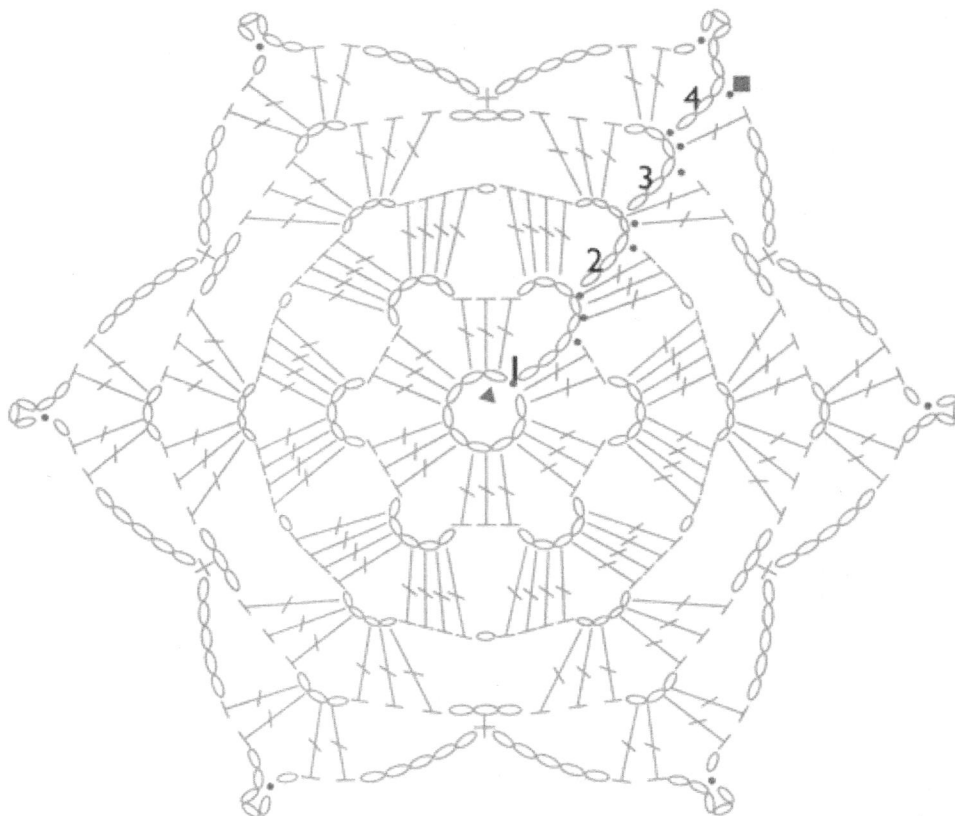

Shape 7

SHAPE 7

Flower pattern

Round 1: Yarn loop, ch 1, 7 sc into loop, Sl st in ch-1.

Round 2: Ch 5, (skip 1 sc, 1 sc in next sc, ch 4) 3 times, Sl st in first ch of rnd.

Round 3: Sl st in next ch, ch 3, 6 dc in ch-loop, ch 2, skip 1 sc, (7 dc in next ch-loop, ch 2, skip 1 sc) 3 times, Sl st in 3rd ch of rnd.

Round 4: Ch 1, 1 sc in same place as last Sl st, (1 sc in each of next 2 dc, 2 sc in next dc) twice, skip 2 ch, 2 sc in next dc, (1 sc in each of next 2 dc, 2 sc in next dc) twice, skip 2 ch, repeat from twice, Sl st in ch-1.

Round 5: *Ch 3, 1 dc in same place as last Sl st, (1 dc in next sc, 2 dc in next sc) twice, 2 dc in next sc, (1 dc in next sc, 2 dc in next sc) twice, turn. ch 1, skip first dc, 1 sc in each of 14 dc, 1 sc in 3rd ch of rnd, turn. ch 1, skip first sc, 1 hdc in next sc, 1 dc in each of next 4 sc, 1 sc in next sc, Sl st in each of next 2 sc, 1 sc in next sc, 1 dc in each of next 4 sc, 1 hdc in last sc, ch 1, Sl st in ch-1, 2 Sl st in side edge of dc below, Sl st in side edge of sc below dc, Sl st in next sc of Round 4. Repeat from 3 times. Fasten off.*

⟳ See a yarn loop.

> **Tip-** Round 5 is worked back and forth in three rows across two petals.

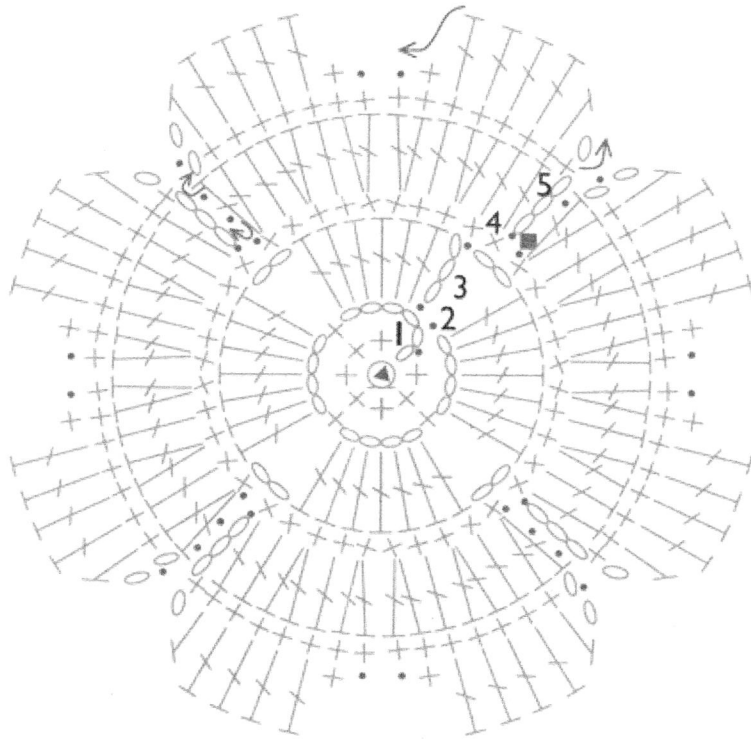

Shape 8

SHAPE 8

Open hexagon pattern

Ch: ch 6, Sl st in first ch to make a ring

Ch 6, (1 tr into ring, ch 2) 11 times, Sl st in 4th ch of ch-6.

Sl st in next ch-2 sp, (ch 3, 1 dc, ch 2, 2 dc) in next sp, 3 dc in next sp, *(2 dc, ch 2, 2 dc) in next sp, 3 dc in next sp, repeat from* 4 times, Sl st in 3rd ch of ch-3.

Ch 1, 1 sc in first dc, *(1 sc, ch 2, 1 sc) in ch-2 sp, 1 sc in each of next 7 dc, repeat from* 5 times, (1 sc, ch 2, 1 sc) in ch-2 sp, 1 sc in each of next 5 dc, Sl st in ch-1.

Ch 3, 1 dc in each of first 2 sc, *(1 dc, ch 2, 1 dc) in ch-2 sp, 1 dc in each of next 9 sc, repeat from* 5 times, (1 dc, ch 2, 1 dc) in ch-2 sp, 1 dc in next 6 sc, Sl st in 3rd ch of ch-3.

Ch 1, 1 sc in each of first 3 dc, *(1 sc, ch 2, 1 sc) in ch-2 sp, 1 sc in each of next 11 dc, repeat from* 5 times, (1 sc, ch 2, 1 sc) in ch-2 sp, 1 sc in each of next 7 dc, Sl st in ch-1. Fasten off.

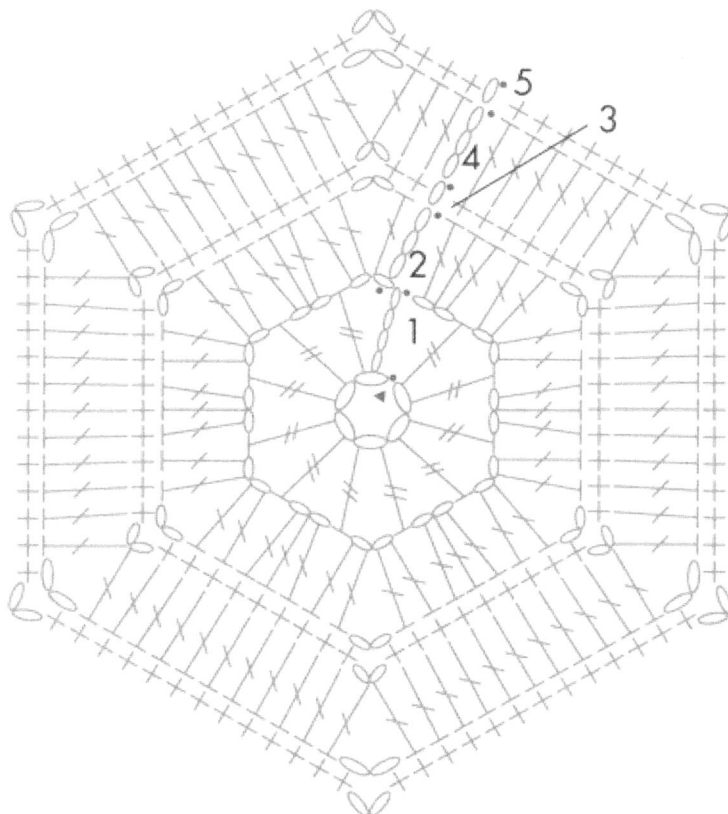

Tip- This pattern can be adapted to make an octagon or any other such shape. For example, to make an octagon, start with an eight-stitch chain, make fifteen treble crochets in Round 1, and do the repeat in Round 2 six times and the repeats in Rounds 3–5 seven times.

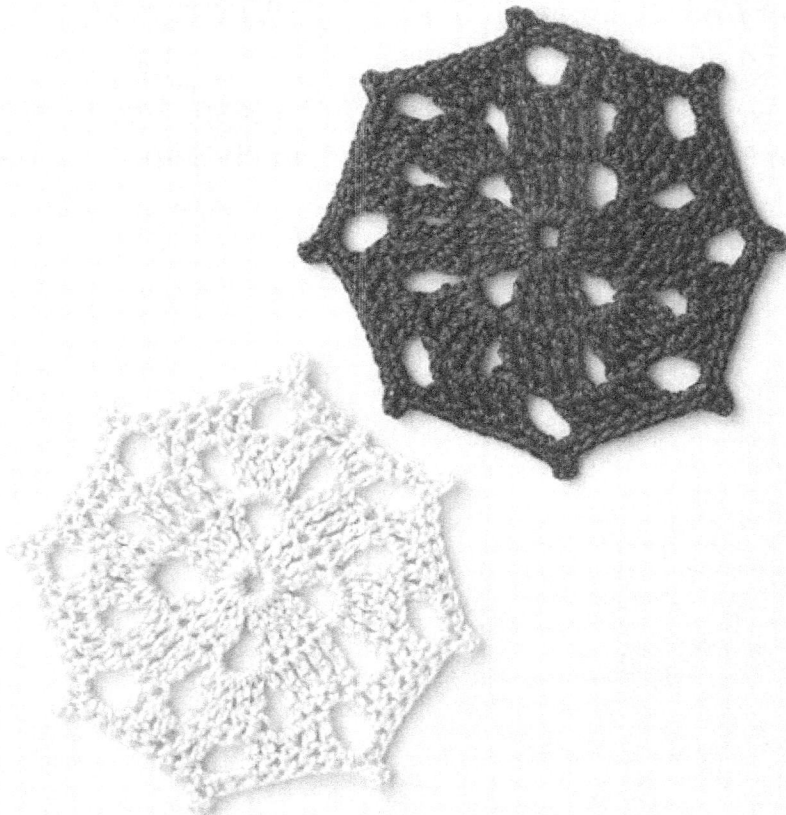

Shape 9

SHAPE 9

Octagon

Picot: chain-3 picot
Ch: ch 6, Sl st in first ch to make a ring

Ch 4, 4 tr into ring, *ch 3, 5 tr into ring, repeat from* twice, ch 3, Sl st in 4th ch of rnd.

Ch 4, 1 tr in each of 4 tr, ch 3, *5 tr in ch-3 sp, ch 3, 1 tr in each of 5 tr, ch 3, repeat from* twice, 5 tr in ch-3 sp, ch 3, Sl st in 4th ch of rnd.

Ch 3, 1 dc in first tr, *ch 3, skip 1 tr, 1 dc in next 2 tr, 1 dc in ch-3 sp, 1 dc in next 2 tr, repeat from* 6 times, ch 3, skip 1 tr, 1 dc in next 2 tr, 1 dc in ch-3 sp, Sl st in 3rd ch of rnd.

Ch 1, 1 sc in next dc, *(2 sc, 1 picot, 1 sc) in ch-3 sp, 1 sc in each of next 5 dc, repeat from* 6 times, (2 sc, 1 picot, 1 sc) in ch-3 sp, 1 sc in each of next 3 dc, Sl st in ch-1. Fasten off.

See work a picot.

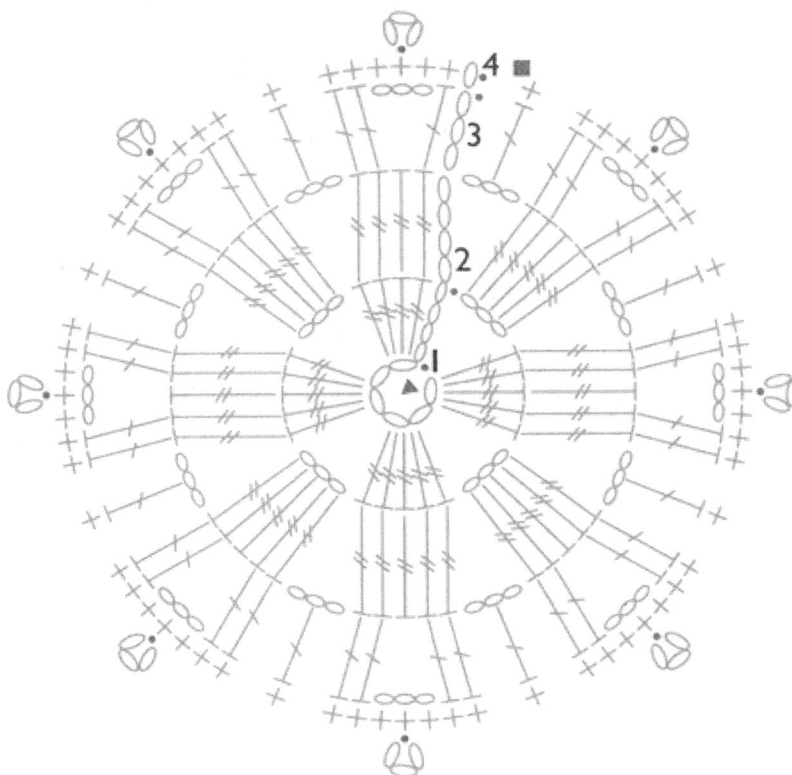

Shape 10

SHAPE 10

Star pattern

Ch: ch 6, Sl st in first ch to make a ring

Sl st into ring, ch 4, work CL of 2 tr into ring, *ch 6, work CL of 3 tr into ring, repeat from* 4 times, ch 6, 1 Sl st in top of first CL.

Ch 6, 1 dc in same place as last Sl st, *ch 2, 5 sc in ch-6 sp, ch 2, (1 dc, ch 3, 1 dc) in top of next CL, repeat from* 4 times, ch 2, 5 sc in ch-6 sp, ch 2, Sl st in 3rd ch of ch-6 at beg of rnd.

Sl st in ch-6 sp, ch 6, 1 dc into same sp, *ch 4, 1 sc in each of next 5 sc, ch 4, (1 dc, ch 3, 1 dc) in ch-3 sp, repeat from* 4 times, ch 4, 1 sc in each of next 5 sc, ch 4, Sl st into 3rd ch of ch-6 at beg of rnd.

Sl st in ch-6 sp, ch 6, 1 dc in same ch-6 sp, *ch 6, skip 1 sc, 1 sc in each of next 3 sc, ch 6, (1 dc, ch 3, 1 dc) in ch-3 sp, repeat from* 4 times, ch 6, skip 1 sc, 1 sc in each of next 3 sc, ch 6, Sl st in 3rd ch of ch-6 at beg of rnd.

Ch 3, *4 dc in next ch-3 sp, ch 5, 1 Sl st in top of last dc, 3 dc in same ch-3 sp, 1 dc in next dc, 3 dc in next ch-6 sp, ch 4, skip 1 sc, 1 sc in next sc, ch 4, 3 dc in next ch-6 sp, 1 dc in next dc, repeat from* 5 times omitting last dc of last repeat, Sl st in 3rd ch of ch-3. Fasten off.

See a cluster (CL).

Shape 11

SHAPE 11

Flower in a circle Cluster (CL) = 5 double treble crochets, each worked into the back loop of a single crochet Ch: ch 5, Sl st in first ch to make a ring

Ch 3, 15 dc into ring, Sl st in 3rd ch of ch-3.

Ch 1, 2 sc in sp before each dc, 2 sc in sp before ch-3, Sl st in ch-1.

Ch 5, skip first sc, dtr4tog worked in back loop of next 4 sc, *ch 9, (work 1 CL, inserting hook in same sc as last dtr then in next 4 sc), repeat from* 6 times, ch 9, Sl st in top of dtr4tog.

Ch 1, 9 sc in first ch-9 sp, *skip 1 CL, 9 sc in next ch-9 sp, repeat from* , Sl st in ch-1. Fasten off.

See work a cluster (CL).

See working into the back loop.

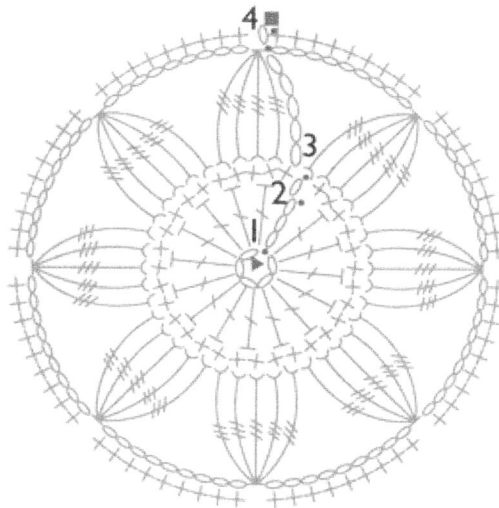

EDGINGS

Crochet edgings are used to give a neat or fancy finish to a piece of crochet or woven fabric. They are worked into the edge of the main crochet piece or into hem-stitched holes along woven fabric (see this page).

Always work with the right side of the fabric facing you and join the yarn at the right-hand end of the piece. Work into the stitches of the edge (or hem-stitched holes). The simpler patterns work well in any yarn, but the more delicate ones should be worked in finer cottons.

TURKISH CROCHET

Crochet work has been a part of Turkish handicrafts since at least Ottoman times, when gold and silver threads were crocheted to edge embroideries. Women's scarves are traditionally edged with crocheted edges called *oya*.

Tip- Reverse single crochet (also known as crab stitch or corded edging) can be used to provide a plain, firm edge on crocheted work. See for instructions.

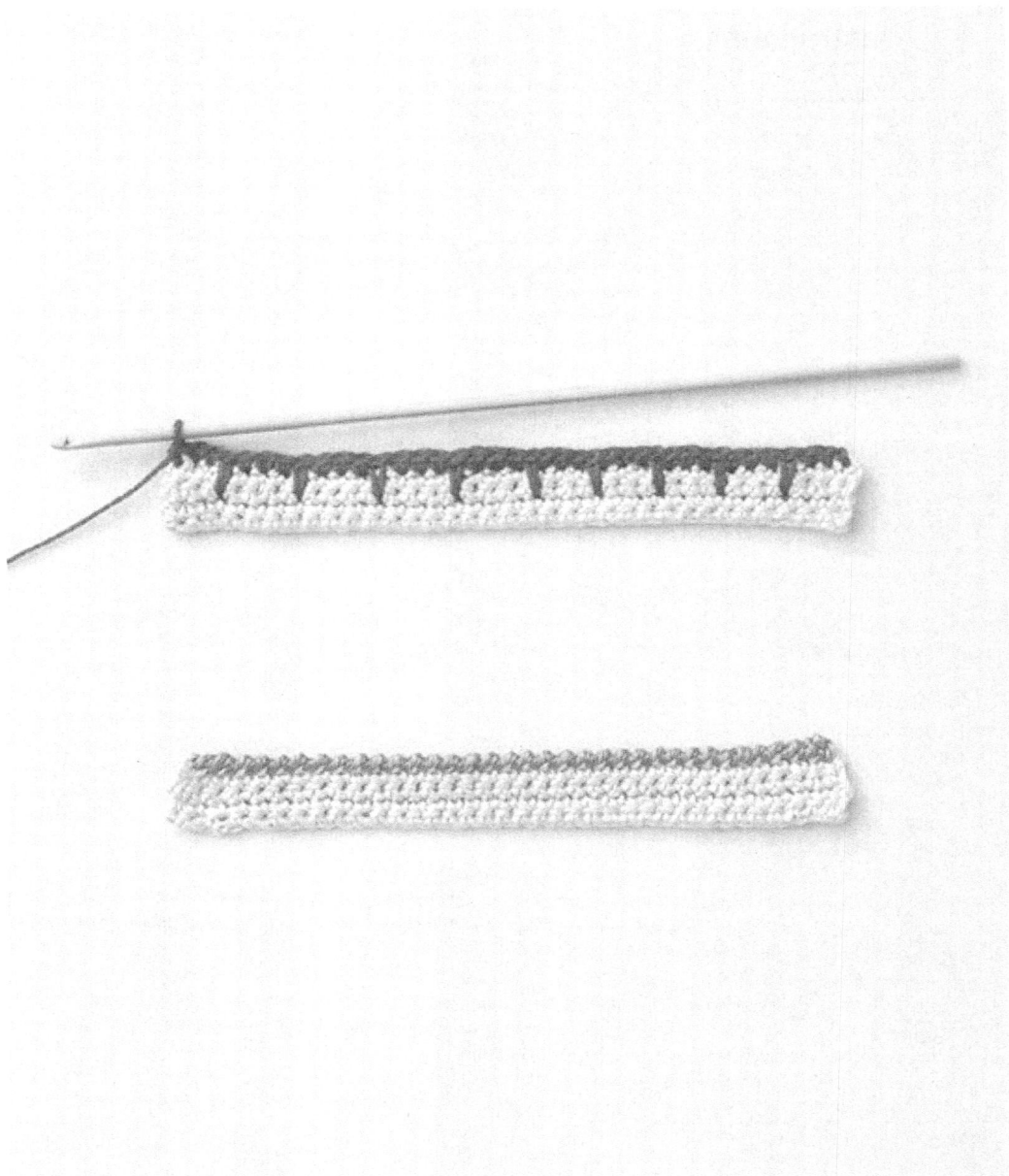

Edging 1 (top) and an edging of reverse single crochet

EDGING 1

Blanket edging

Blanket edging can be worked in crochet as well as embroidery, although crocheted blanket edging is usually only added to crocheted fabric. The spikes may be spaced more widely apart if required.

Spike: Work as for single crochet but insert hook the required depth–usually about ¼ inch (6 mm)–below the edge of the fabric (see this page).
Sts: multiple of 4 + 3

Row 1: Ch 1, 1 sc in each of next 2 sts, *work 1 spike in next st, 1 sc in each of next 3 sts, repeat from* . Fasten off.

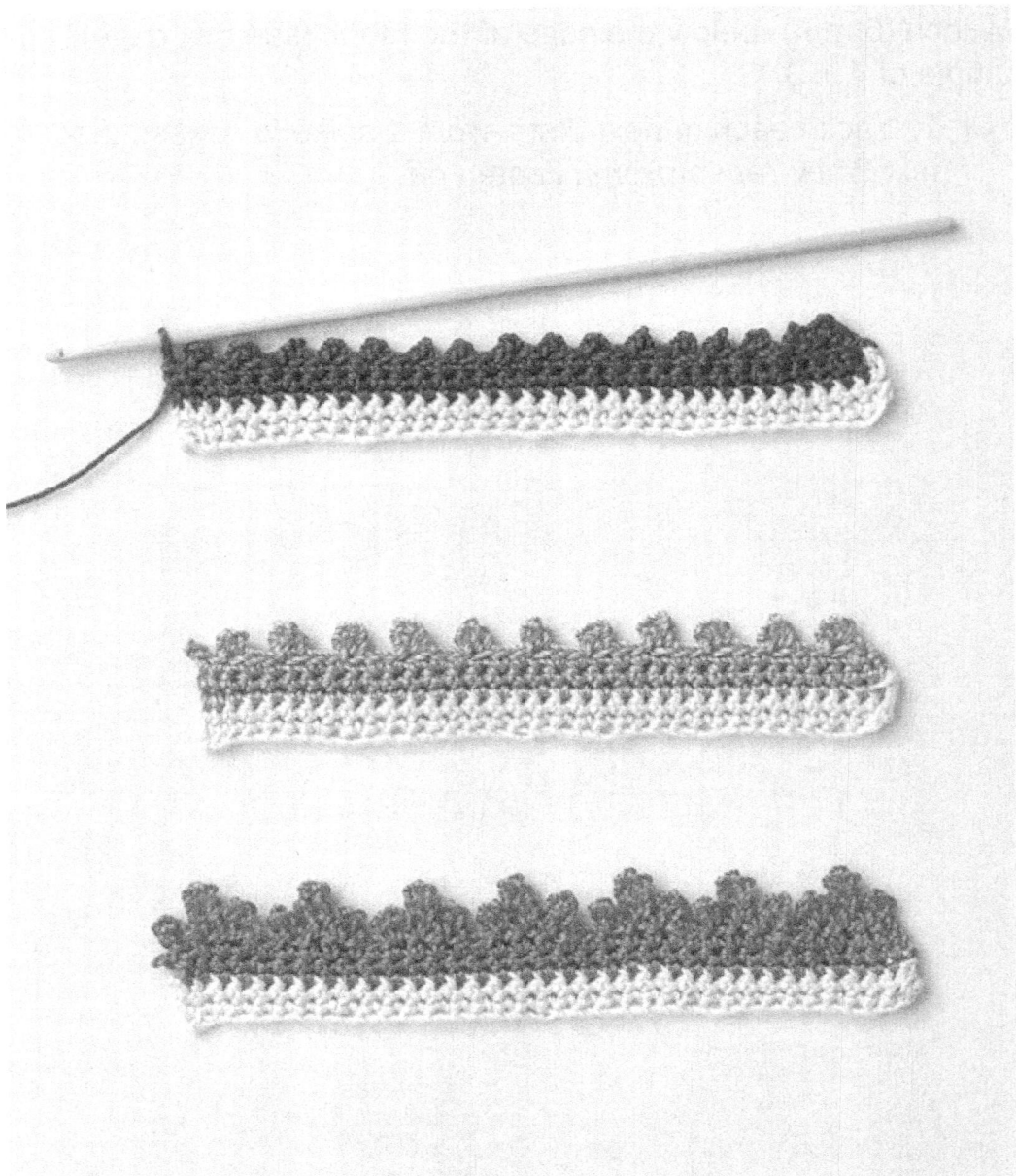

Edging 2 (top), Edging 3 (center), and Edging 4

EDGING 2

Sts or holes: odd number

Row 1: Ch 1, 1 sc in each st (or hole), turn.

Row 2: Ch 1, skip first sc, 1 sc in each sc with last sc in last st, turn.

Row 3: Ch 1, skip first sc, *ch 3, SI st in first ch of ch-3, skip 1 sc, 1 sc in next sc, repeat from* with last sc in last st. Fasten off.

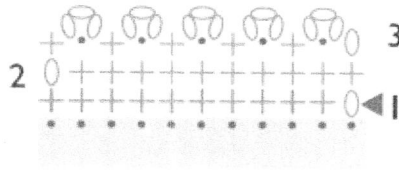

EDGING 3

Sts or holes: multiple of 3 + 2

Row 1: Ch 1, 1 sc in each st (or hole), turn.

Row 2: Ch 1, skip first sc, 1 sc in each sc with last sc in last st, turn.

Row 3: Ch 1, skip first sc, 1 sc in next sc, *ch 5, SI st in first ch of ch-5, skip 1 sc, 1 sc in each of next 2 sc, repeat from* with last sc in last st. Fasten off.

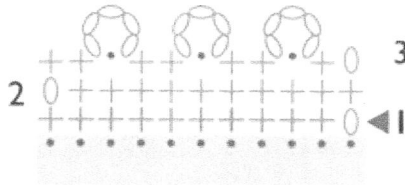

EDGING 4

Small picot: chain-5 picot;
large picot: chain-7 picot
Sts or holes: multiple of 5

Row 1: Ch 1, 1 sc in each st (or hole), turn.

Row 2: Ch 1, skip first sc, 1 sc in each sc with last sc in last st, turn.

Row 3: Ch 1, skip first sc, *(1 sc, small picot) in next sc, (1 sc, large picot) in next sc, (1 sc, small picot) in next sc, 1 sc in each of next 2 sc, repeat from* , ending with (1 sc, small picot) in next sc, (1 sc, large picot) in next sc, (1 sc, small picot) in next sc, 1 sc in last st. Fasten off.

See work a picot.

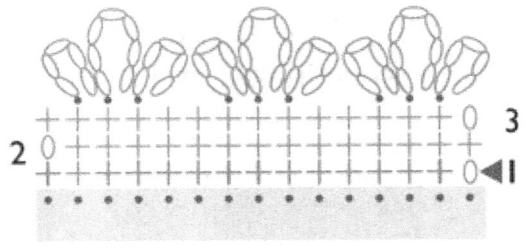

Edging 5 (top), Edging 6 (center), and Edging 7

EDGING 5

Sts or holes: multiple of 8

Row 1: Ch 1, 1 sc in each st (or hole), turn.

Row 2: *Ch 3, skip 3 sc, 2 dc in next sc, ch 6, Sl st back in 2nd ch, ch 1, 2 dc* *in same sc as last dc, ch 3, skip 3 sc, 1 sc in next sc, repeat from* with last sc in last st. Fasten off.

EDGING 6

Sts or holes: multiple of 4 + 1

Row 1: Ch 1, 1 sc in each st (or hole), turn.

Row 2: Ch 1, skip first sc, 1 sc in each sc with last sc in last st, turn.

Row 3: Ch 1, skip first 2 sc, 5 dc in next sc, skip 1 sc, 1 sc in next sc, *skip 1 sc, 5 dc in next sc, skip 1 sc, 1 sc in next sc, repeat from* with last sc in last st. Fasten off.

EDGING 7

Sts or holes: multiple of 4

Row 1: Ch 1, 1 sc in each st (or hole), turn.

Row 2: Ch 1, skip first sc, 1 sc in each sc with last sc in last st, turn.

Row 3: Ch 3, skip first 3 sc, *1 dc in next sc, ch 3, 4 dc around previous dc, skip 3 sc, repeat from* to last 3 sc, ch 3, Sl st in last st. Fasten off.

286

WORKING A CORNER

Crocheting a mitered corner is straightforward. In the first row of the edging, work two chain stitches at each corner, and then in the second row work stitches into the chain stitches. Repeat these two rows as required.

For a sharper corner, work three stitches into the corner stitch or hole, making the center one longer (e.g., in a row of double crochets, the center stitch can be a treble crochet).

Edging 8 (top), Edging 9 (center), and Edging 10

EDGING 8

Sts or holes: multiple of 6

Row 1: Ch 1, 1 sc in 2nd st (or hole), 1 sc in each of next 2 st, ch 5, 1 sc in same st as last sc, *1 sc in each of next 6 st, ch 5, 1 sc in same st as last sc, repeat from* , turn.

Row 2: Ch 1, skip 1 sc, 1 sc in next sc, *ch 10, 1 sc in 2nd sc after ch-loop, 1 sc in each of next 2 sc, repeat from* with last sc in last st, turn.

Row 3: *Work 3 sc in ch-10 loop, (ch 3, 3 sc) 4 times in same loop, 1 sc in center of 3 sc of Row 2, repeat from* in each ch-loop. Fasten off.

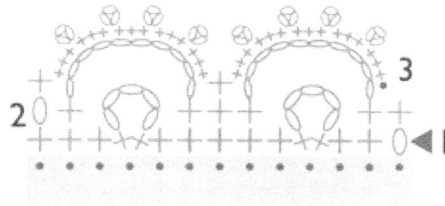

EDGING 9

Sts or holes: multiple of 8

Row 1: Ch 1, 1 sc in each st (or hole), turn.

Row 2: *Ch 3, (1 dc, ch 3, 1 dc) in 4th sc, ch 3, skip 3 sc, 1 sc in next sc, repeat from* with last sc in last st, turn.

Row 3: *Ch 3, Sl st in top of first dc, (ch 5, 1 sc, ch 6, 1 sc, ch 5, 1 sc) in ch-3 loop between double crochets, ch 7, repeat from* to last dc, ch 3, Sl st in last ch of Row 2. Fasten off.

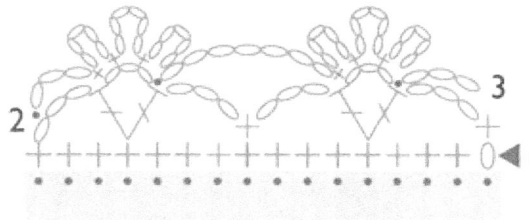

EDGING 10

Bobble = 4 treble crochets
Sts or holes: multiple of 8

Row 1: Ch 1, 1 sc in each st (or hole), turn.

Row 2: *Ch 5, work 1 bobble in 4th sc, ch 4, Sl st in top of bobble, ch 5, skip 3 sc, 1 sc in next sc, repeat from* to end of row. Fasten off.

See work a bobble.

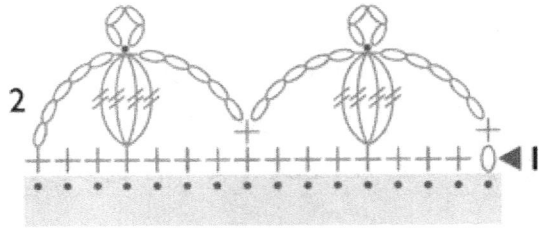

Edging 11 (top) and Edging 12

EDGING 11

Sts or holes: multiple of 8

n 1: Ch 1, 1 sc in each of next 5 st (or holes), ch 6, Sl st back in 4th sc from hook, work 13 sc in ch-loop, 1 sc in each of next 2 st, turn. *Ch 2, 1 tr in 2nd sc of ch-loop, repeat from* 5 times, ch 2, Sl st in first ch worked, turn. †3 sc in ch-loop, ch 3 in dc, repeat from † 5 times, 3 sc in last ch-loop.

Continue to make fans as required, beg each with 1 sc in next 6 st.

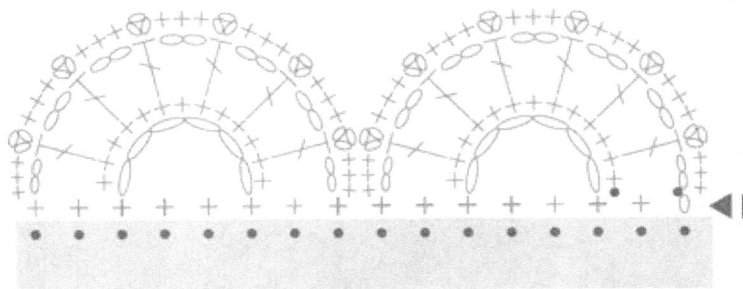

EDGING 12

Sts or holes: multiple of 8 + 6

Row 1: Ch 1, 1 sc in each of next 5 st (or holes), *(2 dc, 3 tr, 2 dc) in next st, 1 sc in each of next 7 st, repeat from* , turn.

Row 2: Ch 1, skip 1 sc, *1 sc in each of next 2 sc, ch 4, skip 1 sc, 1 sc in each of next 2 sc, (ch 1, 1 dc) between dc of Row 1 3 times, (ch 1, 1 dc) in same sp as last dc, (ch 2, 1 dc) in next sp, (ch 1, 1 dc) in same sp as last dc, (ch 1, 1 dc) in next 2 sp, ch 1, skip 1 sc, repeat from* , 1 sc in each of next 2 sc, ch 4, skip 1 sc, 1 sc in next sc, 1 sc in last st, turn.

Row 3: Sl st in 2nd sc, *4 sc in small ch-loop, 2 sc in ch between dc 4 times, (2 sc, ch 4, 2 sc) in top sp, 2 sc in ch-sp 4 times, repeat from* , 4 sc in last ch-loop. Fasten off.

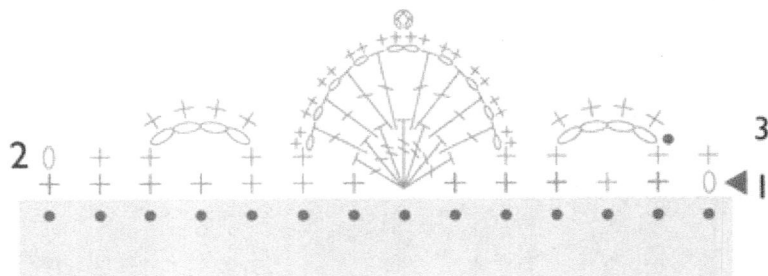

Edging 13

EDGING 13

Sts or holes: multiple of 38 + 1

Row 1: Ch 1, 1 sc in next 19 st (or holes), *ch 5, 1 sc in same st as last sc, 38 sc, repeat from* ending with 19 sc, turn.

Row 2: Ch 1, 1 sc in each of next 14 sc, *ch 4, (1 tr, ch 1) 6 times in ch-loop, ch 3, skip 4 sc, 29 sc, repeat from* ending with 15 sc, turn.

Row 3: Ch 1, 1 sc in each of next 10 sc, *ch 4, (6 dc, ch 2) between first and 2nd dc and between 3rd and 4th dc, (6 dc, ch 4) between 5th and 6th dc, skip 4 sc, 21 sc, repeat from* ending with 11 sc, turn.

Row 4: Ch 1, 1 sc in each of next 6 sc, *ch 4, (10 tr over 6 dc, ch 2) 3 times, ch 2, skip 4 sc, 13 sc, repeat from* ending with 7 sc.

Row 5: Ch 1, 1 sc in each of next 2 sc, *ch 5, (1 dc in each tr, ch 2) 3 times, ch 3, skip 4 sc, 5 sc, repeat from* ending with 3 sc.

Row 6: Ch 7, 1 sc in first ch, 1 sc in next sc, *ch 5, (4 tr over first 2 dc, 1 dc in each of next 2 dc, 4 tr over next 2 dc, 1 dc in each of next 2 dc, 4 tr over next 2 dc, ch 3) 3 times, ch 2, skip 2 sc, 1 sc in next sc, ch 6, sc in same sc, repeat from* working last 2 sc in last st. Fasten off.

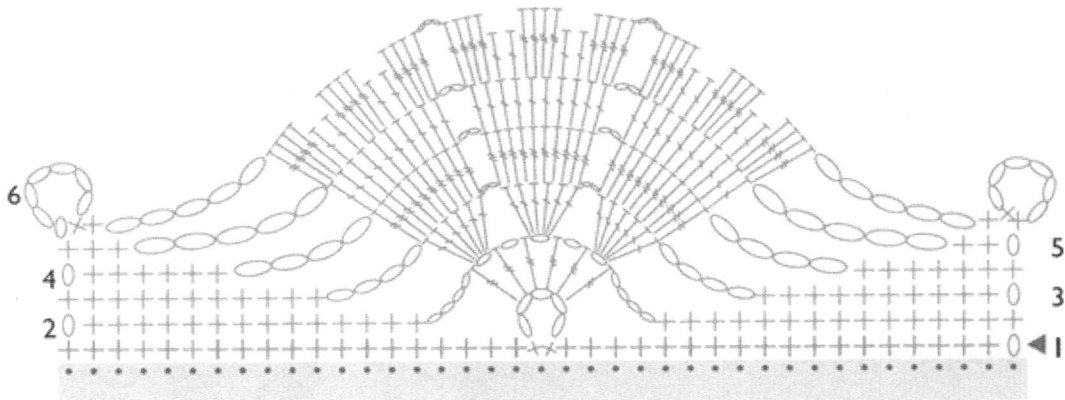

Edging 14

EDGING 14

Cluster (CL) = 6 treble crochets;
Small cluster (smCL) = 3 treble crochets Sts or holes: multiple of 16 + 1

Row 1: Ch 1, 1 sc in each st (or hole), turn.

Row 2: Ch 4, 3 tr in first sc, *ch 4, skip 5 sc, 1 sc in next 5 sc, ch 4, skip 5 sc, (4 tr, ch 3, 4 tr) in next sc, repeat from* ending with 4 tr in last st, turn.

Row 3: Ch 4, 1 tr in first tr, 1 tr in each of next 2 tr, 2 tr in next tr, ch 3, 1 dc in center sc of 5 sc, ch 3, 2 tr in next tr, 1 tr in each of next 2 tr, 2 tr in next tr, *ch 3, 1 tr in ch-loop, ch 3, 2 tr in next tr, 1 tr in each of next 2 tr, 2 tr in next tr, ch 3, 1 dc in center sc of 5 sc, ch 3, 2 tr in next tr, 1 tr in each of next 2 tr, 2 tr in next tr, repeat from* , ending with 2 tr in 4th ch of ch-4, turn.

Row 4: Ch 4, skip first tr, tr5tog in next 5 tr, work 1 CL in next 6 tr, *ch 5, work tog (2 dc in ch-3 sp, 1 dc in tr, 2 dc in ch-3 sp), ch 5, work 1 CL in next 6 tr, 1 CL in next 6 tr, repeat from* , ending with 1 CL in top of last 5 tr and 4th ch of ch-4, turn.

Row 5: Ch 4, 5 tr in top of first CL, ch 4, 6 tr in top of adjacent CL, *ch 3, 1 dc in dc5tog, ch 3, 6 tr in top of next CL, ch 4, 6 tr in top of adjacent CL, repeat from* , turn.

Row 6: Ch 4, 1 tr in each of 5 tr, ch 4, 1 tr in loop, ch 4, 1 tr in each of 6 tr, *ch 2, 1 dc in dc, ch 2, 1 tr in each of 6 tr, ch 4, 1 tr in loop, ch 4, 1 tr in each of 6 tr, repeat from* , ending with last tr in 4th ch of ch-4, turn.

Row 7: Sl st to 2nd tr, ch 4, skip 1 tr, tr2tog in next 2 tr, ch 4, 1 sc in next tr, (4 sc, ch 4, 4 sc) in ch, skip tr, (4 sc, ch 4, 4 sc) in ch, Sl st to 2nd tr, ch 4, skip 1 tr, work 1 smCL in next 3 tr, *skip (1 tr, 2 ch, 1 dc, 2 ch, 1 tr), work 1 smCL in next 3 tr, ch 4, 1 sc in next tr, (4 sc, ch 4, 4 sc) in ch, skip tr, (4 sc, ch 4, 4 sc) in ch, Sl st to 2nd tr, ch 4, skip 1 tr, work 1 smCL in next 3 tr, repeat from* . Fasten off.

To work a cluster (CL) and see work stitches together.

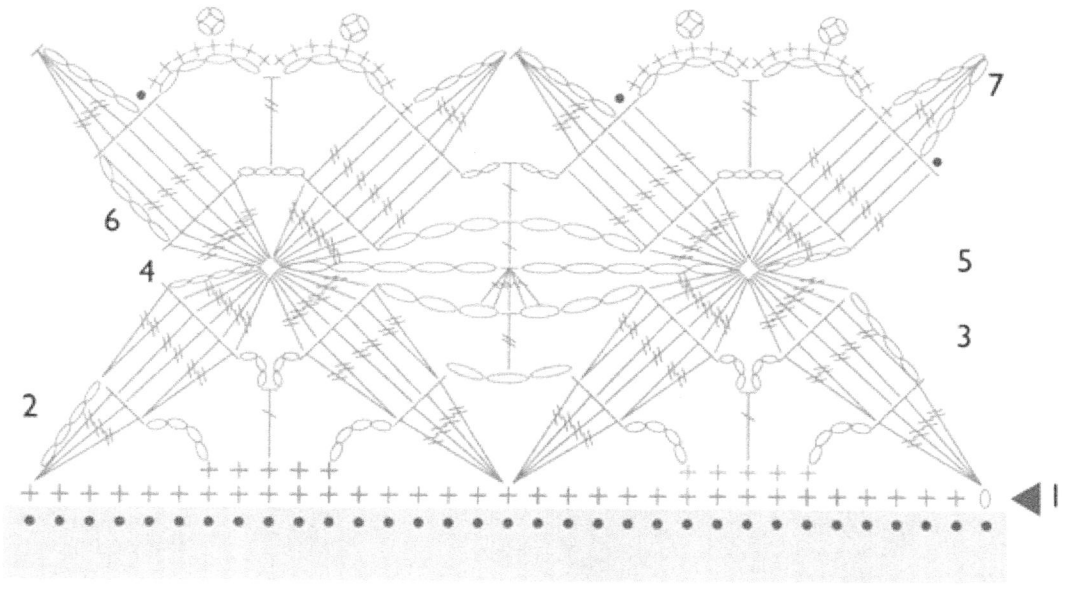

Edging 15 (top), Edging 16 (center), and Edging 17

EDGING 15

Sts or holes: multiple of 4

Row 1: Ch 1, 1 sc in each st (or hole), turn.

Row 2: *Ch 7, skip 3 sc, 1 sc in next sc, repeat from* , turn.

Row 3: Sl st 3, ch 3, *(1 dc, ch 4, Sl st in 2nd ch from hook, ch 1, 1 dc) in center of next ch-loop, repeat from* to last ch-loop, ch 3, Sl st in last ch-loop. Fasten off.

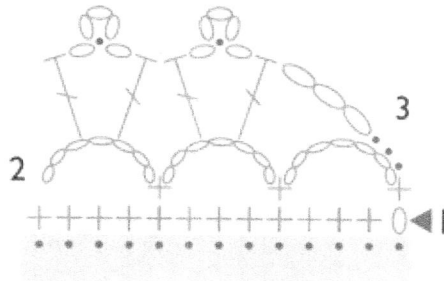

EDGING 16

Sts or holes: multiple of 4

Row 1: Ch 1, 1 sc in each st (or hole), turn.

Row 2: Ch 5, skip first sc, 1 dc in each of next 3 sc, ch 2, *skip 1 sc, 1 dc in each of next 3 sc, ch 2, repeat from* with last dc in last ch, turn.

Row 3: Ch 5, *3 dc in ch-2 sp, ch 2, repeat from* ending with 3 dc, turn.

Row 4: Ch 6, *Sl st in 5th ch from hook, ch 1, 4 sc in ch-2 sp, repeat from* . Fasten off.

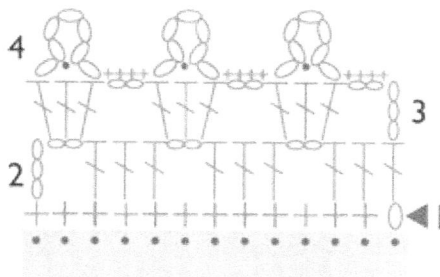

EDGING 17

Sts or holes: multiple of 6

Row 1: Ch 1, 1 sc in next 2 st (or holes), *ch 12, Sl st in 9th ch from hook, ch 3, hold RS and pull thread through 1st ch from hook, 1 dc in ch-loop, ch 2, (5 dc in ch-loop, ch 2) 3 times, 2 dc in ch-loop, pull yarn through where circle began, ch 2, 1 sc in same sp as last sc, 1 sc in* next 3 st, ch 4, Sl st in first ch, 1 sc in next 3 st, repeat from joining circles with Sl st in 3rd dc of first group of 5 dc. Fasten off.

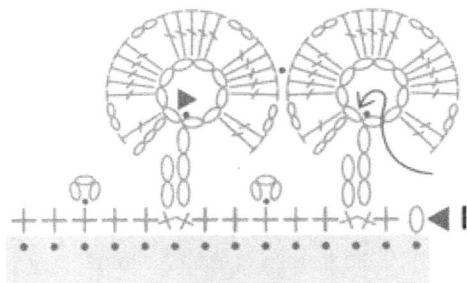

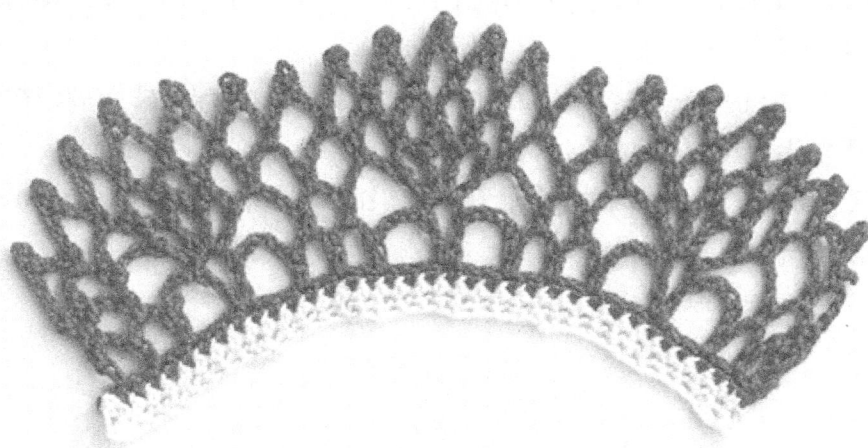

*Edging 18 **(top) and** Edging 19*

EDGING 18

Picot: chain-4 picot

Sts or holes: multiple of 10 + 7

Row 1: Ch 1, 1 sc in each st (or hole), turn.

Row 2: Ch 1, *ch 4, skip 1 sc, 1 sc, ch 4, skip 1 sc, 1 sc, ch 5, skip 2 sc, (1 dc, ch 3, 1 dc) in next sc, ch 5, skip 2 sc, 1 sc, repeat from* to last 4 st, ch 4, skip 1 sc, 1 sc, ch 4, skip 1 sc, 1 sc, turn.

Row 3: Ch 2, 1 sc in first loop, *ch 4, 1 sc in next loop, ch 5, skip ch-5 loop, work (4 dc with ch 3 between each) in ch-3 loop, ch 5, skip ch-5 loop, 1 sc in next ch-4 loop, repeat from* , ch 4, 1 sc in last loop, ch 1, 1 sc in tch, turn.

Row 4: Ch 1, 1 sc in ch-1, ch 5, *1 sc in next loop, ch 5, repeat from* , ch 2, 1 sc in tch, turn.

Row 5: Ch 1, *(ch 2, 1 picot, ch 2), 1 sc in next loop, repeat from* . Fasten off.

See work a picot.

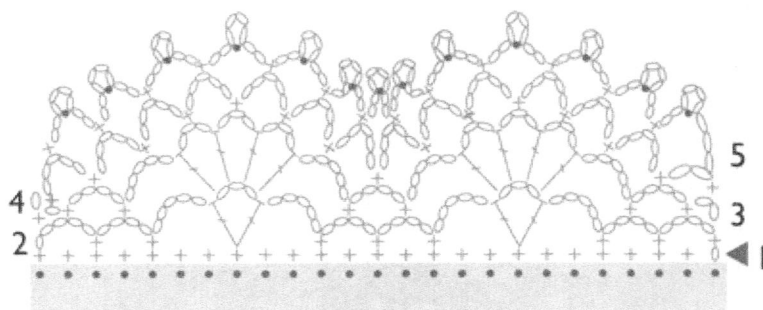

EDGING 19

Picot: chain-7 and slip stitch into last double crochet Sts or holes: multiple of 6

Row 1: Ch 1, 1 sc into each st (or hole), turn.

Row 2: Ch 1, *ch 5, skip 1 sc, 1 sc in next sc, repeat from* , turn.

Row 3: Ch 2, 1 sc in first loop, *ch 5, 1 sc in next loop, repeat from* , ch 1, 1 sc in tch, turn.

Row 4: Ch 4, 1 sc in first loop, *ch 5, 1 sc in next loop, (3 dc, 1 picot, 3 dc) in next loop, 1 sc over next loop, ch 5, 1 sc over next loop, repeat from* , ch 2, 1 sc in tch. Fasten off.

See work a picot.

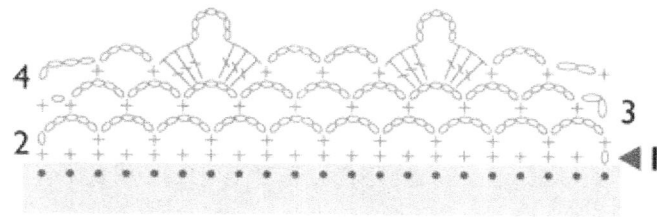

Edging 20 (left) and Edging 21

EDGING 20

Row 1: Ch 11, 1 dc in 7th ch from hook, ch 3, skip ch-3, 1 dc in last ch, turn.

Row 2: Ch 7, skip first dc, 1 dc in ch-3 sp, ch 3, skip 1 dc, 1 dc in ch-6 sp, turn.

Row 3: Ch 5, skip first dc, 1 dc in ch-3 sp, ch 3, skip 1 dc, 13 dc in ch-7 sp, turn.

Row 4: Ch 3, skip first 2 dc, (1 sc in next dc, ch 3, skip next dc) 5 times, 1 sc in next dc, ch 3, 1 dc in ch-3 sp, ch 3, 1 dc in ch-5 sp, turn.

Row 5: Ch 5, skip first dc, 1 dc in ch-3 sp, ch 3, skip next dc, 1 dc in ch-3 sp, turn.

Repeat Rows 2–5 as required, ending with Row 4. Fasten off.

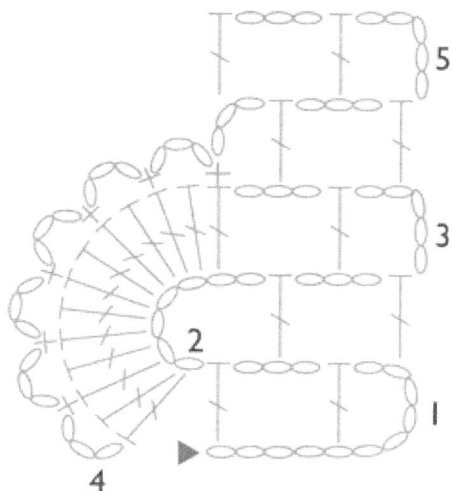

EDGING 21

Row 1: Ch 5, (1 tr, ch 3, 1 tr) in 5th ch from hook, turn.

Row 2: Ch 3, skip first tr, 9 dc in ch-3 sp, skip 1 tr, (1 tr, ch 3, 1 tr) in ch-4 sp, turn.

Row 3: Ch 3, skip first tr, 9 dc in ch-3 sp, skip 1 tr, (1 tr, ch 3, 1 tr) in sp before first dc, turn.

Repeat Row 3 as required, finishing on odd-numbered row. At end of last row, do not turn.

Attachment chain ch 3, *ch 6, 1 sc in 3rd ch of ch-3 at beg of last row, repeat from* and finish with 1 sc at beg of Row 2. Fasten off.

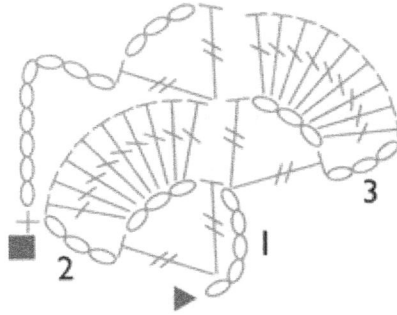

> **Tip-** These two edgings, or trims, are crocheted separately and then stitched to the fabric piece. Be careful when you are working them, as they can easily be stretched and distorted.

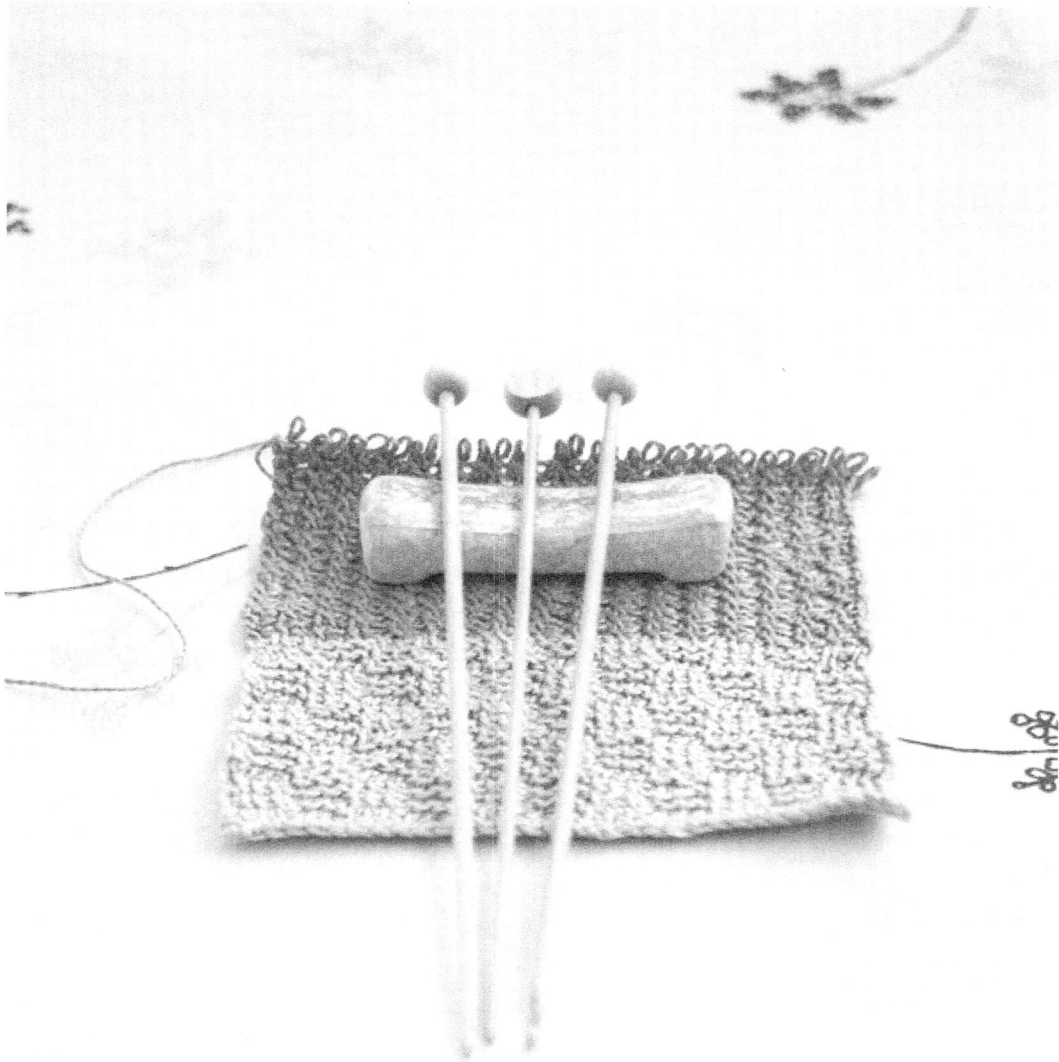

Specialty crochet

Several types of crochet work use special hooks or other tools to create unusual forms of crocheted fabric. The best known of these forms are broomstick lace and Tunisian crochet.

: BROOMSTICK LACE

Broomstick lace (also known as Jiffy lace, as it works up so quickly) can be worked over your finger, but it is easier to keep the loops the same size if you use a pin. The pin has a pointed tip so that the loops can be hooked off. A large knitting needle (about ⅝ inch or 15 mm in diameter) is ideal, but larger pins can be made by sharpening the end of a wooden dowel.

The pin is held in the left hand and the crochet hook in the right, as usual (or the reverse if you are left-handed).

In this section instructions are given for the basic stitches used in broomstick lace, as well as some of the more popular stitch patterns.

BASIC STITCHES

Broomstick loop stitch (ls)

Insert the hook into the stitch at the left-hand end of the row (or as instructed). Yarn over (yo) and pull up a loop (as if making a chain stitch). Lengthen the loop and slip it onto the pin.

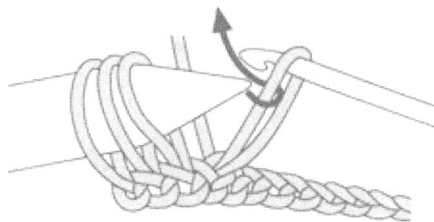

The loops on the pin form the first row of crochet and are worked, as instructed, with the hook.

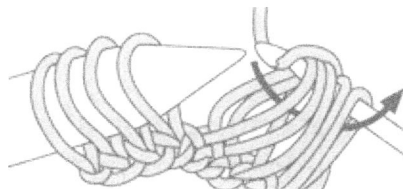

Bouclé loop stitch (bls)

This stitch is usually worked on the wrong side so that the loops form on the right side.

Insert the hook in the required stitch and place the yarn over the pin as shown. Hook both threads and draw the yarn through. There should be three loops on the hook as shown in the diagram below.

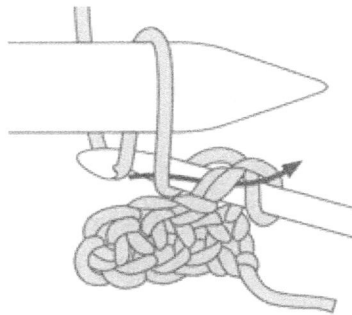

Yarn over (yo) and draw the yarn through all the loops. There should be one loop left on the hook.

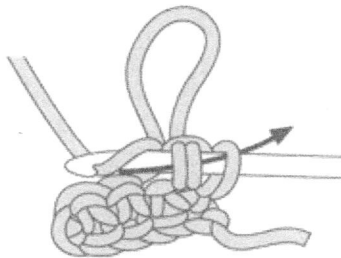

Tip- A single row of bouclé loop stitch can be worked along an edge to form a fringe.

DOUBLE-ENDED CROCHET

Double-ended crochet uses a long double-ended hook that allows you to work stitches off either end. The rows are worked back and forth with the loops left on the hook in one row and removed in the next, in a way similar to Tunisian crochet. Like Tunisian crochet, double-ended crochet produces a soft fabric that looks like knitting. However, it is worked in two or more colors, with the color changed every second row. The yarns are carried up the sides of the fabric so that the result is reversible.

Double-ended crochet is also known as Crochet on the Double, reversible crochet, cro-hooking, and, if a thick yarn and large hook are used, crochenit.

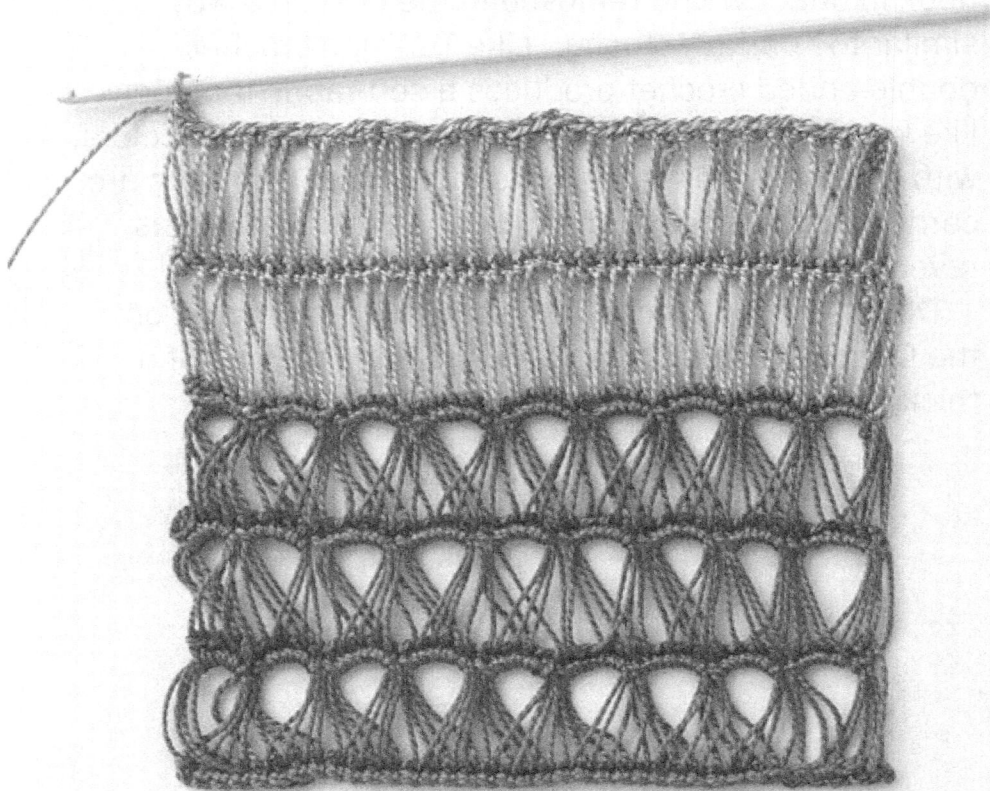

Broomstick loop rows (top) and Broomstick lace

BROOMSTICK LOOP ROWS

Ch: required sts

Work from left to right: skip 1 ch, 1 ls in each ch, work loop in last ch and lengthen it to same height but keep it on the hook. Do not turn work.

Lks 1 in ls on hook, *1 sc in next loop, slipping loop from pin, repeat from* to end. Do not turn work.

Lengthen loop on hook and slip onto pin, skip first sc, 1 ls in each sc to last st, 1 ls in lks, lengthen loop to same height and keep it on hook. Do not turn work.

Repeat Rows 2 and 3.

See locking stitch (lks).

BROOMSTICK LACE

Ch: multiple of 4

Row 1: Work from left to right: lengthen loop on hook, skip 1 ch, 1 ls in each ch, work loop in last ch and lengthen it to same height but keep it on the hook. Do not turn work.

Row 2: Lks 1 in ls on hook, insert hook through loop below hook and next lp3tog (slipping loops from pin) and work 1 sc, work 3 more sc in same place, *inserting hook through next lp4tog (slipping loops from pin) work 4 sc in same place, repeat from* to end. Do not turn work.

Row 3: Lengthen loop on hook and slip onto pin, skip first sc, *1 ls in each sc, lengthen loop to same height and keep it on hook, do not work into lks. Do not turn work.

Repeat Rows 2 and 3.

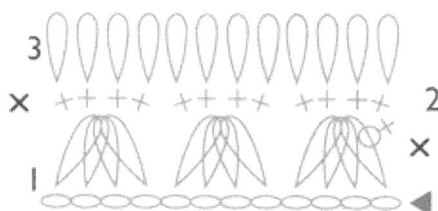

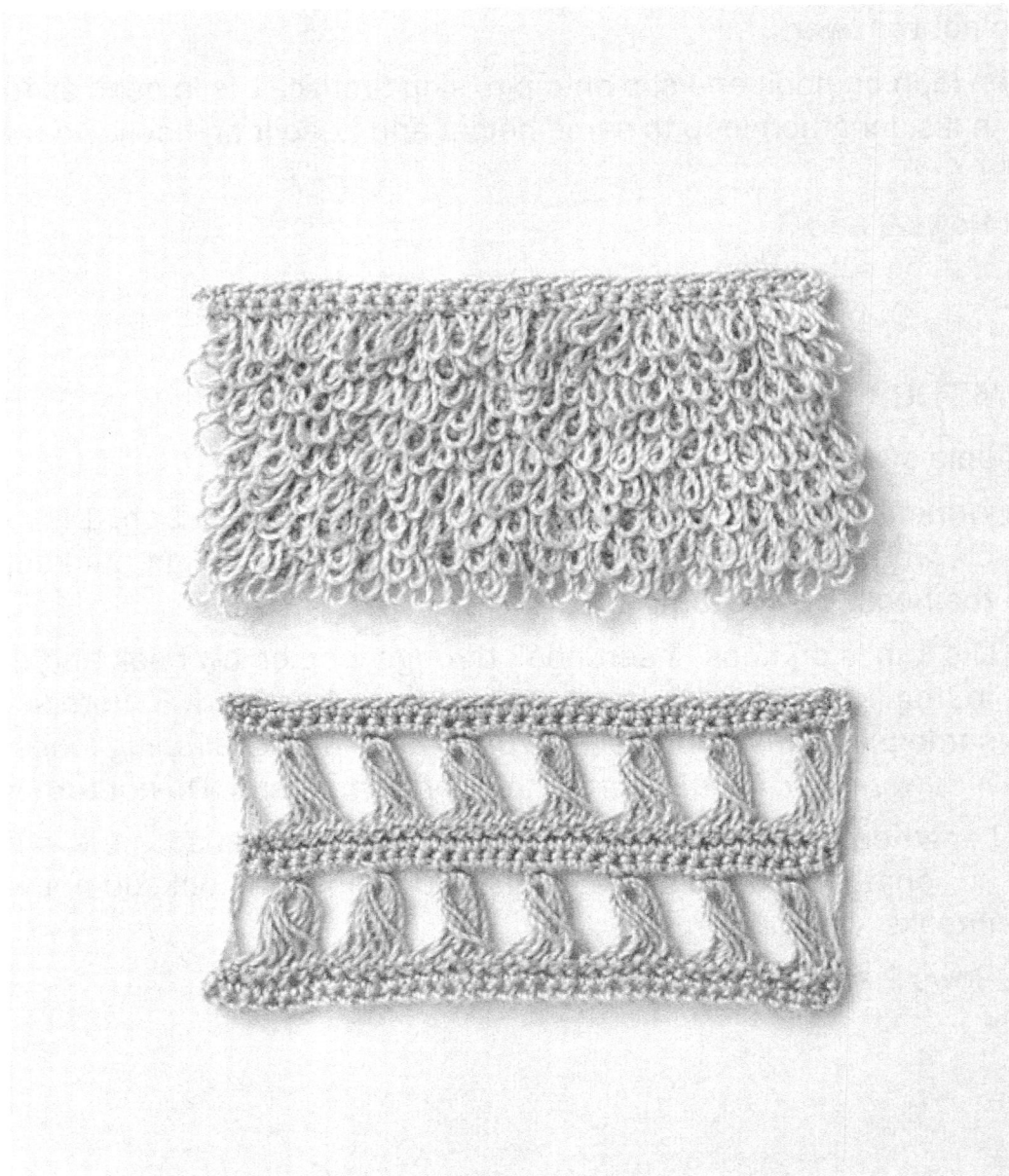

Bouclé loop rows **(top)** *and* *Broomstick clusters*

BOUCLÉ LOOP ROWS

Ch: required sts

Sc in 2nd ch from hook, 1 sc in each ch, turn.

Ch 1, lengthen this ch to height required, skip first sc, 1 bls in each sc, 1 bls in last st, turn.

Ch 1, skip first bls, 1 sc in each bls, 1 sc in last st, turn.

Repeat Rows 2 and 3.

BROOMSTICK CLUSTERS

Ch: multiple of 5 + 3

Row 1: Sc in 3rd ch from hook, 1 sc in each ch to end. Do not turn work.

Row 2: Lengthen loop on hook and slip onto pin, skip first sc, * 1 ls in each sc, 1 ls in 1 ch, lengthen loop to same height and keep it on hook, repeat from *. Do not turn work.

Row 3: Lks 1 in ls on hook, ch 2, *insert hook through next lp5tog (slipping loops from pin) and work 1 sc, ch 4, repeat from *, ending with ch 2, 1 sc in last ls, turn.

Row 4: Ch 1, skip first sc, 2 sc in ch-2 sp, *1 sc in next sc, 4 sc in ch-4 sp, repeat from *, ending with 2 sc in ch-2 sp, 1 sc in lks, turn.

Row 5: Ch 1, skip first sc, 1 sc in each sc, 1 sc in last st. Do not turn work.

Repeat Rows 2–5.

See locking stitch (lks).

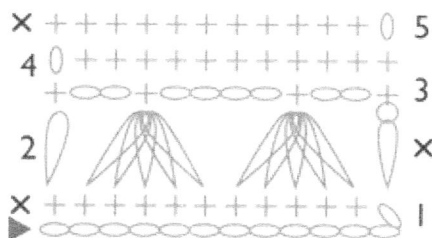

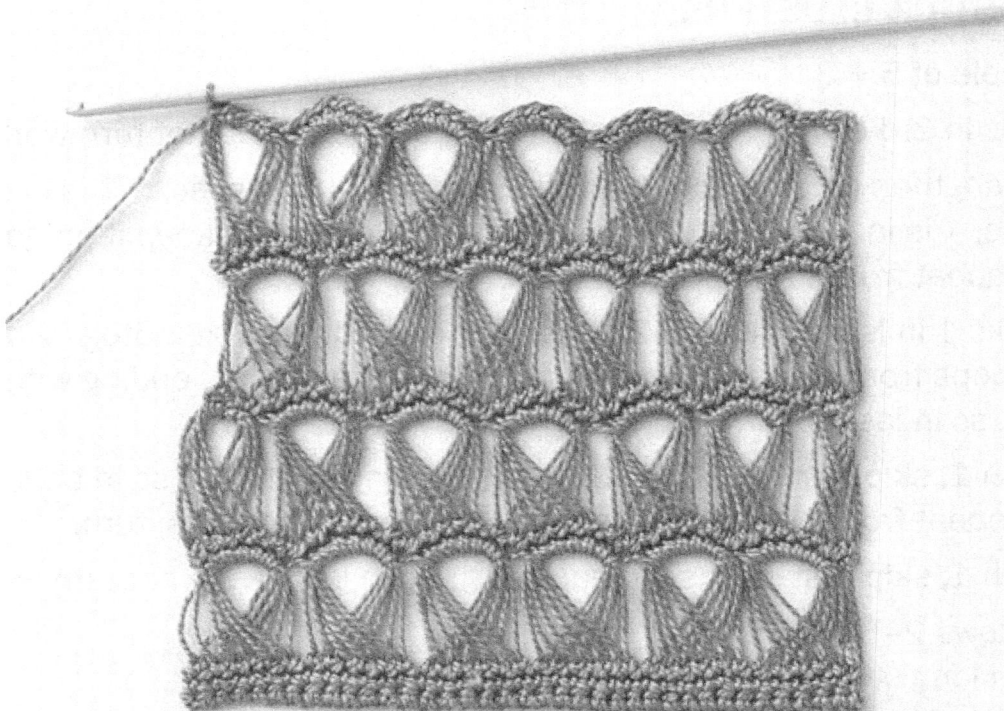

Offset Broomstick Lace

OFFSET BROOMSTICK LACE

Extended loop stitch (Els): Insert hook as directed, yo, pull up a loop, yo, draw yarn through both loops, lengthen loop and slip it onto pin.

Ch: multiple of 6 + 1

Row 1: Sc in 2nd ch from hook, 1 sc in each ch. Do not turn work.

Row 2: Ch 1, lengthen loop on hook and slip onto pin, skip first sc, 1 Els in each sc, 1 Els in last sc, lengthen loop to same height and keep it on hook. Do not turn work.

Row 3: Lks 1 in loop on hook, insert hook through loop below hook and next lp5tog (slipping loops from pin) and work 5 sc in same place, *insert hook through next lp6tog (slipping loops from pin) and work 6 sc in same place, repeat from *. Do not turn work.

Row 4: Ch 1, lengthen loop on hook and slip onto pin, skip first sc, 1 Els in each sc, 1 Els in lks, lengthen loop to same height and keep it on hook. Do not turn work.

Row 5: Lks 1 in loop on hook, insert hook through loop below hook and next lp2tog (slipping loops from pin) and work 2 sc in same place, *insert hook through next lp6tog (slipping loops from pin) and work 6 sc in same place, repeat from *, ending with 3 sc in last lp3tog. Do not turn work.

Repeat Rows 2–5.

See locking stitch (lks).

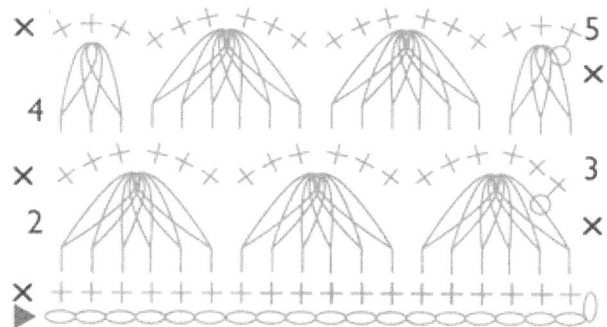

⁝ TUNISIAN CROCHET

Tunisian crochet is worked in rows without turning the work. When working from right to left, all the loops are kept on the hook while they are worked off during the "return" row (working from left to right). The result resembles knitting.

A long, cylindrical hook is used to hold all the stitches (very long ones come in sections that screw together). A knob at the end prevents the stitches from falling off. These hooks are known as Tunisian hooks, Afghan hooks, or tricot needles.

BASE ROWS

Ch: required sts

Insert the hook in the 2nd ch from the hook, yo and the draw yarn through the ch. Repeat to the end of the row, keeping all the loops on the hook.

Row 2: Ch 1, *yo and draw the yarn through two loops, repeat from * to the end of the row. Do not turn the work. The loop remaining on the hook becomes the first stitch of Row 3.

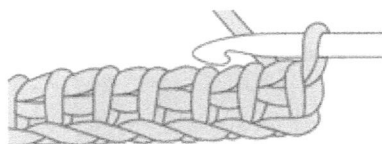

This style of crochet has many names. As well as Tunisian crochet, it is known as Afghan stitch, tricot crochet, hook knitting, shepherd's knitting, and railroad knitting. Although the finished work resembles knitting, Tunisian crochet is classed as a form of crochet because it is produced using a hook instead of two needles.

BASIC STITCHES

Tunisian simple stitch (Tss)

Insert the hook under the leg of the next stitch, working from right to left.

Yo and pull up a loop.

Tunisian knit stitch (Tks)

With the yarn in back, insert the hook under the leg of the next stitch from front to back.

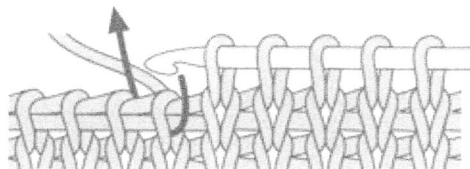

Yo and pull up a loop.

Tunisian purl stitch (Tps)

Bring the yarn to the front of the work.

Insert the hook under the leg of the next stitch, working from right to left.

Take the yarn to the back of the work.

Yo and pull up a loop.

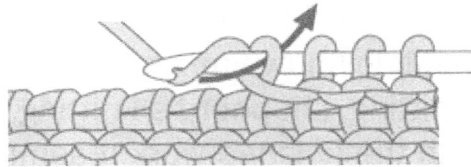

Tip- Tunisian stitches have a very strong diagonal pull. This is not evident with the shorter stitches used in this book, but with longer stitches (e.g., Tunisian double crochet) it is difficult to create a square piece of work, even after blocking. It is best to use longer stitches only where such distortion will not matter.

From the top: Tunisian Simple Stitch rows, Knit rows, Purl rows, *and* Rib pattern

SIMPLE STITCH ROWS

Ch: required sts Work Base Rows 1 and 2.

Row 3: Skip first st, 1 Tss in each st to end. Do not turn work.

Row 4: As Base Row 2.

Repeat Rows 3 and 4.

⟳ See work Base Rows 1 and 2.

KNIT ROWS

Ch: required sts Work Base Rows 1 and 2.

Row 3: Skip first st, 1 Tks in each st to end. Do not turn work.

Row 4: Ch 1, *yo, draw yarn through first 2 loops on hook, repeat from * to end (1 loop on hook). Do not turn work.

Repeat Rows 3 and 4.

⟳ See work Base Rows 1 and 2.

PURL ROWS

Ch: required sts Work Base Rows 1 and 2.

Row 3: Skip first st, 1 Tps in each st to end. Do not turn work.

Row 4: Ch 1, *yo, draw yarn through first 2 loops on hook, repeat from * to end (1 loop on hook). Do not turn work.

Repeat Rows 3 and 4.

⟳ See work Base Rows 1 and 2.

RIB PATTERN

Ch: multiple of 4 + 2
Work Base Rows 1 and 2.

Row 3: Skip first st, 1 Tks in next st, *1 Tps in each of next 2 sts, 1 Tks in each of next 2 sts, repeat from * to end. Do not turn work.

Row 4: Ch 1, *yo, draw yarn through first 2 loops on hook, repeat from * to end (1 loop on hook). Do not turn work.

Repeat Rows 3 and 4.

⟳ See work Base Rows 1 and 2.

*Tunisian Crossed pattern **(top)** and Basketweave pattern*

CROSSED PATTERN

Ch: even number of sts Work Base Rows 1 and 2.

Row 3: Skip first st, *skip next st, 1 Tss in next st, 1 Tss in skipped st, repeat from *, 1 Tss in last st. Do not turn work.

Row 4: Ch 1, *yo, draw yarn through first 2 loops on hook, repeat from * to end (1 loop on hook). Do not turn work.

Repeat Rows 3 and 4.

⟳ See work Base Rows 1 and 2.

BASKETWEAVE PATTERN

Ch: multiple of 6 + 5

Work Base Rows 1 and 2.

Row 3: Skip first st, 1 Tss in each of next 3 sts, *1 Tps in each of next 3 sts, 1 Tss in each of next 3 sts, repeat from *, 1 Tss in last st. Do not turn work.

Row 4: Ch 1, *yo, draw yarn through first 2 loops on hook, repeat from * to end (1 loop on hook). Do not turn work.

Rows 5–8: Repeat Rows 3 and 4 twice.

Row 9: Skip first st, 1 Tps in each of next 3 sts, *1 Tss in each of next 3 sts, 1 Tps in each of next 3 sts, repeat from *, 1 Tss in last st. Do not turn.

Row 10: As Row 4.

Rows 11–14: Repeat Rows 9 and 10 twice.

Repeat Rows 3–14 as required.

⟳ See work Base Rows 1 and 2.

Glossary

back (of work) the side of the piece facing away from you as you work **back loop** the loop behind the top part of the stitch **bar** the horizontal part of the stitch **base chain** the length of chains made at the beginning of the work (also called foundation chain) **beginning group** the group made at the beginning of the row or round; it has one less stitch than the other groups, because the turning chain at the beginning of the row is regarded as the first leg of the group **chain-space** the hole created by a group of chain stitches. Sometimes the stitches in the next row are worked into this larger gap rather than into any individual stitch **cluster** series of stitches worked into a number of stitches of the previous row and joined at the top (e.g., bobble, popcorn, puff) **decrease** reduce the number of stitches **edging** decorative rows of crochet added to the crochet piece or to woven fabric **foundation chain** the length of chains made at the beginning of the work (also called base chain) **free loops** the row of unworked loops that remain in the previous row after working that row into the front or back loops only **front (of work)** the side of the piece facing you as you work **front loop** the loop in front of the top part of the stitch **gauge** the number of stitches and rows to a given measurement **group** several stitches worked into the same place (e.g., fan or shell) **hem-stitching** a method of making holes in woven fabric to prepare it for a crocheted edging. Groups of threads are gathered together to

make gaps on either side

increase add to the number of stitches **leg** vertical part of the stitch (especially in formations such as clusters where there are a number of vertical legs) (also called post) **multiple** the number of chain stitches needed to form a motif **multiple +** the number of chain stitches needed to form a motif plus the extra needed for the turning chain **post** the vertical part of a stitch, which will be larger or smaller depending on the type of crochet stitch used. Raised stitches are worked around the post, rather than into the stitches (also called a leg) **repeat** work the instructions the number of times specified (e.g., "repeat 5 times" means to work the instructions six times, the original time and five more times) **right side** side of the work that will show **round** series of stitches that forms a circle around the work; most rounds join with a slip stitch and the work is not turned **row** series of stitches forming one line of the work; you turn the work at the end of the row (unless instructed otherwise) **turning chain** the chain stitch made at the end of a row; it is the first stitch of the next row unless the pattern says otherwise **wrong side** the side of the work that will not show when the piece is finished

Note to left-handed crocheters

Left-handed people have far fewer problems with crochet than with many other handicrafts. This is because most crochet is double-sided.

To learn crocheting from a right-handed person, sit opposite the crocheter and mirror his or her actions. To use the instructions for the basic stitches in this book, prop the book in front of a mirror so that you can see the illustrations in reverse and still read the instructions directly from the book.

Substitute "left" for "right" and vice versa throughout the instructions.

Stitches will slant or twist in the opposite direction from a right-hander's crochet, but this does not matter as long as you are consistent.

Shaped pieces will be reversed (e.g., if you follow the instructions for the right side of a sweater you will make the left side). Again, as long as you are consistent, this does not matter.

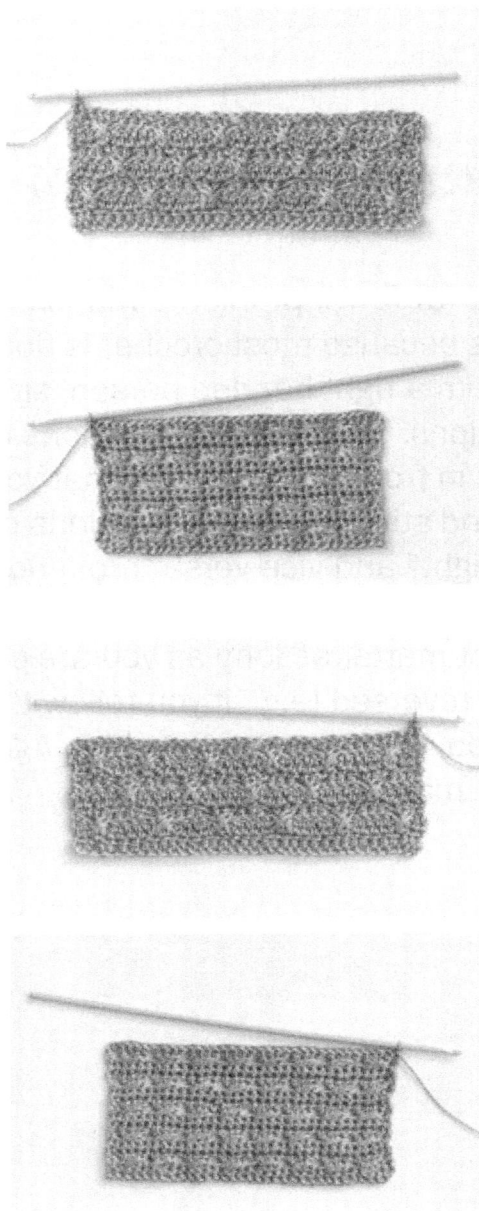

The top two swatches show right-handed work, while the lower two show the same pattern worked by a left-handed crocheter.

Index

Made in United States
North Haven, CT
09 December 2024